READING TEXTS

Reading, Responding, Writing

READING TEXTS

Reading, Responding, Writing

Kathleen McCormick

Gary Waller

with Linda Flower

Carnegie Mellon University

D. C. HEATH AND COMPANY
Lexington, Massachusetts   Toronto

Acknowledgments

Laurie Anderson. "O Superman," reprinted by permission of Difficult Music.

John Ashbery. "And *Ut Pictura Poesis* Is Her Name" from *Houseboat Days* by John Ashbery. Copyright © 1975, 1976, 1977 by John Ashbery. Reprinted by permission of Viking Penguin, Inc.

Italo Calvino. "The Canary Prince" from *Italian Folktales* by Italo Calvino, copyright © 1956 by Giulio Einaudi editore, s.p.a., English translation copyright © 1980 by Harcourt Brace Jovanovich, Inc. Reprinted by permission of Harcourt Brace Jovanovich, Inc.

Emily Dickinson. No. 712-8H [Because I could not stop for Death] and No. 1624 [Apparently with no surprise] by Emily Dickinson. Reprinted by permission of the publishers and the Trustees of Amherst College from *The Poems of Emily Dickinson,* edited by Thomas H. Johnson, Cambridge, Mass.: The Belknap Press of Harvard University Press. Copyright 1951, © 1955, 1979, 1983 by the President and Fellows of Harvard College.

Robert Hass. "Meditation at Lagunitas" copyright © 1979 by Robert Hass. From *Praise* by Robert Hass, published by The Ecco Press in 1979. Reprinted by permission.

John Jump. Abridged selection from "Hamlet" by John Jump, © Oxford University Press 1973. Reprinted from *Shakespeare: Select Bibliographical Guide* edited by Stanley Wells (1973) by permission of Oxford University Press.

Mark Knopfler. "Money for Nothing" copyright © 1985, Chariscourt Ltd. All rights administered by Rondor Music Ltd., London. Administered in U.S. and Canada by Almo Music Corp. (ASCAP), International Copyright secured. All rights reserved.

Robert Lowell. "Skunk Hour" from *Life Studies* by Robert Lowell. Copyright © 1959 by Robert Lowell. Reprinted by Permission of Farrar, Straus and Giroux, Inc.

Gregory Orr. "All Morning" by Gregory Orr from *Gathering Bones Together*. Copyright © 1975 by Gregory Orr. Used with permission.

Dr. Seuss. Excerpts from *How the Grinch Stole Christmas* by Dr. Seuss, copyright © 1957. Reprinted by permission of Random House, Inc.

Dave Smith. "Messenger" by Dave Smith from *Goshawk, Antelope* (University of Illinois Press). © 1978 by Dave Smith. Originally in *The New Yorker*.

William Stafford. "Traveling Through the Dark" from *Stories That Could Be True: New and Collected Poems* by William Stafford. Reprinted by permission of Harper & Row, Publishers, Inc.

William Carlos Williams. "The Great Figure" from *The Collected Earlier Poems* by William Carlos Williams. Copyright 1938 by New Directions Publishing Corporation. Reprinted by permission of New Directions Publishing Corporation.

W. B. Yeats. "Easter 1916" from *Collected Poems* by W. B. Yeats. Reprinted with permission of Macmillan Publishing Company and with permission of A. P. Watt Ltd. on behalf of Michael B. Yeats and Macmillan London Limited. Copyright 1924 by Macmillan Publishing Company, renewed 1952 by Bertha Georgie Yeats.

COVER: Joanna Steinkeller

Preface

We designed *Reading Texts* for use with any course in literary (and related media) studies that takes the interaction of reading and writing seriously. In particular, *Reading Texts* introduces some of the most important insights of recent literary and cultural theory into the literature classroom. Though not primarily designed for courses in literary theory, it does take literary theory seriously. Over the last fifteen years, our understanding of reading and writing has changed dramatically. *Reading Texts* demonstrates how these changes can be adapted to the study of literature in the classroom. It is the first acknowledgment in a textbook that the important insights of literary and cultural theory are appropriate for—and bring excitement to—the classroom.

Reading Texts can be used with a variety of courses, whether organized by genre or period, or by thematic or issue-centered principles. It introduces a number of texts, including complete poems, extracts from stories, plays, and television programs, and references to many familiar texts. Because the assignments and writing suggestions can be applied to any text, however, they can be used in any existing literature course.

The three major divisions of *Reading Texts* indicate its breadth of coverage in reading and writing.

- Part 1, Understanding the Reading Situation, incorporates the central insights of recent *reader-centered* and *culturally focused* criticism to help students become aware of their own reading strategies and the broader cultural forces that influence them.
- Part 2, Understanding the Writing Situation, introduces students to the goals and strategies of process-oriented writing models, which treat writing about literary texts as a cognitive act deeply influenced by broader cultural forces.
- Part 3, Reading, Responding, Writing, introduces the major literary genres and media texts and shows how the reading and writing strategies introduced in Parts 1 and 2 can be adapted to these genres.

Some of the theoretical sources of *Reading Texts* are described in Brief Suggestions for Further Reading (p. 267) for the benefit of those students whose level of interest in literary, cultural, and writing theory may prompt them to read in more depth. But the basis for the adaptation, development, and testing of the theory presented here has been grounded firmly in our own classroom practices.

In particular, *Reading Texts* combines two major strands of recent literary theory that have long needed to be adapted to the classroom. The first is **reader-centered** or **reader-response** criticism, which focuses less on finding meanings ''in'' texts and more on the *process* by which meanings are created through the interaction of texts and readers. The second is **cultural** criticism, in which both readers and texts are studied within the complex cultural dynamics of their time, and are thus not regarded as isolated, purely subjective entities.

But *Reading Texts* is a book of applied theory—a "how-to" book directed to changing the ways readers approach and understand a text. With this emphasis on application, in Chapter 1 we develop a model of how readers create meaning, with clear and detailed examples drawn from research and teaching practices. Because both readers and texts are located within the general and literary ideologies of their culture, they bring particular repertoires into the reading situation, and meanings are created by the *matching* of these repertoires. In Chapter 2, we provide further discussion on establishing the context of both reader and text by analyzing in depth how three major factors—language, history, and culture—influence the reading situation.

In Chapters 3 and 4, we turn to writing, focusing primarily on the development of cognitively and culturally self-aware *response statements*. In Chapter 3, we analyze different ways in which students can write about literature, setting out the reading strategies and writing goals, along with the benefits and costs, of summarizing, free-associating, interpreting, and writing response statements with increasingly detailed cognitive and cultural awareness. In Chapter 4, we set out new criteria for persuasiveness in writing formal papers that emphasize students' critical thinking abilities. Essays are seen as persuasive not if their writers claim that their positions are objectively true, but rather if they acknowledge the situated nature of their positions and recognize the implications of maintaining them. We provide many examples of student response statements and papers in both chapters.

A distinctive aspect of *Reading Texts,* particularly of Chapters 3 and 4, is the perspective provided by the research conducted by Linda Flower, Kathleen McCormick, and their colleagues, both faculty and graduate students, in the Center for the Study of Writing, for which Carnegie Mellon and the University of California (Berkeley) are being funded by the Department of Education through NIE. This five-year project will, its participants believe, dramatically change the ways researchers, teachers, and students come to understand the nature of writing, and the authors of *Reading Texts* are pleased that some of the first fruits of this research are emerging here. Chapter 3, in particular, grows out of collaborative work by Linda Flower, Kathleen McCormick, John R. Hayes, Karen Schriver, and their fellow researchers at Carnegie Mellon.

We envisage *Reading Texts* being of great practical benefit to teachers of literature. We have chapters on the major traditional literary genres—poetry, fiction, and drama—and also a chapter on "reading" media texts, demonstrating how the principles and practices we advocate can be applied profitably to nontraditional areas. In the Appendix, we include a detailed Glossary and a section on Documenting the Research Paper to augment the discussion in the main body of the book.

We contend that the overall goal of studying literary and other texts is to become a *strong reader* and a persuasive, self-aware writer. To achieve this goal, we insist that the study of literature be neither simply text-based nor simply reader-based, but that students can learn strategies that allow them to comprehend and articulate the complex cognitive and cultural forces underlying their experiences of reading literature. To this end, a powerful method and vocabulary are introduced and exemplified from our classroom practice.

Thus *Reading Texts* brings together in a reading-into-writing textbook the most useful theory, research, and practice of both the "new literary theory" and the "new rhetoric." The authors foresee its use with *any* literature class as a guide to developing highly self-aware reading and writing skills. By emphasizing the sociocultural factors that influence both reading and writing about literature, *Reading Texts* provides literature teachers with a guide to developing innovative syllabuses and thought-provoking assignments for any literature course.

This book has been a labor of love for the two principal authors. It has grown out of their close collaboration on *The Lexington Introduction to Literature* (D. C. Heath, 1987) and other projects, and they wish to thank their fellow worker on that anthology, Lois Fowler, for her encouragement and tolerance. They wish also to thank Linda Flower for her vital contributions to *Reading Texts* and for her enthusiasm for their work.

Kathleen McCormick wishes to thank the faculty and graduate students who teach "Reading Texts" and who have tried out some of this material and offered much needed support and criticism. She also wants to thank all her students who have enthusiastically submitted to having their repertoires (both general and literary) exposed and enlarged, and who have, in the process, taught her a great deal. Special thanks, finally, to Bill Sheidley, Lee Jacobus, Mary and Bill Curtin, Edith and Jim McCormick, and particularly to Gary Waller—for difficulties, but no doubts.

Gary Waller wishes to thank his colleagues at Carnegie Mellon who have supported his efforts to set up a model undergraduate curriculum in English that would support the theory and practice outlined in this book. He also wishes to give his collaborator special thanks for her theoretical rigor, her patience with his desire to take short cuts when clearly she was right and he was wrong, and for her willingness to explain how difficult theoretical concepts can be understood and communicated.

All the authors wish to thank the editors at D. C. Heath for their enormous patience and encouragement, especially Paul Smith who saw the possibilities as well as the risks, and Judith Leet who deserves a special award and a great dinner for being so thorough and helpful. Our thanks, too, to Jacqueline Hall and Laurie Walz for deciphering and not being overwhelmed by countless revisions.

Kathleen McCormick
Gary Waller

Contents

Readings Used in This Text   xv

Part 1
Understanding the Reading Situation   1

1 Reading Texts   3

"Reading" and "Texts"   3
"Old" and "New" Methods of Reading   5
   The Old Model: The Author's Meaning Is "in" the Text   5
   The New Model: Readers Interact with Texts   6
   Creating a Reading: The New Model   7
   Arguments Against the Old Model   8
   Arguments in Favor of the New Model   8
Why Read Texts at All?   10
Reading for Multiple Meanings   11
   Polyvalent Versus Monovalent Readings   13
Becoming Aware of Your Own Repertoire   13
The Reading Situation: An Overview   14
Ideology: General and Literary   16
The General Repertoire of the Text   19
   Dominant and Counter-Dominant Views   19
   "Universal Themes" Are Historically and Culturally Produced   20
The General Repertoire of the Reader   22
The Literary Repertoire of the Text   24
The Literary Repertoire of the Reader   25
Strong Readings   27
   Arguments for Developing Strong Readings   28
   Are There Limits to Interpretation?   29

2 Language, History, Culture   32

The Pull of Ideology   32
The Reader's Context: Language, History, Culture   33
Language   34
   Language Both Is "Written by" and "Writes" Its Users   34
   Language Pre-Exists Its Users   35
   Language Is Always Value Laden   36

Poetry and the Indeterminacy of Language   38
Exploring the Poem's Argument   40
Deepening Your Reading Experience   41
History   41
    The Pespectival Nature of History   41
    Reading with Historical Perspective   45
    Reading for Absences   47
Culture   49
    The Shift from Literacy Studies to Cultural Studies   49
    The Significance of Studying Contemporary Literary Texts   51
Conclusions and Suggestions   53

Part 2
Understanding the Writing Situation   55

3   Reading to Write Response Statements   57

Reading Situations and Task Representations   57
A Reading and Writing Assignment: Robert Lowell's "Skunk Hour"   59
Task Definitions   61
Text-Based or Reader-Based Task Definitions   61
    Summarizing   61
    Reading Strategies and Writing Goals for Summarizing   62
    Benefits and Costs of Summarizing   62
    Free-Associating   65
    Reading Strategies and Writing Goals for Free-Associating   65
    Benefits and Costs of Free-Associating   66
    Interpreting   67
    Reading Strategies and Writing Goals for Interpreting   67
    Benefits and Costs of Interpreting   69
Moving Beyond These Preliminary Task Definitions   70
The Interactive Response Statement   71
General Guidelines for Writing Response Statements   73
Interactive Task Definitions   76
    Self-Consciously Responding to the Text   76
    Reading Strategies and Writing Goals for Responding to the Text   77
    Benefits and Costs of Responding Self-Consciously to the Text   77
    Analyzing Your Response Cognitively   81
    Reading Strategies and Writing Goals for Analyzing Your Response
        Cognitively   81
    Benefits and Costs of Analyzing Your Response Cognitively   82
    Analyzing Your Response Culturally   84
    Reading Strategies and Writing Goals for Analyzing Your Response
        Culturally   85
    Benefits and Costs of Analyzing Responses Culturally   86

4 From Response Statements to Formal Papers 92

Dispelling Common Assumptions About Formal Papers   92
Four Major Goals for Formal Papers   93
Reading and Writing Are Always Processes   94
From Response Statements to Formal Paper: Kafka's "The Metamorphosis"
      and Calvino's "The Canary Prince"   95
    Response Statement Assignment on "The Canary Prince": Exploring Your
      Repertoire   96
    Response Statement Assignment on "The Metamorphosis": Expanding
      Your Repertoire   101
    The Formal Paper: Comparing Responses to the Two Meta-
      morphoses   102
    Sample Student Paper: "Changing Conventions and Changing Inter-
      pretations"   107
Learning to Read Literary Criticism: Responding to Criticism on
      Hamlet   118
Writing a Formal Research Paper   128
    Research Paper Topic   128
    Sample Student Paper: " 'Unending Dreams of Commentary': How Critics
      Engage with Doris Lessing's *Summer Before Dark*"   131

Part 3
Reading, Responding, Writing   149

5 Reading Poetry   151

Creating Your Text   151
Poetry Is a Way of Reading   152
    Poetry as Playing with Language   154
    Involving the Reader   155
Reading Poetry and Reading Rock Lyrics   156
    The Context of Poetry Today   158
    Connotative Richness   159
A Common Pattern for Reading Poetry   161
Reconstructing the Poem's Argument   162
Formulating Your Initial Response: Filling in Gaps   165
Personal Associations   166
Expanding Your Knowledge of a Poem's Repertoire: Discovering Contra-
      dictions   167
    Ideological Conflict in the Text   168
Analyzing Your Repertoire   170
A Strong Reading: Developing a Differing Perspective   172
    Historical Research   174
    Implications Beyond the Classroom   175
Enjoying Poetry Together   175
    What Is the Poem "About"?   177

Bringing Associations to the Poem   178
Blackberry or "Blackberry"?   179

6 Reading Fiction   181

Fiction in Our Lives   181
    Why Do You Read Fiction?   181
    Reading Fiction as "Natural"   183
Conventional Reading and Text Strategies for Fiction   184
    Plot   184
    Character   185
    Point of View   186
    Theme   187
Unconventional Reading and Text Strategies for Fiction   188
    Plot   188
    Naturalizing Strategies   189
    Character   191
    Character in "The Hitchhiking Game"   191
    Point of View   194
    Theme   196
Mixing Traditional and Untraditional Reading and Text Strategies with a
    Traditional Story   198
    A Symptomatic Reading of "The Lady with the Dog"   199
Mixing Traditional and Untraditional Strategies with a Contemporary
    Story   203
The Interconnection of Your Literary and General Repertoires   206
    The Interaction of the Reader's and the Text's General Repertoire: A
        Layering of Historical Periods   207
Gender-based Differences in Reading Fiction   210
Enjoying Fiction More—and Differently   212

7 Reading Drama   215

The Distinctiveness of Drama: The Text as Performance   215
    Visualizing a Scene   216
    A Play Is Not a Novel   217
    Drama Is Found in Everyday Life   218
    Acting Spaces and Audiences   219
    Acting Spaces and Styles Through History   220
Cultural Influences on Theatrical Productions   222
    Shakespeare's Plays in Performance   222
How Plays Change Through History   224
    Ideological Contradiction in *Doctor Faustus*   225
    Cultural Influences on the History of Production   225
    Ideology Is Always Contradictory   227
Scripts, Actors, Audiences: The Interactive Nature of Performance   228
    Text Strategies and Reader Expectations: Comedy and Tragedy   228

The Blurring of Distinctions Between Entertaining and Serious
    Theater   229
"Entertaining" Plays and Provocative Productions   230
"Problem" Plays   231
Intellectual Theater as Entertainment   231
Brecht's Influence on Modern Productions   233
Beckett's Influence on Contemporary Productions   234
The Open-Ended Nature of Drama   235
Entertainment and Seriousness in Brecht and Beckett   236
Student Responses to Brecht's *Galileo*   236
Student Responses to Beckett's *Waiting for Godot*   239

8   Reading Media Texts   243

Expanded Definitions of "Reading" and "Texts"   243
A Media-Saturated Culture   244
Reading Television   246
The Economic Motivation of Network Television   248
Analyzing the Effect of "Flow" in the Television Text   249
What the Media Text and the Viewer Bring to the Reading Process   250
Ideological Analysis of Sitcoms   251
Developing Cognitive and Cultural Awareness: *How the Grinch Stole
    Christmas*   254
How the Grinch Stole Christmas as Bardic Television   257
Analyzing Rock Music: Participation in Ideology   258
Rock Lyrics and Ideology   259
Writing About Rock Music   260
Summarizing, Free-Associating, Interpreting   261
Response Statements: Cognitive and Cultural Awareness   263
Reading Other Media Texts   265
Conclusion   266

Brief Suggestions for Further Reading   267

Documenting the Research Paper   271

Glossary of Terms   281

Index   293

Readings Used in This Text

The following readings, either complete works or excerpts, are discussed at length in the text or are used for writing assignments.

Chapter 1

EMILY DICKINSON, *Because I Could Not Stop for Death*   3
STEPHEN CRANE, *The Open Boat*   7
EDMUND WALLER, *Go, Lovely Rose*   9
WILLIAM CARLOS WILLIAMS, *The Great Figure*   12
ANNE BRADSTREET, *To My Dear and Loving Husband*   21

Chapter 2

GREGORY ORR, *All Morning*   38
JOHN ASHBERY, *And* Ut Pictura Poesis *Is Her Name*   39
WILLIAM BUTLER YEATS, *Easter 1916*   42

Chapter 3

ROBERT LOWELL, *Skunk Hour*   59
GARY WALLER, *Culture and Anarchy*   63
SIR ROBERT SIDNEY, *Song 17*   67
WILLIAM WORDSWORTH, *I Wandered Lonely as a Cloud*   70
DAVE SMITH, *Messenger*   78
ANDREW MARVELL, *To His Coy Mistress*   82
WILLIAM WORDSWORTH, *She Dwelt Among the Untrodden Ways*   87

Chapter 4

ITALO CALVINO, *The Canary Prince*   96
FRANZ KAFKA, *The Metamorphosis*   101, 103
STEPHEN VANDERFHOOF (Student), "Changing Conventions and Changing Interpretations"   107
JOHN JUMP, "*Hamlet*"   120
JENNIFER EVEN (Student), " 'Unending Dream of Commentary': How Critics Engage with Doris Lessing's Summer Before the Dark"   131

Chapter 5

MARK KNOPFLER, *Money for Nothing*   156

WILLIAM STAFFORD, *Traveling Through the Dark*   159

WILLIAM SHAKESPEARE, *Sonnet 65* (Since brass, nor stone, nor earth, nor boundless sea)   161

JOHN DONNE, *A Valediction: Forbidding Mourning*   162

WILLIAM BLAKE, *London*   168

EMILY DICKINSON, *Apparently with No Surprise*   170

RICHARD LOVELACE, *To Lucasta, Going to the Wars*   172

ROBERT HASS, *Meditation at Lagunitas*   176

Chapter 6

DONALD BARTHELME, *Views of My Father Weeping*   188

JOHN BARTH, *Lost in the Funhouse*   194

ANTON CHEKHOV, *The Lady with the Dog*   200

JOYCE CAROL OATES, *The Lady with the Pet Dog*   200

GABRIEL GARCÍA MÁRQUEZ, *The Incredible and Sad Tale of Innocent Eréndira and Her Heartless Grandmother*   203

NATHANIEL HAWTHORNE, *The Maypole of Merry Mount*   207

Chapter 7

OSCAR WILDE, *The Importance of Being Earnest*   216

WILLIAM SHAKESPEARE, "All the world's a stage" (from *As You Like It*)   218

Chapter 8

DR. SEUSS, *How the Grinch Stole Christmas*   254

LAURIE ANDERSON, *O Superman (For Massenet)*   261

READING TEXTS
Reading, Responding, Writing

Part 1
Understanding the Reading Situation

ℋ Chapter 1
Reading Texts

"Reading" and "Texts"

Reading . . . texts. That sounds familiar enough, doesn't it? *Reading* is an activity you've performed from your very early years. It is a skill, or a set of skills, by which you process written information or by which you follow written instructions.

When we say here *reading texts,* we generally mean the reading of literature. This implies that the skills of reading are directed to a very specific kind of experience. When you read "literature," in addition to gaining information, you expect to gain some pleasures that you associate with reading literary texts—emotional uplift, humor, insights into the human condition, and so forth.

Over the years, as you have learned to study literary texts in more depth, you have extended the meaning of the word "reading" to something *you* write or sometimes speak—as when you say, "I have to do a reading of this poem by Emily Dickinson for class tomorrow." This statement really means that (most likely) you will be *writing* something to be read by a teacher or that you will make an oral presentation in class that will be heard and responded to by your fellow students.

Let's see what this involves. One of Emily Dickinson's poems, for instance, is this suggestive piece:

EMILY DICKINSON (1830–1866)

Because I Could Not Stop for Death

Because I could not stop for Death—
He kindly stopped for me—
The Carriage held but just Ourselves—
And Immortality.

We slowly drove—He knew no haste
And I had put away
My labor and my leisure too,
For his Civility—

We passed the School, where Children strove
At Recess—in the Ring—
We passed the Fields of Gazing Grain—
We passed the Setting Sun—

Or rather—He passed Us—
The Dews drew quivering and chill—
For only Gossamer, my Gown—
My Tippet—only Tulle—

We paused before a House that seemed
A Swelling of the Ground—
The Roof was scarcely visible—
The Cornice—in the Ground—

Since then—'tis Centuries—and yet
Feels shorter than the Day
I first surmised the Horses' Heads
Were toward Eternity—

When you do a "reading" in the sense we mentioned—that is, when you speak or write something "on" or "about" this poem for your instructor or fellow students—what do you do? Probably something like the following:

1. You read over the poem for its general sense, checking out unfamiliar words—for instance, *tippet, tulle, cornice.* You consult footnotes or a dictionary to help you.

2. You then might try to respond to the "voice" you hear speaking in the poem, which you probably identify with the "I" the poem mentions. You might ask yourself questions such as these: Who is the "I"? And how do I, the reader (you, me, whoever reads the poem), relate to the "I" of the poem?

3. You then extend your reading by focusing on the issues, the questions, the interests you perceive the poem is raising for you, based on *your* own experiences. Clearly, Death might appear to you, as it does to many readers, to be a major concern of the poem. What do I, the reader—you might ask yourself—feel or believe about death? Do those beliefs agree or overlap with the poem's assumptions? Do I find the poem's views relevant to me? Part of your reading starts to focus on such questions and how they relate to your own experiences, or to what you might even see as universal, or at least very common, experiences. Our society has a number of dominant ways of discussing the significance of death that are most likely part of your beliefs and feelings. How is your reading of this poem affected by them?

A reading of a text, therefore, not only *explains* the text's meaning but also analyzes your experiences while reading it and their broader cultural implications.

4. Finally, of course, you start to organize your thoughts and reactions into a coherent and, you hope, persuasive argument, traditionally called an "interpretation." You try to explain why your experience of the poem took the shape it did, why it had the impact on you it did. You might focus on the poem's formal features (its meter, rhyme scheme, voice, and so forth), how it holds together, what kind of statement on the human condition it might be making. Such an interpretation would be *text-centered*. Or you might take a more *reader-centered* approach. You might comment on the fear or mystery of death in your own life; on how the poem's eerie suggestiveness works on your feelings; or on how the depiction of life as a journey affects you. Such comments focus on *your* experiences, evoked by the poem as you read and think about it. Or you might try to generalize a little more, perhaps considering the questions of death and eternity in a religious or philosophical context. Or you might focus on your surprise when you found the serious subject of death treated ironically, even playfully, in the poem.

Those are typical procedures you might employ when you develop a "reading" of a text. Over the course of this book, we want to show you ways you can develop and deepen your reading experiences. At this point, note how the procedures we have outlined involve "writing" as much as they do "reading"— both writing as, literally, writing down your ideas and questions, and also "writing" understood metaphorically, as expressing or articulating the poem in different words. As a *reader*, you *rewrite* the poem.

"Old" and "New" Methods of Reading

The Old Model: The Author's Meaning Is "in" the Text

We have just described some of the things people do when they do a "reading" of a literary text. In this book, we want to introduce you to ways you can both deepen your experience of reading texts and understand something of the reading process. It seems commonsensical that when you read, something is communicated or transferred *to* you *from* the text. Because texts are written *by* somebody, it seems equally commonsensical to assume that what is communicated comes "from" a person somewhere "behind" the text, the author. We can represent this model (what we call the "old" model of reading) this way:

Author → Text → Reader

According to this model, the reader's job is to understand the "meaning" (sometimes expressed as the "message") contained "in" the text. We put quotation marks around "meaning," "message," and "in" because they are metaphors, not literally true—and somewhat confusing metaphors at that, as you will see.

The New Model:
Readers Interact with Texts

In fact, rather than "finding meaning in" or "getting meaning out of" a text (familiar expressions in our language that imply that meaning is somehow "contained in" texts), readers use their knowledge of the language system and literary conventions, and their general assumptions about the world at large, to *make* sense of those black marks on the page. In other words, reading is not a passive activity in which you just take in information; rather it is always an active one in which, whether consciously or not, you *create* your version of the text. What is literally "in" a text is, of course, a lot of pages with black marks on them, pages of what linguists call *signifiers* that you, the reader, attach to *signifieds*. The signifier "blackberry," for example, is attached to the signified, those big juicy fruits you find on bushes, or in pies or jams. (Why we have chosen "blackberry" will become clear in Chapter 5.)

It is up to *you* to make those signifiers significant. And you do so because of what you have learned, often seemingly unconsciously, about "reading." Those marks on the page only have significance to you because you are part of a particular linguistic and cultural community that has taught you to associate certain words with certain concepts or things. If you spoke a different language, not only would you have different words or signifiers, but also in some cases you would have different signifieds as well. If you know a foreign language, you have probably discovered that on occasion a certain word, such as the French *jouissance,* can't easily be translated into English because we don't have a parallel word in our language. Similarly, the Eskimos have many words for snow, the fine distinctions of which we can't understand, not because our snow is different but because our language is different. Thus, without the signifier (the word) we cannot understand the signified (the concept).

The new model of reading we advocate emphasizes three points in relation to signifiers and signifieds:

- no one-to-one correspondence exists between signifiers and signifieds, that is, words have *multiple meanings,* no one of which can be said to be "correct"

- different readers attach different signifieds to the signifiers in a text, and *thereby readers help to create the texts they read*

- the relationship between signifiers and signifieds is *cultural* (and the existence of different signifieds in different languages can lead to marked differences in the ways different language users perceive the world)

Creating a Reading:
The New Model

Here is another text to work with—the opening of the well-known story, "The Open Boat," by Stephen Crane (1871–1900).

> None of them knew the color of the sky. Their eyes glanced level, and were fastened upon the waves that swept toward them. These waves were of the hue of slate, save for the tops, which were of foaming white, and all of the men knew the colors of the sea. The horizon narrowed and widened, and dipped and rose, and at all times its edge was jagged with waves that seemed thrust up in points like rocks.
>
> Many a man ought to have a bath-tub larger than the boat which here rode upon the sea. These waves were most wrongfully and barbarously abrupt and tall, and each froth-top was a problem in small boat navigation.
>
> The cook squatted in the bottom and looked with both eyes at the six inches of gunwale which separated him from the ocean. His sleeves were rolled over his fat forearms, and the two flaps of his unbuttoned vest dangled as he bent to bail out the boat. Often he said: "Gawd! That was a narrow clip." As he remarked it he invariably gazed eastward over the broken sea.

This passage certainly gives its readers some information, but it invites a much more complex experience than merely recording facts. The words are evocative and can trigger multiple emotional suggestions—look, for instance, at *foaming, jagged, thrust, barbarously*. These words are not there primarily for information. They are chosen for their *affective* power, that is, their power to sway the emotions of their readers.

How would you do a *reading* of this passage? In other words, what kinds of things might you say about it? You might say that it creates a certain kind of atmosphere. But when you try to be more precise about that, you look for evidence not so much in the text as in the impression that reading the text makes on you. You might use your own memories of boating. You might recall other experiences in which you have been afraid. In doing so, note that you are almost automatically bringing your own experiences to bear upon your reading. You are attaching your own signifieds to the signifiers of the text, and your signifieds may be vastly different from those of other readers. In this book we advocate that you do this very self-consciously and deliberately—that whenever you read, you call upon your own appropriate experiences and knowledge as much as possible. Reading is not merely the transfer of information from an author to a reader: it is an activity in which you, as an individual and a member of a particular society, are deeply and actively involved.

But, you might say, you aren't an expert reader. Some of you might even be afraid that developing your *own* interpretation might cause you to "miss the point" of the text. But who is to say what the "point" of a text is? Such a notion implies that a literary text contains a "true" or "correct" meaning, often thought to be "what the author intended."

Arguments Against the Old Model

The notion of a single, or true, meaning intended by an author is quite problematic for a number of reasons. First, literary texts not only seem ambiguous, but in fact they *encourage* multiple, different readings. Because literature is *polyvalent,* it can always mean more than one thing, and its polyvalence makes it enjoyable to read. Different readers and critics frequently develop quite diverse, often contradictory, interpretations of literary texts, all of which can be justified and supported by evidence from the text. Consequently, it seems difficult to assert that literary texts possess a single or "true" meaning given to them either by their author or by one "expert" reader.

Second, when asked, authors frequently say that they don't know exactly what their own texts mean, or that the meaning of a text has changed for them since they wrote it. Further, an author often writes without an explicit intention, or with multiple, often contradictory, intentions. Even if an author did have a single intention, how are you, as a reader, to know when you have discovered it? So using the argument "I know what Shakespeare meant when he wrote *King Lear*" to support one interpretation as the only correct one is in fact to argue: "I have my interpretation of *King Lear,* and I assume that Shakespeare read his play in the same way that I am reading it." Whenever you say "the author intended," you may be really saying simply, "I think." In this book, we encourage you to say "I think . . ." and to explore the social, cultural, and literary assumptions and values underlying your own interpretations of texts.

Arguments in Favor of the New Model

Literary theorists and reading researchers have recently modified the old model of reading that asserts that texts simply communicate authors' meanings to readers. The new model of reading argues that texts do not contain meanings but that *readers actively make meanings.* Further, the new model argues that texts cannot be said to have a single "correct" meaning because the meanings readers assign to texts are produced by social and cultural forces that change over time. Readers, like the texts they interpret, do not exist in isolation but are, rather, strongly influenced by their cultural context. Thus in the new model it becomes important to study not only the text and not only the reader, but also the broad cultural situation in which texts are written and are read. You may have noticed this cultural emphasis in our discussion of the Emily Dickinson poem that we glanced at briefly. We suggested that an important question was whether the issues raised in her poem about death overlap with or are different from *your* beliefs or feelings about death and from those of your culture.

In this book you will find an approach to reading texts (and not just literary texts but also the "texts" of film, songs, television, and other systems of signs that surround you in this message-saturated world) that stresses the following points:

1. Reading is an *interactive process,* produced by the interaction of readers and texts.

2. Reading has both *cognitive and cultural dimensions,* that is, it is both an intellectual procedure that requires certain mental strategies and skills, and a cultural procedure, contingent upon your wider beliefs and assumptions.

3. The making of meaning is not merely a "subjective" or individual experience because both readers and texts are deeply influenced by their sociocultural contexts. Readers and texts alike are produced by (that is, they are the products of) their history and culture. Or as some theorists like saying, metaphorically, they are "written" by their culture.

4. As a consequence of point 3, and because relationships between signifiers and signifieds are always culturally derived, certain readings might seem "correct" or even "intended by the author" in one sociocultural context but will not seem so across *all* cultural contexts. Thus no text can be said to contain a single, fixed meaning since readers' determinations of meaning are dependent on social, cultural, and literary assumptions that are in a continual state of change.

5. The readings readers develop from the texts have *implications* for the other parts of their lives outside the classroom: there is no such thing as a purely "literary" reading.

Writing Suggestions

1. (*a*) Do a reading of the Emily Dickinson poem "Because I Could Not Stop for Death" (p. 3) according to the old model, and then do another according to the new model of reading.
(*b*) Explain two major differences between your two readings.
(*c*) Which model of reading do you feel more comfortable with? Why?
(*d*) Which model is more like the kinds of writing about literature you have done in the past?
(*e*) Which model gives you more freedom as a reader?

2. Using the following poem (or a text of your own choosing), compare and contrast some aspects of the old and new models of reading.

EDMUND WALLER (1606–1687)

Go, Lovely Rose

Go, lovely Rose,
Tell her that wastes her time and me,
    That now she knows,
When I resemble her to thee,
How sweet and fair she seems to be.   5

Tell her that's young,
And shuns to have her graces spied,
    That hadst thou sprung
In deserts where no men abide,
Thou must have uncommended died.   10

Small is the worth
Of beauty from the light retir'd:
    Bid her come forth,
Suffer herself to be desir'd,
And not blush so to be admir'd.   15

    Then die, that she
The common fate of all things rare
    May read in thee,
How small a part of time they share,
That are so wondrous sweet and fair.   20

Why Read Texts at All?

Why does anyone read "literary" texts at all? When asked such a question, teachers and educators often reply that reading the great texts of one's culture gives readers a sense of history, a sense of belonging to a tradition, a means of sharing a common inheritance.

Another explanation of why literature is taught in school (and one compatible with the first reason) is that it reveals human language at its most intense. According to this view, in the "great" poems or plays or stories of our culture, the highly charged language stimulates our feelings and thinking in unaccustomed ways and so gives us uniquely valuable experiences.

A more cynical (or is it realistic?) view is that educational institutions use literature to discipline students, to put them under society's control by presenting them with its dominant values and assumptions. Certainly, every society assumes that its young people need to be integrated into its common ways of thinking and introduced to its shared beliefs and problems. According to this view, studying literature is a way to indoctrinate people into how reality is perceived or constructed in their society—now and in the past.

An alternative to this last explanation is that reading literature encourages readers to question, or to try to change, the norms of their culture. According to this view, the pleasure of reading literature (rather like the experience of listening to music, watching movies, and so on) is that it allows people to discover sides of themselves or to have enriching experiences that the dominant structures of their society try to control, repress, or trivialize. So reading literature can also be seen as a *counter-dominant* practice, in that it opens up experiences counter to those dominant in society.

Yet another view, an apolitical one, sees literature as giving readers experiences that are solely aesthetic, that help them to escape from the utilitarian and goal-oriented dynamics of their society. Many works of literature suggest that readers should cultivate other, more contemplative ways of seeing—of seeing inwards, of seeing into themselves, or maybe of just seeing ordinary things in new ways but without immediately measurable benefits.

Perhaps the most widespread reason given for reading literature is that it teaches readers about themselves. Readers learn to become more sensitive to and more aware of themselves, to share in the common and exciting experiences of being human, or to become more morally or politically aware. The Roman poet Horace wrote that the dual function of art was to teach *and* amuse. Sometimes the teaching is direct and aggressive; such literature is called *didactic*. It has, as the poet John Keats put it, "a design upon us." It wants its readers to behave or act in a certain way, and it lets them know what that way is. Other texts invite their readers to discover their own insights: they use language that is evocative and open-ended, asking their readers to bring their own experiences to mind as they read. Many of Shakespeare's plays and poems are often felt to have the resonance and deep emotional power to draw in their readers and to make them think about their own comparable experiences. In reading this way, you are not analyzing the writer's experience so much as *your own*. The pleasure of reading texts implied here is something beyond what you get when you understand the "message" of a text; it is, rather, the intense kind of pleasure that you might get from a deep personal experience—one that envelops you, making you feel joyful, abandoned, shocked, or ecstatic.

Such an explanation points up the seriousness of the experience of reading literary texts. But sometimes reading is more like playing than looking for deep philosophical insights. This is the "amuse" or "entertain" of Horace's phrase. With some detective stories, for instance, readers guess, speculate, follow clues, playing as if in a child's game. Many kinds of fiction start off with a mystery that slowly unravels. Part of the pleasure of this kind of reading is puzzling out the mysteries.

So while sometimes the experience of reading will be serious, difficult, even tormenting and anguished, at other times it will be sheer pleasure, fun, a diversion from serious matters—and sometimes it will be both simultaneously. What you make of your reading of texts—whether or not you agree with texts politically, whether you revel in the beauty of their language, whether you use them to escape from life for a while or use them to guide your life—depends on the context in which you are reading, your mood, your goals, and your cultural background. Bear in mind that there is no one correct way to read a given piece of literature.

Writing Suggestions

1. Either using some reasons we have given here or developing some reasons of your own, explain why *you* read literary texts.
2. Sometimes a person reads different literary texts (such as poems, short stories, plays) for different reasons. Compare and contrast your reasons for reading any two literary texts of your choice, and discuss the effects of those reasons on your overall reactions to the two texts.

Reading for Multiple Meanings

In discussing the variety of effects that literature can have on its readers' lives, what should be stressed is that most of these effects will be brought about by what the individual reader brings to his or her experience of reading. When we read a text as literature, we do not assume there is a single meaning that readers simply absorb passively: to read a text as literature is to read it in a *polyvalent* way (polyvalent means "having many meanings"). When read in this way, a text can awaken many different readings and experiences. Here is an example.

WILLIAM CARLOS WILLIAMS (1883–1963)

The Great Figure

Among the rain
and lights
I saw the figure 5
in gold
on a red
firetruck
moving
tense
unheeded
to gong clangs
siren howls
and wheels rumbling
through the dark city.

In many ways this poem is very precise in its details. It gives its readers certain information. Yet it requires very active readers—to create a picture in their minds not just from information "in" the poem but from the associations they all have with lights and noises of the city and with speeding fire trucks. All readers have different, emotionally charged, views of cities. They appeal to some people as vibrant and wonderful, whereas to others they are threatening and oppressive. When you read Williams's poem, you can become aware of its polyvalence: it will be read as exciting and alluring by some, as evoking danger and disorder by others. Still other readers will find that it provokes in them simultaneously a sense of energy *and* oppression. No single reading is the "correct" one. The poem's appeal lies in the multiplicity of readings that are possible—and in the subsequent discussion it provokes.

Now let's take a more complex case. When readers discuss a play like Shakespeare's *Macbeth,* they may find they agree on its overall, general effect—that it is gloomy, frightening, and "tragic." But they can take many points of view to explain this effect. Different parts of the experience of reading (or viewing) the play appeal to different readers (or spectators), and these are therefore valued differently. One group of people might see *Macbeth* as the study of a noble, ambitious, but flawed hero; another group may see it as a study of a pernicious murderer and his vicious wife; yet a third group may see the play as raising questions about corruption in a politically destructive society. As a literary text, the play should be read *polyvalently*—to allow it to produce a variety of responses and interpretations.

Writing Suggestions

1. Develop two different readings of Williams's "The Great Figure" in order to illustrate its polyvalence.
2. Choose a text you are reading in class and indicate ways in which it is polyvalent.

Polyvalent Versus Monovalent Readings

Let us contrast a *polyvalent* reading with a *monovalent* reading. In a monovalent reading situation, ambiguities that could lead to polyvalent readings are regarded as hindrances. If, for example, readers feel that the instructions for assembling a bookcase encourage them to read polyvalently, they would call them "unclear" or "ambiguous" and would probably end up with a pile of timber and a sore thumb—and no bookcase! After all, instructions and manuals have an overriding purpose—to help their readers get a particular task done. Of course, you can—if you want—choose to read any text (including instructions on how to build a bookcase) polyvalently or monovalently. If you are reading the instructions for operating your new personal computer, and you read the sentence "move the mouse across the tabletop" as referring to a small furry rodent instead of a piece of equipment, you may show how funny you are, but your computer isn't going to work. Reading monovalently in such circumstances is more conducive to getting your computer functioning efficiently. On the other hand, if you were in fact trying to make a joke, you might well decide to interpret the word "mouse" as a small furry rodent.

So readers generally distinguish "literary" from "non-literary" modes of reading by the degree to which they allow for multiple interpretations. When we come to deal with different literary *genres* later in this book, we will return to the concept of reading generically—poetically, fictionally, and so on.

Writing Suggestion

Bear in mind that while you frequently read literary texts polyvalently and non-literary texts monovalently, it is possible to read any text either way. Take a short passage from a literary and a non-literary text and suggest ways in which each can be read both polyvalently and monovalently.

Becoming Aware of Your Own Repertoire

Students often come into a college literature class convinced that (contrary to the assertions being made here) they have *no* views to bring to the text they are reading. Often that is because they have been taught that their views are irrelevant, uneducated, or confused, and that their literature class is a place where they are supposed to learn to read "properly." It is true that everyone can learn to read *better*—in order to have more interesting reading experiences. But all readers, even the most inexperienced, in fact have a **repertoire** of knowledge about literature and about beliefs, and they bring this repertoire to their reading. All readers bring to their experience of reading a complex (and perhaps never fully analyzable) set of expectations, desires, prejudices, and former experiences (both literary and non-literary), which we are calling their *repertoire*.

In explaining this fundamental notion of repertoire, we have asked our students to analyze the repertoire of assumptions they brought to reading two widely anthologized stories, Anton Chekhov's "The Lady with the Dog," and Joyce Carol Oates's, "The Lady with the Pet Dog" (which is an adaption of the Chekhov story). One student began by saying, "My values really had nothing to do with my reactions to the stories." And yet as she looked more deeply into her response to the stories, she spoke of "identifying" with the characters' dilemmas and of "taking offense" at some of the values that Gurov, the main character in the Chekhov story, embodied: "I found my intelligence insulted by the old-fashioned male point of view. The ways in which he treated and described women made me angry." This student discovered that she was indeed bringing her own values and beliefs to bear on her reading—and that her interpretation of the stories was dramatically affected by them. She was asking *her* own questions of the text—or, more precisely, those questions that her cultural background, her gender, and other socially produced beliefs influenced her to ask.

In Chapters 3 and 4, we will describe the ways a *response statement* (one of which provided us with this student's remarks) can be used very effectively to show the ways that all readers do what she was doing. All readers bring values, prejudices, and assumptions acquired from their social and cultural backgrounds to their readings—and these to a large extent determine the ways they develop their readings of texts. Personal involvement is a crucial and inevitable part of the experience of reading literature. Yet in our experience many students report that they have rarely been asked whether—or even more important *why*—they enjoy reading a text, though they may have been told that they *should* enjoy it. We hope you will be encouraged in this book to do both—to enjoy your reading and to analyze what is going on as you read.

The Reading Situation: An Overview

In the course of this chapter, we will be introducing some important terms. Here we will define and clarify the most important of them. They have arisen from trying to answer such questions as these: What happens in the act of reading a text? What is the relationship between a text's and a reader's general assumptions and beliefs about the world?

Here we will set out, in rather bare fashion, the most important of these terms. If the discussion seems a little abstract, we explain it in more detail in the sections following, giving a number of specific examples.

Our model of the reading process stresses that reading is always **over-determined;** that is, it is the product of multiple factors that work in different combinations to produce different readings. First, what does the *text* bring to the reading situation? When a text is written, it incorporates both explicit and implicit material that is derived from its place within the society's ideology. The term **ideology** refers to the shared though very diverse beliefs, assumptions, habits, and practices of a particular society. Some of these are specifically literary matters, such as whether the author is seen as a unique genius or as a spokesperson for society, what literary genres and conventions are most highly valued, whether women's writing is acceptable, and so forth. We refer to such aspects as the **literary ideology.** We refer to all other, non-literary, matters as the **general ideology.**

Any individual text is written out of its society's general and literary ideology. We call the text's particular appropriation of ideology its repertoire, a term that refers to the particular combination of ideas, experiences, habits, norms, conventions, and assumptions that allows the text to be written. We further divide the repertoire of the text into two kinds. Because we are interested in literary analysis, we can distinguish that part of the repertoire that refers to literary matters as the **literary repertoire.** This would include such matters as literary form, plot, characterization, metrical pattern, and so forth. The non-literary repertoire we term the text's **general repertoire.** This includes such matters as moral ideas, values, religious beliefs, and so forth.

We can represent this scheme by the following diagram:

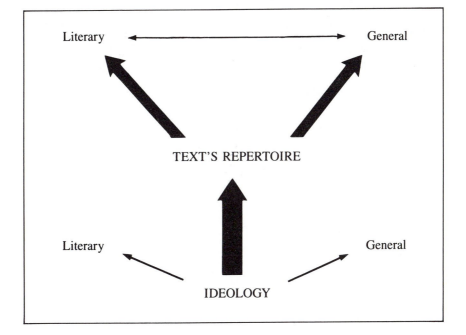

The literary and general repertoire provide the text with its interface with its readers—to whom we now turn.

Readers too are inhabitants of particular sociocultural formations and partake of their society's **ideology**, both **literary** and **general**; they appropriate from that ideology their particular **repertoires.** Likewise, their repertoires consist of specifically *literary* matters—assumptions and beliefs about literature, previous literary experiences, strategies of reading—as well as *general* matters. Again, it is the combination of the literary and non-literary repertoires that provides readers with their interface with the text. We can now add the reader to our representation (see page 17). The ways readers respond to texts will depend on how their general and literary repertoires interact with those of the text. We will term this process a **matching of repertoires.**

Ideology: General and Literary

The most important term relevant to the study of literature is one that we are adapting from political philosophy—*ideology.* This very important (and often very misunderstood) word means those common values, practices, ideas, and assumptions of a particular society that, in fact, hold it together—the deeply ingrained, sometimes only partly conscious, habits, beliefs, and lifestyles of a particular time and place. What we are terming **general ideology** is all those practices that most of a society's inhabitants take for granted as "natural," or "universal," or always true, even if (as we can show by comparing diverse cultures or different historical periods) they are not natural or universal but rather are very specific to a particular culture. Ideology emerges in such ordinary practices of a society as marriage, family arrangements, religious beliefs, education, the value of the individual, the political organizations, and in very ordinary details of lifestyle. Ideology is always characterized by the acceptance of certain ways of living as true or universal or more natural—and the rejection of, even the incomprehensibility of, alternatives.

Writing Suggestions

1. (*a*) List as many characteristics as you can about one aspect—religion, education, the role of women, the family, sexual practices—of your culture's **general ideology.**
   (*b*) Do all these characteristics support one another or do some conflict?
   (*c*) If you have found some conflicts in your culture's general ideology, explore ways in which you think those conflicts might influence the members of the culture.
2. Contrast one aspect of your generation's ideology with that of your parents'. How do such differences affect your and their perception of what is "right," "correct," or "natural" behavior?
3. Contrast one aspect of your culture's ideology with that of another culture.

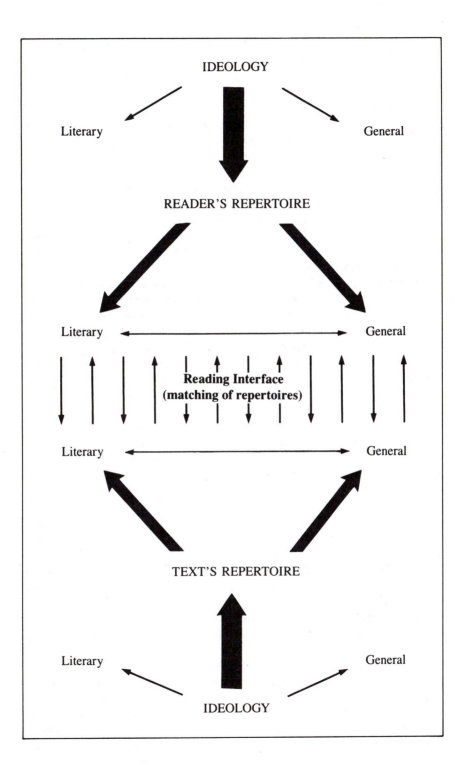

Literary ideology is closely related to a society's general ideology. The term refers to the particular assumptions and practices each society has in relation to literature. All societies have distinct and often quite different sets of ideological presuppositions about literature. Is the writing of novels or poems an important part of the society's life? Is poetry believed to express the personal and individual thoughts of the poet or to voice the common beliefs of the community? Is literature seen as subservient to political orthodoxy or is it felt to be an area of mental and emotional freedom? Is drama considered a religious ritual or just escapist entertainment? Is literature seen as "reflecting" reality?

These are not just technical questions or questions of personal taste. They are questions to which different societies give different answers. Together, the answers reflect the distinctive assumptions of a particular society about the writing and reading of literature. They show us the ways by which a society's **general ideology** is articulated through its literary practices, and they help to determine the particular shape these literary practices take.

Sometimes a period's literary ideology is expressed through the forms by which literature is written. Just because the text that you are now reading takes the form of the book, with three authors listed on the title page, a copyright statement, a preface and so forth, does not mean that texts have always appeared in such form. The form this book takes is one very specific to our culture. In earlier periods, books were also published commercially, but there have been very many different methods of producing "literature," all of which make a difference to the kind of text typical of a given society. Some kinds of fiction (for instance, in the nineteenth century) were serialized (or published in short segments) in magazines before being published completely in book form. In some societies, private publication was the rule. In some cultures, works were not written down at all. Many stories in the past were retold orally for many generations (for example, the works of Homer), and many of the lyrics written in the Renaissance (for example, by Sidney or Donne) were never printed in their authors' lifetimes.

All of these ways in which texts are produced affect the kinds of literature that are dominant in a particular period. They also affect the expectations readers will have of their reading experiences. Readers of Dickens's serialized novels, for example, knew that the story's climax would follow a certain pattern, created to fit its publication in magazines. Poets in an oral culture compose with repeated, easily memorizable formulae. Playwrights working for the commercial theater will try to create works that their audiences will appreciate and buy tickets to see. All of these methods of production affect the characteristics of the literary texts of their period.

Or take poetry. Today poetry is often published by small presses in limited editions; it can also (though rarely) be given mass publication. Most typically, it appears in little magazines—like *Poetry, Slipstream, Yankee,* or thousands of others. But in the past it was often not published at all: it might have been simply distributed by hand among a small group of the poet's friends (as was usually the case in Shakespeare's time). Or take drama. For much of the past, plays were not thought of as "literature" at all but merely as popular entertainment. Consider the differences between a Shakespeare play as a *script* for a theater performance and the play as a piece of *literature* in a textbook.

Likewise, different kinds of readings seem to be preferred by different historical periods. We can see this, for example, in the ways Shakespeare's plays have changed their meanings over time. During the eighteenth century, Shakespeare's comedies were generally regarded as "true to life" and natural, and were usually preferred to his tragedies, the emotions of which were felt to be rather excessive and contradictory. From the late nineteenth century on, the tragedies, particularly *Hamlet* and *King Lear,* have been preferred. *King Lear* is today often regarded as one of the greatest works of art ever created—usually because it seems to raise, most powerfully and painfully, questions central to our experiences and our fears in this century.

The general and literary ideology of one's culture are important influences on the reading (and writing) of texts. They don't have to be discussed fully and exhaustively whenever you do a "reading" of a literary text. That would certainly spoil the fun of, say, lying in a hammock with a good book, or listening to a poet give a reading in a restaurant or an auditorium. But when you want to understand the importance of a text and the potential impact of literature upon its readers and upon your society, then you need to consider them.

Writing Suggestion

The **literary ideology** of any culture is made up of conflicting attitudes. For example, many people today think that "best sellers" are the most interesting fiction written. They consider themselves well read if they buy and read the latest Book-of-the-Month Club selection. Other people, in contrast, frequently disdain best sellers, assuming (perhaps without reading them) that they must be "trash," about sex and violence if they appeal to "the masses." Discuss similar contradictions and their effects on *your* reading choices in relation to science fiction, pulp romances, "good literature," poetry, drama, or pornography.

The General Repertoire of the Text
Dominant and Counter-Dominant Views

Every time you read a work from the distant past, you encounter assumptions, beliefs, and perspectives that differ from your own. The perspectives of the text—its attitudes about moral values, social practices, and so forth—make up its **general repertoire.** As a reader, you too have a general repertoire, that is, a set of values, assumptions, beliefs, and expectations that influence the questions you put to literature. The interaction of the text's general repertoire with your own can help make you aware of cultural differences between your time and the time the text was written.

For example, when reading Sophocles' play *Antigone,* you may be a little shocked to discover that the bodies of traitors to the state were, by custom, not allowed to be buried but were displayed in public until they rotted and turned to bones. The general repertoire of the text simultaneously accepts this practice (by the actions of Creon) and challenges it (by the actions of Antigone). The repertoire of a text, like your own, can often be complex and contradictory. Or you become aware from Shakespeare's *Romeo and Juliet* that the dominant views in Shakespeare's age took for granted that a father had virtually complete control over his daughter's life—especially over whom she married. Yet, like *Antigone, Romeo and Juliet* also introduces the *counter-dominant* view that such practices are cruel and destructive. When reading texts from an earlier period, you can recognize the historical distancing between the original time the work was written and the time it is being read: the views that were counter-dominant in these two texts are now *dominant.* Does this mean you find the work unapproachable or irrelevant? Should such matters be ignored, or should you concentrate on more seemingly "universal" matters?

Writing Suggestions

1. (*a*) Examine the general repertoire of an older text you have read, and discuss ways in which it embodies both the dominant and counter-dominant views of its time.

   (*b*) Are the counter-dominant views of this older text dominant or counter-dominant in your own time?

"Universal Themes" Are Historically and Culturally Produced

The question of "universal" meanings in literature is a commonly discussed one. It's often thought that "great" works of literature are somehow timeless and universal, that they include values and experiences shared by most men and women in all times and places. According to this view, outdated aspects of a work should be ignored and instead the "universal" concerns or themes stressed. But the more specifically you analyze so-called universal themes, the more you may realize that they are historically and culturally produced variables. The ideas and feelings we have about love, say, are not the same as those of Chaucer or Shakespeare or Milton. You may talk about love with a common vocabulary, yet you often mean quite different things and have quite different assumptions.

Anne Bradstreet's poem "To My Dear and Loving Husband," for example, was written in America in the middle of the seventeenth century and addresses feelings and attitudes that are particular to her society. You can still recognize them in part (even though they might seem a little old-fashioned) because our society still praises marriage, still looks favorably on husbands and wives who love each other:

ANNE BRADSTREET (1612–1672)

To My Dear and Loving Husband

If ever two were one, then surely we.
If ever man were lov'd by wife, then thee;
If ever wife was happy in a man,
Compare with me ye women if you can.
I prize thy love more than whole Mines of gold,   5
Or all the riches that the East doth hold.
My love is such that Rivers cannot quench,
Nor ought but love from thee, give recompence.
Thy love is such I can no way repay,
The heavens reward thee manifold I pray.   10
Then while we live, in love let's so persevere,
That when we live no more, we may live ever.

While you may still understand such attitudes, the views of marriage in this poem—which are part of the general repertoire of the poem—are in some ways very different from those dominant today. Some investigation into the place and period in which the poem was written (colonial America) can show you important historical differences. Marriage was not seen as a matching of equals as it generally is today, so that the assertion that "if ever two were one, then surely we" is not assuming the same kind of equality that readers of today probably would. It might, in fact, be quite a daring assertion. A woman was (literally) her husband's property; marriage was sanctioned not simply by society but by God. Once readers learn such information about marriage in colonial America, the way in which their and the text's repertoires match may well change significantly. The poem might be somewhat diminished in readers' eyes if they see its repertoire as sexist or retrogressive; on the other hand, it might make them admire Bradstreet's assertions of a certain degree of equality in an age when it was not taken for granted.

Another aspect of the poem that might be either familiar or unfamiliar to you, depending on your general repertoire, is its religious ideas. The poem's last line contains the appropriately pious hope that a Puritan would have, that when the loving couple die, they will live forever in a life after death. Do you share such views? When a modern lover swears that he or she will love someone "forever," is the meaning the same as in Bradstreet's prayer? Does the secularization of the Western world since the seventeenth century affect your reading of those lines? Once again, historical differences between the general repertoires of the text and the reader may produce quite different readings today.

Either way, with love and religion alike, you become aware that you are not dealing with "universal" or "timeless" themes when you read a literary text; you are, rather, encountering real historical and cultural differences. The ways in which your general repertoire intersects with that of the text will determine your response to the poem.

Writing Suggestions

1. (a) How did you respond to Bradstreet's poem, both before you read our discussion of it and after?

   (b) Do you see it as embodying both dominant and counter-dominant views of its time? What aspects of its general repertoire do you find yourself agreeing with? What aspects do you disagree with?

2. (a) Discuss what you consider to be "universal themes" or attitudes in the general repertoire of another text you are studying.

   (b) Explain why those "universal themes" are really culture-specific either by discussing a cultural situation in which they would not seem "true" or by explaining some ways in which different cultures have *translated* these themes to suit their own purposes.

The General Repertoire of the Reader

Different readings arise in part because each reader brings to a text a different general repertoire—a set of culturally conditioned experiences, beliefs, knowledge, and expectations, about such matters as politics, religion, morality, lifestyle, love, education, and so forth. Whenever you read, you test—often unconsciously—whether your repertoire matches or intersects with that of a text. The influence of your repertoire on your reading is often invisible to you until you encounter interpretations that differ from your own. For example, you may sympathize with the narrator in Gilman's story "The Yellow Wallpaper" because you believe that people with psychological problems should be treated with dignity and respect, and not with patronizing disdain as her husband seems to treat her. Another reader, who believes that many psychological problems could be avoided if self-indulgent people only disciplined and controlled themselves, might be annoyed with the narrator's inability to maintain a grasp on reality. In neither instance can these reactions to the narrator be said to be solely dependent on the information given about her in the story. You may at first think that your sympathy toward the narrator is dictated by the text, but when you discover that other readers respond quite differently to her, you then recognize the role of your general repertoire—in this case, your beliefs about the nature and treatment of mental illness—in creating your response.

Many different repertoires can therefore develop within any society's general ideology. After all, there's probably never been an issue on which everyone thought exactly alike. But the *dominant* ideology of any period makes some beliefs seem more plausible than others and also necessarily *excludes* certain interpretive possibilities from consideration. For example, none of you would probably interpret the narrator in "The Yellow Wallpaper" as speaking either in the voice of god or in the voice of the devil, although these interpretations of madness would have been quite possible—indeed the norm—in an earlier historical time.

Many of the texts you read in a literature course come from a distant historical period. You may consult reference books, books of criticism, biographies, dictionaries, or histories to enlarge your repertoire—to give yourself clues about the characteristic beliefs and lifestyles of a given time. But enlarging your repertoire in this way doesn't mean that somehow you move back in time. After all, you live in the late twentieth century, not in Shakespeare's England or Nathaniel Hawthorne's New England. You read a text in your own time, not in the time in which it was written. So you read it with questions and interests that come into existence because of your particular place in history. The text offers you clues and perspectives by which you may put meanings together, but it is always you, the reader, not the author, and not the author's original audience, who formulates that meaning, who decides what perspective to adopt. A good writer tries to employ as many strategies as possible to attract a reader's curiosity, interest, and involvement, and in that way influences his or her readers. But you and you alone establish the meanings of the texts you read on the basis of your repertoire. You bring your own associations to help make meanings from the text, and your readings will therefore often be quite different from the writer's or the original audience's. You may be female or male, black or white, middle-aged or young, and these factors will influence your readings. You bring many gender-specific, race-specific, generation-specific, and culture-specific questions to your reading. You often respond immediately (positively or negatively) to certain reading experiences you feel strongly about. And, of course, you can change your readings of texts very drastically if your life experiences change. Everyone at some time has had the experience of rereading a novel or a poem and interpreting it quite differently because of what has happened in the interim.

Our fundamental point is that the beliefs you have as a person affect you as a reader: reading is not something you do independent of your historical situation. Perhaps the most persuasive of the reasons for reading literature we discussed earlier is to make readers look at themselves, their society, and their history in fresh, stimulating, and sometimes disturbing ways.

Writing Suggestions

1. Frequently when you enjoy reading a text, it is because your general repertoire—your attitudes and beliefs—matches those of the text. Discuss a text that you like and analyze two ways in which your general repertoire and that of the text interact.
2. Discuss a text that you did *not* like or one that disturbed you. Analyze two ways in which your general repertoire clashed with that of the text and explore the ways in which your cultural situation influenced you to develop views that conflicted with those of the text.

3. Give an example of how, either inside or outside of class, you have enlarged your repertoire about a particular text, by learning more about its historical setting, its initial reception, the ways it has been interpreted by other readers, and so forth. In what ways, if at all, did enlarging your repertoire change your response to the text?

The Literary Repertoire of the Text

What are the specifically *literary* aspects of the text's repertoire? What are the text features that interact with the reader's *literary* repertoire? The text's literary repertoire is made up of the literary **conventions** it follows and its formal **text strategies.** For example, stories have *plots* and *characters* and are often told from particular *points of view*. Many traditional poems have formal rhyme schemes and meters. Plays are often divided into acts and frequently follow the convention of rising action, climax, and falling action. Essays follow certain rhetorical structures whereby an argument is introduced, expanded upon, contradictory points refuted, and the argument restated. When you investigate your responses to a text, you may find that certain text strategies greatly influenced you. For example, Dave Smith's poem "Messenger" (see page 78 for text) is told from the first-person perspective, although the "I" shifts back and forth from a child to an adult. The poem also describes a severe storm and a landslide, events that can be read either literally or figuratively. The shift in ages of the "I" of the poem and the ambiguity of the storm imagery are both text strategies.

Older models for reading literature often emphasized the study of these formal features—plot, rhyme scheme, point of view—to the exclusion of everything else. But when you read, you can never examine all the strategies of a text, and we do not advocate that you examine any of them purely for the sake of noting their existence. While your reading of a text can be enhanced by paying attention to the fact that it is, say, a sonnet written in iambic pentameter, such matters constitute only part of the text's repertoire. What is important is how text strategies influence the way you read and respond to the text.

Another part of the text's literary repertoire is its **blanks** or **gaps**—absences of connections—that readers must fill in order to make sense of the text. Obvious gaps occur between the end of one chapter and the beginning of the next in a novel where readers must use their imaginations to decide what happened in between. Another more subtle gap is the *theme* of a story, which is never explicitly stated. Characters are described and conflicts occur, but "what it's all about" is a gap that the reader must fill in. The lack of exact directions to actors in a play also constitutes a gap. In Shakespeare's *Hamlet*, for example, Hamlet tries to trick King Claudius into revealing his guilt by having a group of actors perform a mime and a play, both of which are fairly obvious in their meaning to an audience. The text, however, does not specify what the king is doing while Hamlet's two little plays are being acted. Does the king get the point at first? Does he understand the trick? Why does he wait for the second play? The director and actors must fill in these gaps and decide what the king's facial expressions will be, how he will move, where he will sit. And no two directors will fill these gaps in exactly the same way. Gaps in any text allow readers much interpretive freedom.

Texts also contain **indeterminacies** or ambiguities—words, phrases, idioms so general in their application that they need to be filled out with the reader's own personal meanings. When you read Robert Burns's line "O My Luve's like a red, red rose," what is "my love"? More particularly as *you* read that line, who is *your* love? Is she aggressive, intelligent, excitable, personable, witty, flirtatious? Is he strong, carefree, sensitive, considerate, bad-tempered? As readers read "my love," they bring their own meanings to that *indeterminate* phrase.

Another kind of indeterminacy is the description of a character or a setting: the text once again gives readers certain details, but not all. In Hawthorne's romance *The Scarlet Letter,* the forest where the two tragic lovers, Hester Prynne and Arthur Dimmesdale, meet is sometimes described in detail and sometimes in generic rather than specific terms. A reader must fill out the setting both in terms of specific details and of its significance.

The literary repertoire of the text, therefore, affects your response to a greater or lesser extent depending on your degree of attunement to it. While you cannot be attuned to all the conventions, strategies, gaps, and indeterminacies of a text, you must be attuned to a number of them if you are to develop a persuasive and original reading of it.

Writing Suggestions

1. (*a*) List as many text strategies in a particular poem or a short story as you can.
   (*b*) What particular text strategies, such as kinds of rhyme or certain points of view, are you most likely to notice when reading?
   (*c*) Compare and contrast the effects on you of two different formal text strategies.
2. (*a*) Discuss a text you have read that has an apparent gap in it.
   (*b*) In what ways did you fill in this gap?
3. (*a*) Discuss a poem you have read that has a number of ambiguities in it.
   (*b*) How did you read these ambiguities?
   (*c*) Is your reading monovalent or polyvalent?

The Literary Repertoire of the Reader

As we discussed the text's repertoire, it became obvious that it was impossible to ignore the reader's part in responding to it. A *matching of repertoires,* that is, the intersection of the text's features and the reader's expectations, occurs whenever readers read. Readers' **literary repertoires** are their assumptions and knowledge about what literature "is" or "should be" based on their previous reading. Most readers, for instance, assume that a story will have certain conventions such as clear characterization, some degree of tension that will eventually be resolved, and a good plot. Readers expect to find these conventions in a story because the majority of stories have them and because they are often those aspects of a story discussed in English classes.

Some readers have a narrow repertoire that is based on a combination of their reading experiences and their personal taste: they may think that poetry means only formal rhymed verse because that is the only kind of poems they have read. As you will see later, it is possible to enlarge your repertoire by exposing yourself to new and different types of texts from those you usually read, but how you respond to any text—familiar or unfamiliar—will always depend on the assumptions that you bring to it. If you expect all stories to be realistic, you will probably find yourself puzzled by Kafka's "The Hunger Artist": it seems senseless if you try to read it as a realistic story. One way to try to understand it is to enlarge your literary repertoire to include the conventions of *absurdism* as well as *realism*. Familiarizing yourself with absurdism may not help you like "The Hunger Artist," but it will broaden the expectations you have for reading and categorizing stories.

Readers' **cognitive styles** and **reading strategies** also affect their literary repertoires. Cognitive style is the general way in which people take in, process, and react to what they perceive. For example, some people temperamentally have developed a much higher tolerance for *ambiguity* than others. They enjoy opening up multiple meanings of texts and are happy to read a text without reducing it to a single meaning. They tend to read connotatively much more readily than others. In texts and in general conversation, they may frequently see many possible meanings, enjoy *double entendres,* and like to pun. Other people, with contrasting cognitive styles, tend to read literally: whether they are reading a poem or a letter from a friend, they do not so readily "read between the lines." But keep in mind that whatever your cognitive style, you can always enrich it by expanding your assumptions about reading and your reading strategies.

Reading strategies are the various techniques you use to process a text. You may, for example, use some of the following reading strategies:

- create themes
- identify with characters
- look for a consistent point of view
- create literal-figurative distinctions
- fill in gaps
- relate the text to other texts you have read
- relate the text to personal experiences
- respond to certain *text strategies* (such as viewpoint, tone, meter, mood)
- read playfully for multiple meanings
- relate your "personal" response to the text to larger aspects of your culture

Some readers, for example, will feel challenged by a complex and ambiguous story such as John Barth's "Lost in the Funhouse." They will read and reread it slowly and carefully, trying to make sense of it. Other readers might choose to ignore its ambiguities by paying attention only to those parts that make sense to them immediately. Others might try to understand the story by placing it in a larger context of other similar texts they've read.

Some of your reading strategies will develop as a response to certain text strategies that you encounter. In the approach to reading we advocate here, we suggest that, regardless of what kind of text you are reading, you actively adopt strategies that will "open" the text up to multiple meanings and place it in larger cognitive and cultural contexts. To do this, it is often necessary for you to read texts "against the grain," that is, to use reading strategies that defy text strategies in order to develop—what we call in the next section—strong readings.

Writing Suggestions

1. (a) Define, in as much detail as you can, your *cognitive style,* that is, the processes by which you read texts of any kind. Do you skim? Do you read slowly and carefully? Do you try to "get the gist"? Do you work to develop counter-arguments?

   (b) Do you like certain formal text strategies more than others? Why, for instance, might you like *first-person* narration better than *third-person?*

   (c) Do you like poems to use a lot of images or to be abstract? In novels, do you like long descriptions of what characters look like?

   (d) Do you like texts with many gaps?

   (e) Do you like poems with many ambiguities?

   (f) What do your likes and dislikes tell you about your reading processes and cognitive style?

2. Of the reading strategies listed on page 26, which are you most likely to adopt when reading a poem, a play, or a short story?

3. (a) Analyze your response to a literary text of your choosing, explaining what reading strategies you used to match particular text strategies.

   (b) What does your choice of particular reading strategies tell you about your expectations of what literature should be and about your cognitive style?

4. In what ways do you feel you need to, or would like to, enlarge your literary repertoire?

Strong Readings

There is never a perfect fit in the matching of repertoires between reader and text. As you build up your reading of a text, you ask your own questions of the text, establishing a dialogue with it on both literary and more general issues.

Some texts provide their readers with very explicit directions on how they wish to be read. You can resist them, fight back as it were, but often your best enjoyment comes, initially at least, from following the directions in which the text wants to take you. An insistent text often has a powerful literary repertoire: it may have a very concentrated argument or use very forceful accumulated metaphors. Such strategies may be designed to guide or limit your readings—to give you definite "boundary conditions" by which your reading is to some extent controlled. You may, in such a situation, be content to adapt your repertoire to that of the text.

In contrast—and this becomes increasingly true as texts raise disturbing questions for you—you may want to acknowledge that your repertoire does not exactly match the text's, and you may choose to explore those differences. For example, you may find that you are not sympathetic to the character of Hedda in Ibsen's play *Hedda Gabler,* even though you feel that the text wants you to be. You may argue that anyone silly enough to marry such a dull man as Tesman, and anyone cruel enough to burn the manuscript of a man she loves, deserves her fate. In other words, you may refuse to see Hedda as a victim of circumstance because your general repertoire suggests to you that people are responsible for their own destinies. We emphatically encourage you to develop such interpretations—to create what we term **strong readings.**

A strong reading of a text is a clearly articulated reading that self-consciously goes "against the grain" of a text. A strong reading is *not* a misreading. Nor is it perverse or imperceptive. It can only develop if a reader is aware of the dominant text strategies and chooses, for various reasons, be they literary or cultural, to read the text differently. You can recognize that a text may want you to respond in a given manner, but you may *choose* to use your cultural awareness to resist that prescribed way of reading. You become thereby a strong, independent reader. This kind of reading is one we wish very much to encourage—where you define a particular perspective on a text, develop it persuasively, and articulate its implications.

Such an approach requires you to become very self-aware of what you are doing. You become like an interrogator or a detective. This text has designs on me, you might say. How did the text become as it is? And what effect does its demands have on me? Do I agree with it or do I want to argue with it? Are the issues it raises ones I recognize?

In a passage in John Fowles's novel *The French Lieutenant's Woman,* the narrator imagines himself sitting in a railroad car opposite one of his own characters. He looks across at the character and asks himself: "Now, what can I do with you?" Fowles presents that attitude as the *writer's,* but it also should be a *reader's* attitude. What can you do with the texts you read that is interesting, that will stimulate other readers?

Arguments for Developing Strong Readings

Readers may choose to construct strong readings for various reasons. First, you may discover that your repertoire or your ideological perspective is at such odds with that of the text that you cannot passively accept the text's position, and you feel you must read the text "against the grain." You may find a well-known love poem so sexist in its assumptions that you have to read it from a feminist perspective (see page 172 in Chapter 5).

Or you may see significances in a text, particularly an older one, that you know were not part of the author's repertoire but that are so relevant to your culture that you feel they need to be articulated. For example, you may interpret the "tyger" in William Blake's poem "The Tyger," written in the late eighteenth century, as suggesting the power of nuclear energy, even though it could not have meant that for Blake. Or else you may deliberately try to read like someone else, from perspectives other than your own seemingly natural one, say, from a feminist, a political, or a fundamentalist position. In that way, you learn what it is like to read from a particular perspective different from your own.

Are There Limits to Interpretation?

Becoming a strong reader does not mean one should produce a bizarre or "subjective" reading of a poem for its own sake. For example, we do not advocate an approach in which readers arbitrarily decide that all poems they read are about baseball just because they are baseball fans. *Strong* readings, because they go against the grain of the text (or against the readings of many of your classmates), must be justified by a clear analysis of how your own interests, beliefs, and preoccupations demand the quite different reading you are presenting. To learn to produce strong readings often involves hard work. You must look at your assumptions closely; you may have to do research and defend your position in detail. But the more you do these things, the more your readings become powerful—and your own.

At this point we ask a familiar question: What limits are there to interpretation? Can, in fact, one say just *anything* about a text? How can one tell a good from a bad interpretation? There is a very serious sense in which *no* interpretation of a poem can be ruled out so long as it is presented logically, well developed and supported, and engaging to hear or read. Those characteristics alone will usually mean that your interpretation isn't too bizarre. Except as a joke, you aren't likely to say that Shakespeare's Sonnet 18 is about the 1987 World Series! But let us look at a less extreme example of a reading of Shakespeare's Sonnet 18, which begins:

Shall I compare thee to a summer's day?
Thou art more lovely and more temperate.

What if someone says that these lines are about the weather forecast? Well, you might say, that's stupid and impossible. But clearly such a response is based on something—on the presence of the words "summer" and "temperate," probably. What you should do is ask such a reader to account for his or her reading—to analyze how both the text and the reader contributed to it and how it is to be elaborated and extended further. What inevitably happens if the reader attempts to make such an elaboration is that the reading can't be taken any further, in which case it is recognized as merely trivial—or else if it can be elaborated, with prompting and discussion, it may turn into something more interesting. For instance "summer" can start to be seen not only literally as the subject of the lines, but metaphorically as a way of trying to explain human emotions by analogy with the seasons. And that is an interesting topic, one that poets and readers have brooded over for many centuries.

So rather than think that your own tentative readings might be "wrong" or "misreadings," try to develop them and see where they lead. Analyze the reading strategies (page 26) you're bringing to the text: maybe you need to try additional strategies. Analyze also the text strategies that are prompting your reading and—perhaps above all—talk and argue about your reading of the text with others. You may, in fact, discover that your original hunch was a productive one—it just needed further development. Part of the fun of reading is the community it creates. In fact, it's the existence of a community of readers that will prevent your own reading from becoming too bizarre or boring. Maybe you *can* justify a reading of Shakespeare's poem as being about the 1987 World Series: weird as that sounds, equally bizarre readings of literary texts have been made by reputable critics and writers.

In practice, some readings will certainly seem more bizarre or less acceptable than others. This is so not because they are necessarily less "correct" but because they are less dominant in our culture. Thus, if you choose to give a text a bizarre reading, you must be prepared to justify it in relation to more dominant readings of your classmates. And who knows? Your strange or unusual or marginal reading might eventually become the dominant reading.

When you find yourself choosing the kind of reading you want to do of a poem—when you can justify and elaborate it in detail and persuade *your* audience of its interest—then you are becoming a strong reader.

Writing Suggestions

1. Have you ever done a strong reading of a text? If so, what reasons did you have for doing it?
2. What advantages and disadvantages do you see for yourself in trying to do a strong reading of a text?
3. (*a*) Select a text that you have read in an English class, preferably one about which the class reached a consensus reading that you might not have completely agreed with.

   (*b*) Explain what the consensus reading was and, as much as possible, analyze the repertoires (literary and general) and the reading strategies that helped to produce that reading.

   (*c*) Develop your own strong reading that goes against the grain of the class's reading.

   (*d*) Justify your reading by explaining ways in which your general and literary repertoire differed from that of the class.

Checkpoints for Chapter 1

1. Reading involves the contributions of *both* reader and text.
2. There is no one "correct" meaning of any text.
3. Reading and writing are both cognitive and cultural processes, not purely individual matters.
4. People read literary texts for many reasons, but reading is always an interactive process.
5. Literary texts lend themselves to *polyvalent* readings—that is, they encourage diverse readings.
6. Reading involves a matching of repertoires, literary and general.
7. A person's general and literary repertoires derive from society's general and literary ideologies.
8. The most interesting kinds of readings are *strong* readings that take a self-conscious position.

℟ Chapter 2
Language, History, Culture

The Pull of Ideology

Sigmund Freud once said that when a man and woman marry, they always bring other people with them into the marriage bed—most notably, of course, their parents. The point is that everything that any of us does is interconnected with the rest of our lives, especially with our biological and cultural inheritances. And the more emotionally charged any particular experience is, the more complex that interconnectedness will be.

Reading literature can be such an experience. So can listening to music, watching a movie, or even (for some people) watching a football game. One can say that when a text and reader "marry," they are no more alone than Freud's husband and wife. They each bring with them interconnections with their society's ideology. But these interconnections are always multiple, a situation sociologists call **overdetermination**—an interaction, perhaps never fully analyzable, of the forces affecting all people: social, cultural, political, psychological, as well as literary.

When you read or write, you are inevitably affected, perhaps only partly consciously, by assumptions, desires, and habits derived from your society's **general** and **literary ideologies.** Nobody can escape the pull of ideology, which is what defines everyone's place in history. You can certainly extend your knowledge of other places, other histories, other ideologies—as well as your own. That is an important part of what education is for. But you can never take wings and somehow stand above your own place in human history.

The assumptions you bring to your reading from your society's general ideology make a real difference to the kinds of readings you do of texts. If you write a response statement on an Elizabethan love poem, for instance, in which a woman is praised for her beauty, it is important to become aware of how your assumptions about sexual equality and gender differences may affect your reading. Do you read the poem differently if you are a man or a woman? Or consider political beliefs. Milton's epic *Paradise Lost* raises many questions about the nature of political authority and obedience. As someone living in the late twentieth century, how do your political beliefs influence the kind of reading you choose to do of that poem? Such questions, you should note, avoid entirely the old issue of "right" and "wrong" readings. They focus instead on your *choosing* to do certain kinds of readings and on your taking responsibility for your readings, as indeed you must for other actions you take in the world at large.

Writing Suggestions

1. Do you think men and women read and write differently because of their gender?
2. Choose a literary work written before the twentieth century. What political or religious issues that you find interesting today would influence your reading of it?

The Reader's Context: Language, History, Culture

In this chapter, we suggest ways in which you can enrich your understanding of how general ideology affects the reading and writing of texts. Often this is the most difficult aspect of reading to analyze. When you read a poem in a textbook, it may not seem that it needs to be connected to the underlying ideas, beliefs, assumptions that shaped it. There it is, right on the page! Reading it just seems to be a matter of the text and you. Similarly, while it is relatively easy to recognize that each reader has distinctive beliefs, ideas, and assumptions, it is much more difficult to see how these are relevant to the reading process. To try to isolate the text as a container of meaning or to isolate the reader as a unique individual is to pretend that texts and readers can escape the pull of ideology. It also turns reading into a less interesting affair. The dynamic nature of reading can only be recognized if it is studied in a cultural context.

In this chapter, we develop a model for you to explore the different contexts in which you read. The model is made up of three interlocking components:

1. Language
2. History
3. Culture

This model provides a way of structuring the kinds of questions that readers bring to bear on literary texts, of systematizing the issues that affect you as you read and write, and of studying the repertoires of texts and readers.

We see the human **subject** (you, Pam Horn, David Sokolow, William Shakespeare, or Bruce Springsteen) as the conjunction of these three factors, *language, history,* and *culture.* That is, no one is separate from the values and traditions that have produced him or her. There is no "unique" or "essential" *me* that I can somehow detach from language, history, and culture. While each person possesses specific and often very varied and interesting—even quirky—characteristics, none of these characteristics can be said to be purely "individual." They all derive from the subject's being situated in larger contexts, whether social, cultural, biological, or gender-related. You are, perhaps, the descendant of Irish immigrants or German-Dutch farmers; you may be middle class or the son of a western Pennsylvania steelworker. Your supposedly unique or personal character traits have been developed and reinforced in you by your immediate family context as well as broader cultural contexts of education and society. You may rebel against this background, but it is there, something that has helped make you what you are.

Ours is a society saturated with many, often contradictory, languages and codes (sometimes called **discourses**), from television to school texts to politics. More broadly, you exist in a particular conjunction of social and cultural forces, variously called twentieth-century, Western, or American civilization. That all these factors bring you into being does not, however, make you simply an automaton. In fact, the effect is just the opposite. Because so many varied, and frequently contradictory, forces produce all of us as subjects, none of us is exactly the same. Some people's orientation will overlap, some won't. It is the very multiplicity of our culture that makes us different. Our "freedom" (to use the word we Americans admire so much, which is so centrally a part of *our* dominant ideology) is precisely the product of the multiple contradictory forces, the *overdetermination,* of our lives.

In this chapter, therefore, we will examine each of these three factors, *language, history,* and *culture,* to show how they apply to the reading of literary and other texts.

Language

Language Both Is "Written by" and "Writes" Its Users

An older (but still prevalent) view of language saw it as a kind of tool. According to such a view, language is something people can learn to control, something that lies around like a pair of pliers or a tennis racket that can be picked up and used whenever a speaker feels like it. If people don't use it well, they can try to improve: they try to serve like Boris Becker or return serve like Martina Navratilova. This view of language as an *instrument* says:

1. You first have ideas.
2. You then find language to express them.
3. Some word or phrase will *exactly* fit what you want to say.

But language doesn't work like that. Without language, there would be no ideas. Recall our discussion in Chapter 1 of the relationship between signifiers and signifieds. One word (or *signifier*) not only can mean many things (or *signifieds*) but it is the very existence of signifiers, of language, that enables people to perceive the world the way they do. When speakers of different languages are given a spectrum of colors from blue to green and are asked to locate where the blue shifts into green, they draw the boundary between blue and green in different places. One then cannot say that blue is *objectively* this color and green *objectively* that color: the perception of differences in blue and green depends on a person's culture and language system.

We can therefore say that people's perceptions of the world are contingent upon their knowledge of language, not that they simply use languages as a tool to describe what they perceive. In this sense we say that people both are *written by* and *write* their language and their culture; that is, they in one sense form statements in language, but in another powerful sense are formed by their language.

Language Pre-Exists Its Users

Language, in the broadest sense, pre-exists its users: people are born into language communities; that is, they are *given* words, symbols, and codes to live by. We say "given" because language comes to people from their societies, families, and other communities, which (like language) they did not create, and within which they are taught to communicate and conceptualize.

Yet language is also the means by which people find their places within their world and by which they are defined. Although it is a continually changing set of words, codes, and symbols, language allows its users to articulate their striving for coherence, communication, and communion. When you try to communicate to other people such concepts as love, justice, integrity, or violence, you do so in language that you did not invent yourself, that belongs to society as a whole, not to you as an individual, but that allows you, nonetheless, to communicate your ideas.

Every word that you use has been used by millions of other people before you, and you often use words that carry with them assumptions you're not aware of. When you fall in (or out) of love and say things like "My heart is broken," or "She was as cold as ice," you probably aren't aware that these phrases come from deep in your cultural past, that they developed in a culture with very different views about love from your own, where people perhaps *did* believe the loss of love literally broke one's heart. Or when you say "I can see the sun rise," you forget that people once believed that the earth stood still and the sun rose (and set) around it. When you use the word *individual* in such a sentence as "The individual is more important than the group," you may not know that an earlier dominant meaning of "individual" was precisely "a member of a group."

Thus signifiers that you now use have had different signifieds throughout history: while the words or expressions have remained the same, their meanings have changed. Similarly, within any particular historical period, signifiers will also have diverse signifieds. The sentence, "Yanks seek victory over Reds," for example, will mean one thing to a baseball fan and something very different to a post-war geopolitical expert. Changes in context will also change what a sentence signifies. Look at the simple sentence, "The tree fell!" and imagine how you would react to it at Christmas time ("Oh, no! How many ornaments broke?") versus after a storm ("Get out the chain saw."). People use language, but it does not belong to them. They can never make it mean one thing because it is part of a system much larger than they are.

To study language is to study the ways by which people are written by the codes of their world. It is simultaneously to study how people try, literally, to make *their* marks in the world and how you can acquire and use the power that language offers you. You can do this systematically by studying *semiotics*—the ways language systems and codes operate in written and spoken language, in music, advertisements, journalism, fashion. You can also study language through literature, which is often described as language at its most intense and evocative. People are created as social beings by all these systems of signs. That makes them *subjects:* both *subject to,* in the sense of being formed and controlled by these systems of signs; and the *subject,* in the sense of the "I" or agent of a sentence, the user of these systems of signs. All the discourses of a culture envelop its members in a network so total that people can't express themselves outside it. Language is not a reflection of a non-linguistic reality—our use of language *creates* that reality for us.

We conclude with three statements that counter the traditional view of language as a tool:

1. Language precedes all of us.
2. Without language, we could not have ideas.
3. No one-to-one correspondence exists between a signifier and a signified either across or within cultures; thus no word or phrase will *exactly* fit what you want to say.

Language Is Always Value Laden

In our classes, we constantly draw our students' attention to the ways in which the most (seemingly) innocent language carries deep ideological values, even in newspapers, on television, on the radio, and in ordinary conversation. In all these contexts, language may at first seem more like a simple means for communicating ideas rather than a value-laden purveyor of ideology. But because language is always used in social contexts, there is *no* value-free language. To show this, we give students four similar sentences:

1. Ronald Reagan is the leader of the American government.
2. Ronald Reagan is the leader of the American regime.
3. Daniel Ortega is the leader of the Nicaraguan government.
4. Daniel Ortega is the leader of the Nicaraguan regime.

We ask students to focus on the differences among these sentences and to state which sentences, if any, are objective, and why. Their initial reaction is generally that "American regime" sounds peculiar, even wrong, and certainly not "objective," whereas "Nicaraguan regime" is a familiar phrase; it sounds less biased and more objective. Likewise, whereas "American government" sounds neutral and therefore objective, "Nicaraguan government" seems slightly less so, as if "we were favoring their political system," as one student put it.

What surprises students is that the dictionary or *denotative* meaning of the two words is virtually the same. What differentiates the words are the *connotations,* the culturally produced, ideologically laden associations that different speakers bring to them. As one student wrote, "I have always associated the word 'regime' with systems of government that both I and my family find unacceptable." In our country, the word *regime* is seen as pejorative whereas *government* is not. As to whether any of the sentences were objective, one student wrote: "Objectivity depends on where you are standing." Other students expressed similar viewpoints: "Since I am a patriotic American, I am biased toward the democratic idea of our government. *Our* use of the word *government* is equated with our own system." This student argued further: "What might seem to us to be a fair and objective statement concerning the American government might be a farce to someone else." Still another student wrote: "Objectivity depends on each system wanting to make itself look good and the other bad."

What emerged from this assignment was the realization that all language is value laden. Since words always occur in context—alongside other words and in varying situations—words are never "objective." One student wrote after a class discussion of this assignment: "As part of the American public raised to regard the media as objective, I am disturbed to find out how words can be manipulated." This recognition may be disturbing to you as well, but it is not as sinister as this student implies. Language, like the human subjects using it, is always within ideology. Thus in speaking and writing, you cannot choose whether to be objective or biased: your language is always already biased. What you have to decide is whether to investigate those biases—not in order to get rid of them but to begin to understand the complex relationship that exists between your culture and your use of language.

Writing Suggestions

1. Reread the opinions expressed by our students on the differences between "regime" and "government." Which do you agree with?
2. What parts of your **general repertoire** are relevant to your reading of *regime* and *government?*
3. Find and discuss other commonly used political words—from a newspaper or network news—that carry contradictory values.

Poetry and the Indeterminacy of Language

If *all* language is value laden, what of the special use of language in literary texts? Of all the types of literature, poetry often contains the most highly charged and suggestive words and so can demonstrate just how powerful language can be. In other words, the meaning of a good poem can never be permanently pinned down because each line, perhaps each word, has so many possible connotations.

But as we will explain in Chapter 5, poetry is just as much a way of *reading* as a way of *writing*. As Terry Eagleton notes in his book *Literary Theory,* you can choose to read even simple declarative statements, such as "Refuse to be put in basket," as poetry by playing with what we called in Chapter 1 their *polyvalence*. "Refuse" can be read either as a noun or as a verb. But you are probably ready to assert with some confidence that "Refuse to be put in basket" was not intended to fortify people against those who seek to put them in baskets. "Refuse," you probably will argue, is a noun here, not a verb. But in some cases you can't be sure because language is always overdetermined. It is this very slippery nature of language that makes people try, as you might have done, to establish contexts in which certain meanings will be seen as dominant and therefore "correct." To suppress that desire to have one meaning dominate is to learn to read poetically, to let the multiple meanings of language, its undecidability, come to the foreground.

Look, for example, at this little poem by a contemporary poet.

GREGORY ORR (b. 1947)

All Morning

All morning the dream lingers.
I am like the thick grass
in a meadow, still
soaked with dew at noon.

These four short lines, designed to make its readers produce their own little dream, create a mood of reverie, of fantasy, of nostalgia. What is the lingering dream about? A girl? A boy? A sunset? It can be almost anything. You create *your* own text from reading the poet's, and you are stimulated to do so by the undecidability, the multiple possibilities, of the words. The more closely you read the poem, the more meanings it begins to develop. Close reading does not mean merely following a poem word by word and working out the *denotations* or dictionary meanings of each word; it also means letting the poem's words suggest multiple, detailed connotations to you. To do so means paying attention both to the words *and* to the diverse and possibly contradictory reverberations they set up in you. Close reading should not *close off* possible readings but should rather *open* them up.

A more complex poem is the following one by the American poet John Ashbery. As you read it—and preferably read it aloud—speak it in as ordinary a voice as possible. Pause between sentences as if you were thinking through an argument.

JOHN ASHBERY (b. 1927)

And *Ut Pictura Poesis* Is Her Name[1]

You can't say it that way any more.
Bothered about beauty you have to
Come out into the open, into a clearing,
And rest. Certainly whatever funny happens to you
Is OK. To demand more than this would be strange   5
Of you, you who have so many lovers,
People who look up to you and are willing
To do things for you, but you think
It's not right, that if they really knew you . . .
So much for self-analysis. Now,   10
About what to put in your poem-painting:
Flowers are always nice, particularly delphiniums.
Names of boys you once knew and their sleds,
Skyrockets are good—do they still exist?
There are a lot of other things of the same quality   15
As those I've mentioned. Now one must
Find a few important words, and a lot of low-keyed,
Dull sounding ones. She approached me
About buying her desk. Suddenly the street was
Bananas and the clangor of Japanese instruments.   20
Humdrum testaments were scattered around. His head
Locked into mine. We were a seesaw. Something
Ought to be written about how this affects
You when you write poetry:
The extreme austerity of an almost empty mind   25
Colliding with the lush, Rousseau-like foliage of its desire to communicate
Something between breaths, if only for the sake
Of others and their desire to understand you and desert you
For other centers of communication, so that understanding
May begin, and in doing so be undone.   30

This complex poem is very self-conscious about the power that *language* has to evoke multiple responses. We will go over it systematically and provide some suggestions on how to pay close attention to language.

---

[1] *Ut Pictura Poesis:* as in painting, so in poetry.

Exploring the Poem's Argument

First, when you start to do a reading of a poem, it is a good idea to concentrate on exploring the poem's argument—getting the *gist* of the text. This means not merely reproducing it faithfully but also constructing *in your own words* the set of issues the poem raises, so you can then go on to do your own strong reading of it.

Here is one experienced reader's attempt to do so.

> The title refers to the interaction of poetry and painting, the "poem-painting" of line 11. It's often thought that a poem should create a picture in the mind. But the opening line seems to deny that we can "say it that way" in quite the way we're used to or would like to. Language gets old; it no longer fits the experiences we want it to evoke. Or we have to search for new words. Sometimes the new experiences we have themselves generate a new vocabulary. But the language of love and beauty is notorious for getting worn out, sounding trite and therefore boring. So when you are, as line 2 puts it, "bothered about beauty" (*bothered* is an especially good word, with its sense of irritation, frustration, of someone nervously looking around and being fussy about something), then you feel the need to get free of all the old ways of saying things.

So far the experienced reader has constructed the gist of the poem down to about line 4. Notice how long this explanation is. The poem is much more succinct, much more suggestive, much more open-ended. Notice how instead of saying all this as our reader just did in a rather prosaic way, Ashbery gives a vivid picture in his metaphor, paradoxically exactly the thing his poem is complaining can't be done: "you have to/Come out into the open, into a clearing,/And rest. . . ."

The poem suggests that even when you try to get into that clearing and pin down meaning, you cannot escape all the pressures and forces that work to open language to multiple meanings. So when a poet gets down to his "poem-painting," what happens? Let us go on.

> At this point, the poem becomes both playful and serious. It is playful in the sense that while the tone is self-deprecating, amusing in its assertion of failure and in its puzzlement that language can't say what you want it to say, the poem is, paradoxically, a triumphant expression of that failure. The poem ends with a wonderful articulation of what it states cannot be articulated. Although every word does not make sense to me in the poem, I feel that it communicates beautifully— if not altogether clearly—the impossibility of communicating. The *problem* of language's inadequacy is expressed with serene confidence. We do not know whether to believe the poet or his poem.

As you can readily see, such a supposed summary is not a "faithful reproduction" of what the poem "says." Inevitably it moves away from the language of the poem itself and into the *issues* the poem raises. The summary is less evocative and more coherent than the poem. It also incorporates material that comes from the reader, not the poem—or perhaps from the reader as stimulated *by* the poem.

Deepening Your Reading Experience

The second part of any good reading, after summarizing, is to deepen *your* own involvement in the experience of reading. You choose an issue that the poem raises for you—expressing beauty, the poem as painting, the frustration of language, whatever it may be—and bring *your* ideas and associations to bear on the poem. You don't have to worry about being "faithful" to the poem because it is so open-ended that it would be impossible to follow it in every direction it might potentially lead. You start a kind of dialogue, taking your cues from the text you are reading, and you let that be the stimulus for your ideas—for *your* new text. You become part of a flow of language that includes poem, gist or summary, personal associations, response, self-conscious contextual analysis, and finally a new text that you are producing from the whole experience. You do this because you recognize the quality of indeterminacy that all language has but that poetry in particular brings to the foreground.

Writing Suggestions

1. Compare your own reading of lines 1–4 of Ashbery's poem with that of our reader. What different emphases do you have?
2. What in your **literary** or **general repertoires** helps to account for these differences?
3. (*a*) Paraphrase a poem you have studied. Which—the poem or the paraphrase—is more easily understood?
   (*b*) Which is more interesting? Justify your analysis.

History

The Perspectival Nature of History

We are not only beings-in-language but also beings-in-history. The second of our three organizing concepts is, therefore, *history*.

You can find an infinite number of examples of historical references in literary texts. For instance, John Berryman's poem "1 September 1939" refers to the date World War II broke out. Norman Mailer's novel *The Executioner's Song* refers in great detail to the life of Gary Gilmore, the convicted murderer whose trial aroused wide comment in the late 1970s. Shakespeare's two *Henry IV* plays refer to many events in the early fifteenth century, even though Shakespeare rearranged them for his own purposes. It is often helpful to do a little research on the historical repertoire of a text, the events or people it refers to, especially when, as in Shakespeare's plays, they come to today's readers from a very different era or culture. When you familiarize yourself with a text's general repertoire, you enlarge your own general repertoire and thereby increase the potential depth of your response. Familiarizing yourself with a text's repertoire does not ensure that you will like the text, but it does allow you to respond to it from a more informed position.

Let's look at a poem that refers to an important political event in the history of Ireland.

WILLIAM BUTLER YEATS (1865–1939)

Easter 1916

I have met them at close of day
Coming with vivid faces
From counter or desk among gray
Eighteenth-century houses.
I have passed with a nod of the head   5
Or polite meaningless words,
Or have lingered awhile and said
Polite meaningless words,
And thought before I had done
Of a mocking tale or a gibe   10
To please a companion
Around the fire at the club,
Being certain that they and I
But lived where motley is worn:
A terrible beauty is born.   15

That woman's days were spent
In ignorant good-will,
Her nights in argument
Until her voice grew shrill.
What voice more sweet than hers   20
When, young and beautiful,
She rode to harriers?
This man had kept a school
And rode our wingéd horse;
This other his helper and friend   25
Was coming into his force;
He might have won fame in the end,
So sensitive his nature seemed,
So daring and sweet his thought.
This other man I had dreamed   30
A drunken, vainglorious lout.
He had done most bitter wrong
To some who are near my heart,
Yet I number him in the song;
He, too, has resigned his part   35

In the casual comedy;
He, too, has been changed in his turn,
Transformed utterly:
A terrible beauty is born.

Hearts with one purpose alone   40
Through summer and winter seem
Enchanted to a stone
To trouble the living stream.
The horse that comes from the road,
The rider, the birds that range   45
From cloud to tumbling cloud,
Minute by minute they change;
A shadow of cloud on the stream
Changes minute by minute;
A horse-hoof slides on the brim,   50
And a horse plashes within it;
The long-legged moor-hens dive,
And hens to moor-cocks call;
Minute by minute they live:
The stone's in the midst of all.   55

Too long a sacrifice
Can make a stone of the heart.
O when may it suffice?
That is Heaven's part, our part
To murmur name upon name,   60
As a mother names her child
When sleep at last has come
On limbs that had run wild.
What is it but nightfall?
No, no, not night but death;   65
Was it needless death after all?
For England may keep faith
For all that is done and said.
We know their dream; enough
To know they dreamed and are dead;   70
And what if excess of love
Bewildered them till they died?
I write it out in a verse—
MacDonagh and MacBride
And Connolly and Pearse   75
Now and in time to be,
Wherever green is worn,
Are changed, changed utterly:
A terrible beauty is born.

Obviously this poem refers to a variety of historical events and personages. The woman mentioned in stanza 2 was the Countess Markiewicz, a leading supporter of the Irish Revolution; Patrick Pearse, the revolutionary leader, "had kept a school"; the "lout" is Major John MacBride who married Yeats's great love, Maud Gonne, and also (in Yeats's eyes) acquired a new dignity by his part in the uprising. So each of these individuals takes his or her place in a public event, the "terrible beauty" of the 1916 uprising that was eventually to free at least part of Ireland from British rule.

Or more accurately, each of these individuals becomes a part of a *version* of history. To say that a literary text provides a "version" of history rather than an "accurate" account probably makes sense because literary texts are fictional rather than factual; they offer interpretations, not objective truths. All historical texts, however, offer only versions of history—interpretations, not objective "facts." Historical events acquire meaning only as part of an interpretation, a "reading" of history. Yeats's poem, so obviously sympathetic to the rebellion of 1916, is one version, but others would be possible: from the perspective of the British government, the Irish people involved in the uprising were traitors.

Writing Suggestions

1. What details in Yeats's poem show that he is constructing a *version* of history rather than an "objective" view of history?
2. Choose a different poem or one you have studied that contains detailed historical references. Show how these are also part of an *interpretation* of historical events rather than an "objective" view.

One of the effects of reading historical literature is that it brings into question the whole notion of objective facts, even those presented in history books. If, for example, you were to read supposedly "accurate" historical accounts of the Vietnam War from the perspective of the North Vietnamese, the South Vietnamese, the American Right, and the American Left, you would get four different readings of the war, some obviously having more in common than others. Even such seemingly objective facts as the number of people killed during a particular month of the war would differ depending on whom you were reading. Thus while historical literature itself blurs the distinction between fact and fiction, it also helps to point out that the distinction was already—indeed as is sometimes said, always already—blurred.

Since we are all situated in a particular historical context, it is impossible for any of us to ever get outside our own perspective and gain direct access to events in the world. Acquiring knowledge about historical texts enlarges your repertoire and enables you to have more detailed and more powerful insights into the texts you read, but it does not give you "objective" knowledge or access to a "true" reading. A historical background helps you understand better the problems and pressures to which the text was a response when it was written and also helps you formulate more clearly your own perspective. Recognizing the perspectival nature of history, therefore, enables you to avoid both a false objectivity and a false subjectivity. Developing historical awareness and perspective is a crucial factor in becoming a strong reader of texts.

Reading with Historical Perspective

Whatever you read, you "translate," to some extent, into your own words. But it is all too easy to project your own prejudices and assumptions upon a text from the past. You can simply read an unfamiliar text in terms of what is already in your repertoire—instead of using its unfamiliarity as a stimulus to expand your repertoire.

Remember that the more distant in time a text was produced, the greater the historical changes between its time and your own—and the greater the need to enlarge your repertoire. Beliefs, fashions, and general ideas about the world change in many complex ways—to such an extent that the general and literary repertoire of a text may be quite different from your own. To explore these differences means that your repertoire about the past (and, paradoxically, your understanding of the present) will be greatly increased.

When you read a text from another period, very little in it may at first seem relevant to you. After all, the understanding of physics, biology, society, life-styles, and pretty much everything assumed by, say, Shakespeare in *Macbeth* is all very different from that of your own period. If your repertoire includes some historical background, some knowledge of Renaissance philosophy, political history, art, or other literature, then you will have less difficulty in reading the play. But you just have to lift your eyes from the page to realize that you live in a totally different world.

You don't live in the sixteenth century when *Macbeth* was written—let alone in the mythical medieval time when the play is set. *Macbeth* takes for granted a world of kings, nobles, witches, and ghosts. Its understanding of the human subject, the nature of desire, politics, ambition, hierarchy, and power are all very different—and in very specific details. *Macbeth* comes from a world we have lost, and it is foolish to pretend that we can read it the way any of its original audience did.

How, then, can you read it? You want to get as informed a perspective about the historical situation of *Macbeth* as possible. When Malcolm and Macduff discuss the nature of kingship in Act IV, you need to know something of the reverence that the dominant ideology of the time bestowed on kings. You need to be aware of the reasons why Macduff is so indignant about what he sees as Malcolm's cowardice. But information of this kind does not lead you to the "correct" interpretation because you still, and inevitably, pose questions of the play from your own concerns. Such information does, however, empower you as a reader to consider the particular perspective you wish to take on the issues raised. To become a strong reader yourself, you need to know something of the issues that might have been seized upon by earlier readers.

You might, for example, interpret the play as opening up a discussion of conscience, integrity, whether ends justify means, and so on. But remember the warning we gave you about "universal themes" in Chapter 1. There is no undistorted, timeless, universal meaning somehow buried in *Macbeth*. Its issues are not the same today as in Shakespeare's time (nor are the solutions you might give them). Yet some degree of continuity exists over time in readers' reactions to the play: many of society's moral or political concerns have remained fairly constant, although the solutions offered in different periods differ vastly. You, therefore, necessarily interpret these issues from the intellectual and moral perspectives *you* have absorbed from your time.

Are you distorting *Macbeth* by reading it (as is inevitable) from your twentieth-century perspective? In part, the answer to this question is yes, because every interpretation focuses on certain aspects of a text and deemphasizes or ignores others. But this distorting quality of reading is always present whether you are reading a text from the distant past or one that was written yesterday. As we discussed in the previous section, all reading, however informed, is always perspectival. The issue, therefore, is not whether you should divest yourself of all your twentieth-century assumptions so that you can perceive the *essential Macbeth*. This is impossible. But if you are reading with historical perspective, you will try to analyze the historical reasons underlying why you respond strongly to some aspects of an older text and not to others. Your strong interest in the political issues, for example, rather than in witchcraft or the divine right of kings in *Macbeth* might in part be explained by the relative continuity of political and moral issues between Shakespeare's England and today. In fact, if some continuity did not exist between the two periods, that is, if there were not some intersection between your repertoire and the text's, you would probably find little in the play to respond to.

The process of ideological change within a society continuously affects literary interpretation. Once again, Shakespeare's plays provide us with excellent examples since they have been so widely read, produced, and written about. In Chapter 4, we will describe how *Hamlet* has been interpreted in vastly different ways over the past four hundred years. Shakespeare's comedies provide us with other examples. In the eighteenth century, they were seen as realistic and moral. *The Merchant of Venice,* for instance, was widely regarded as a triumphant and joyful celebration of Christian virtue. Plays that seemed ambiguous or cynical, however, like *Measure for Measure* or *Troilus and Cressida* were reinterpreted, or ignored, or even rejected from the canon. In the twentieth century, as people have learned more about the mixture of motives and the play of the unconscious in human behavior, they have developed much darker and cynical readings of the comedies, with a play like *The Merchant of Venice* now widely reinterpreted as exposing the intolerance and bigotry of the dominant Christian merchant class. These differences in interpretation are not arbitrary, nor do they seem unjustifiable from the text. They are instances of strong readings arising from the changing general and literary repertoires of different generations of readers.

Writing Suggestions

1. Choose another Shakespeare play (or any other text) and write on the most important differences in the **general repertoire** of the time in which the text was written and your own.
2. Which areas of belief or lifestyle do you think have changed *least?*

3. What historical *event* that you have studied has had widely different interpretations? Briefly discuss the issues on which they differ.

Reading for Absences

At times you may feel at a disadvantage when you read historically remote texts because you do not understand various local allusions, or because certain words seem to be used strangely or certain customs and social practices seem alien to you. It is often necessary for you to do some research to expand both your literary and general repertoires so that you can interact more fully with those of the text.

From a certain perspective, however, you are at a distinct advantage in reading a text from an earlier period. You live in a time that may have resolved or at least recognized and found a way to articulate the tensions and contradictions that were part of that earlier period. Consequently, as a reader with a later historical perspective, you might very well be able to discover and analyze some of an older text's ideological struggles that its author, caught in his or her own historical period, could only hint at but didn't yet have the language to articulate.

Keep in mind that a work of literature is written with the preconceptions and the language afforded by its particular period of history—especially by the *ideological* presuppositions of its time. The writer who produced the work did not produce the language in which he or she wrote. Writers write in a language and an ideology whose laws, contradictions, and particular interests they did not invent. An author's writing, therefore, is always governed by the system of language within which he or she writes—without which nothing could be written. A great writer is generally thought to be one who takes, wrestles with, and extends the possibilities offered by the language of his or her society. And the most interesting works are often those in which readers sense a struggle going on to articulate pressing contradictions and tensions in a language that, because it is necessarily culture-bound, never seems quite adequate to the task.

A work of literature, then, shows us language in conflict with itself. That is why great, or even merely interesting, works reveal to us far more than just what their authors knew or "intended." Texts are frequently read by their later readers for things their authors *didn't* intend—perhaps for what they had no idea they were saying. Readers can read texts—however strange this must sound—for what is *not* "in" them as much as for what is. We call this kind of reading **symptomatic**—that is, we look for "symptoms" of underlying ideology in the text.

Let us try to explain this carefully since this notion of "absence"—what is *not* "in" a text—is a crucial one. A writer and a literary work are deeply influenced by ideology. Literary works can be an index of the tensions that characterize a particular society. These tensions are inevitably complex, subtle, and contradictory, and are often the cause of the energy that you, as a reader from a later period, may find in a work but about which the author may have been only partly conscious. It is the work's later readers who may be able to spot and identify these "symptoms" and thereby help the work say what it couldn't perhaps quite express in an earlier period. This probing of works from the past, looking for the symptoms of their period's struggles and battles, is what makes historical analysis so interesting. John Bunyan's *Pilgrim's Progress,* for example, presents itself as the work of an uneducated craftsman, a tinker, who lived in a small town in England in the seventeenth century. But speaking through his work we can see the struggles of a whole class of underprivileged men and women who did not have even Bunyan's language to express their ideals and yearnings. Bunyan depicts these yearnings in religious terms, seeing experience in terms of a pattern of guilt and salvation; today most readers would see a desire for social and political freedom or a cry for justice emerging through the religious language Bunyan uses.

Likewise we can look back to many symptoms in literature of what we now see as emotional disturbance or repression but what would at the time have been seen as possession by the devil. Many of Nathaniel Hawthorne's stories and novels seem radically divided in their treatment of dark-haired (or "evil") women—as at once alluring and yet doomed. Hester Prynne in *The Scarlet Letter,* who is both adulteress and angel, both proud and humble, both saved and condemned, is clearly built out of unresolved tensions in the ideology of the nineteenth-century American culture in which Hawthorne lived. Today you may read the novel and say that there is nothing wrong with Hester Prynne, that the problems lay in her repressive culture. But in so doing, you are developing a reading at which the text seems only to hint.

Twentieth-century readers can develop such readings, finding things "in" a text that were not seemingly put there by its author, because they have acquired new kinds of knowledge that can help them articulate what earlier texts could not. For example, it is much easier for us in the twentieth century to view social practices as repressive since our thinking is so heavily influenced by Freud. You can, therefore, fill the *absences* in the texts—in different ways, according to the different questions you bring to bear from your own time.

To summarize: how can you become better readers of historical texts? How can you allow texts from the past to speak to you in surroundings that may be very alien to the ones in which they first appeared? You must avoid two equally limiting delusions. One is that "objective," historically verifiable, "true" readings of texts can be found. The other is that recreating the past is simply a matter of your finding your own immediate interests in it. To read with historical perspective is to recognize the ways in which the ideology of your culture influences you to respond more forcefully to some aspects of older texts than to others. Research is crucial to developing historical awareness, but remember that the questions you ask will help determine the answers you discover.

Writing Suggestions

1. Explain what is meant by "absences" in a text.
2. (*a*) Choose a work from another period of history and point to what you see as important "absences" in it.
   (*b*) How would your reading of that text bring out the absences?

Culture

Language points to the interconnected systems by which we all speak and write and (in a sense) are spoken and written. *History* is an inescapable dimension of the real, material world in which we all live. Even after it has disappeared, the past nonetheless still determines much of the present. *Culture,* the third of our terms, suggests, first, that reading literature takes place in the context of the present, within contemporary culture. And, second, *culture* suggests that "literary" texts are not the only texts that people read, interpret, and act upon, and that affect their lives; rather, all the texts of their society—movies, television, popular music, advertising, fashion—profoundly influence its members and are all worthwhile subjects of study in and outside of the classroom. The recent trend in which "literary studies" (the study of literary texts) is becoming part of "cultural studies" (the study of the textual practices of a culture) is, we think, an inevitable and welcome one. To study textual practices in general, as opposed to only literary texts, is to situate part of your ideological inquiry among the most influential "texts" of this culture, and consequentially to broaden your own understanding of what it is to live in America in the later part of the twentieth century.

The Shift from Literary Studies to Cultural Studies

No society has ever been subjected to so many systems of signs and meanings the way ours has. People today grow up saturated by the texts of the media— radio, television, rock music, advertisements, newspapers, magazines. Some of these are written texts, like literature. Others, like rock music, mix spoken language with the new electronic media. All are texts in the sense that they are produced by the codes of our culture and articulate its ideological contradictions. Hence, like literary texts, they can all be "read" and written about. As a student of cultural as well as of literary studies, you can see that the skills and insights you can gain from reading *literary* texts are relevant and crucial for reading the other textual practices of our culture, all the way from *Masterpiece Theater* to *Sesame Street,* from Miller Lite advertisements to *Star Wars* movies.

Many people spend hours watching MTV on cable television: it provides an intriguing mixture of song, drama, and documentary, combining artistic, literary, and musical effects and state-of-the-art electronic technology. Most people see more television drama than stage drama. The cryptic, evocative songs of Bob Dylan or Bruce Springsteen are better known—more widely read, more part of the consciousness of our time—than those of "serious" poets like Fred Chappell or Linda Pastan. All of these experiences are, no less than reading a poem or a novel, *reading texts*.

And yet you would probably say that watching MTV, going to the movies, or reading the newspaper has a somewhat different "feel" for you from reading a poem. This is due, in large part, not to intrinsic differences in the texts themselves but to the differences in their *reading contexts*. Most of you go to the movies for pleasure and read literature for school. This doesn't mean that you don't necessarily enjoy reading literature but rather that you often don't have as much choice about what and when to read it or as much freedom about whether and how to interpret literary texts as you do the texts of popular culture. Further, the texts of popular culture generally maintain a certain amount of both entertainment and comprehensibility that you may feel serious literature does not have. In fact if texts of popular culture are just for entertainment, do they even need to be analyzed?

We are not making a case for the greater (or lesser) cultural value of these "texts" of our culture. But because they are so powerful a cultural force for our time, they demand serious analysis. If you are to investigate how your culture operates, you need to probe all the ways its texts are situated in ideology and all the ways they speak for and to you. Frequently texts of popular culture seem uncomplicated and easy to understand because on the surface they reflect some aspect of the dominant ideology. If you analyze these seemingly simple texts more deeply, however, you often discover that they are formed by many of the same conflicts and contradictions that underlie serious literary texts. For example, one beer company briefly adopted as its slogan, "You can have it all." The company ran a male and a female version of the commercial, which at least superficially suggested that they were giving equal treatment to men and women. But while the men who "had it all" were depicted in a professional work setting and in a sports or leisure setting, such as fishing or camping, the women who "had it all" were depicted in a professional work setting and then in a home setting engaged in some form of domestic work. The notion of "having it all," therefore, differed significantly for men and women. Neither has it all, but the men at least have a balance of work and leisure (although they seem to have no domestic life), while the women have only professional and domestic work— and are depicted as having no leisure at all.

Many viewers of this commercial were probably not conscious of its sexism because on the surface it suggested the possibility of a full life for all. Nonetheless, these viewers may have been subtly influenced by the sex-role stereotypes depicted, especially since these stereotypes are still so dominant in most of our culture. Obviously this beer commercial is "written" by two contradictory discourses: one that seeks to liberate women and the other that seeks to exclude them from certain male privileges and to tie them to a role of "home-making."

Unlike many literary texts, the texts of popular culture—music, film, television dramas—are seemingly not threatening. The study of them often is disturbing, however, because it points up that nothing, not even a simple beer commercial, can be seen as "natural," in the sense of its being uninformed by certain ideological pressures. It is often easier—and less disturbing—to see the ideological position of texts from an earlier period because you are not so immediately or fully implicated in the ideological struggles of a time that is not your own. Even when you read a text from an earlier period knowing that you are situated in a *different* context, you may still tend to believe that your position is not only different but somehow *truer*, more correct, than that of the text because yours came after the text's. When reading an older text, you also may have a tendency to see your own repertoire of beliefs as *the* primary beliefs of the later part of the twentieth century, and by extension to see your position and your culture as monolithic or unified. Studying contemporary cultural texts prevents you from either distancing yourself from the text or assuming the existence of a unified cultural position by stressing the conflicts inherent in your own social context.

Writing Suggestions

1. Choose a favorite TV rock video and show how it reflects current ideological preoccupations.
2. Reread the passage on the concept of "absence" (page 47) and apply it to the TV rock video you chose in question 1.

If you want to become more conscious of the conflicts and contradictions inherent in our culture, you must include in your study texts that reach the largest number of people. In Chapter 8, we will discuss how you can adopt methods from literary analysis to study texts from contemporary culture. The aim of a literary education, after all, is not only to appreciate what is called "literature" but to understand yourselves, your society, your history. To study the characteristic texts produced by your culture is to enter further into what is called a "liberal" or liberating education. We suggest therefore that you look for ways of studying contemporary literary texts *alongside* the texts of such contemporary media as film, television, music. These texts, both literary and non-literary, reveal a kind of "unconscious" to the culture (in the Freudian sense), and you should not ignore all of our culture's distinctive textual practices.

The Significance of Studying Contemporary Literary Texts

Part of the gain of a shift from purely literary to cultural study applies to the analysis of literature itself. You read literary texts from your own time and culture in part to learn about yourself—how you are produced by your own culture, how the most significant texts of your time struggle to interpret the characteristic hopes, fears, and possibilities of your lives. From contemporary texts you can sense most closely the major conflicts of today's society.

Contemporary literature, paradoxically, often seems more difficult for college students to read and interpret than slightly older works. In some cases, students have not been exposed to much contemporary literature in high school, perhaps because of teachers' or school authorities' concerns that much contemporary writing is difficult or, more likely, provocative or controversial. Educational institutions tend to prefer older "classic" works, and so students grow · up more familiar with, say, the novels of Hemingway, Steinbeck, or Fitzgerald (written between forty and seventy years ago) than with those of Updike or Oates or Atwood, who are more their contemporaries. Or students are taught the "classic" poets like Whitman, Dickinson, or Eliot rather than their contemporaries like Robert Hass, Maxine Kumin, or Dave Smith.

Because contemporary texts are selected less frequently as reading in English classes, many students have the impression that contemporary literature is not "good" literature. One student, for example, wrote in an initial response statement on D. M. Thomas's best-selling novel *The White Hotel*, "I was taught not to read popular fiction except in my spare time. I don't think my parents would like to know they were paying for me to be taught to read books like this." Her literary repertoire, of course, had been limited by this unexamined assumption. Thomas's novel not only provides, we think, a magnificent, disturbing, and powerful emotional experience, it also provides its readers with a provocative examination of some crucial historical and psychological questions regarding the contemporary world, and it challenges its readers to grapple with these questions. After we had finished discussing *The White Hotel* in class, however, this same student commented:

> When I first saw that this book was a best seller, I assumed we would read it only for entertainment. But all of our class discussions on it have been about the impossibility of distinguishing fact from fiction, about the human desire to believe in a unified self, about the impact of Freud and the Holocaust on the world today. All this has made me realize that contemporary literature can raise as many interesting questions as the "classics"—and even more urgent ones.

Because she hadn't had much exposure to contemporary literature and because she "knew" that many popular books are quite trivial, she assumed that no contemporary literature was really "worth reading."

But contemporary texts are hard for many students to read for reasons that go well beyond a prejudice against them for not being "classics." Readers cannot easily distance themselves from the tensions they perceive in contemporary texts. The tensions readers discover in older texts might already have been resolved in today's society, but those that readers perceive in a contemporary text are likely to be a part of their ongoing experiences and hence can be quite threatening because they can't be resolved. How is today's reader to gain a perspective on the challenge to the notion of rationality or of life as purposeful, presented in Samuel Beckett's play *Waiting for Godot?* After all, you read (or see) that play in a world in which the threat of nuclear war looms large, in which terrorists are indifferent to the identity of their victims, in which a spaceship can suddenly explode five miles above the earth. How is a reader to respond to the dislocated man and woman in Milan Kundera's story "Hitchhiking Game," particularly to the woman who asserts desperately at the end, "I am me," in a culture in which suicide is the major cause of death among teenagers, in a culture which simultaneously praises and denounces chastity? How is a reader to connect the series of fragments that make up Italo Calvino's novel *If on a Winter's Night a Traveler*, when all that the reader ever sees on television is a series of disconnected fragments?

None of these is an easy question to answer. It is hard for any reader to know how to respond to a text that presents some of the major conflicts of his or her own time. Most contemporary literature is trying to find ways to ask important questions about our own cultural situation, but most of it provides no answers or resolutions. To exist in the same time period, the same cultural context, as that from which the questions of the text derive is to be implicated by them—challenged, even profoundly disturbed.

That degree of relevance can make a text seem difficult and threatening to read. But the sense of being implicated in questions that as yet have no answers in our culture also makes it very important for you to persevere in reading contemporary literature. If you want some insight into your world, you can learn much from the texts of your culture, as they struggle to depict the experiences and the conditions of all our lives. Just as older texts tell us about those forces that made people what they were in the past, contemporary texts reveal our current ideological struggles and human possibilities.

Writing Suggestions

1. Choose a best-selling novel you have read and analyze its major ideological preoccupations.
   (a) What do you think makes it typical of our time rather than of another?
   (b) Reread the passage dealing with the concept of "absence" (p. 47) and apply it to the novel you have chosen.
2. Choose an example from literary history in which one society's "popular" culture has become part of our "high" cultural tradition. Examples might include Renaissance "revenge tragedies" (such as the *Duchess of Malfi* by John Webster) and eighteenth-century fiction (such as *Moll Flanders* by Daniel Defoe). Discuss the particular historical factors that have influenced this development.

Conclusions and Suggestions

We have suggested that literature can be studied very usefully in terms of three interconnected contexts. Here we offer some brief practical suggestions, which we will develop in subsequent chapters, on how to apply these concepts.

You can use each of these categories—*language, history,* and *culture*—as a checklist when you study a work of literature, or any other kind of text, in terms of both general and literary repertoires. *Language* may seem to relate most directly to the matching of text strategies with reading strategies. But when you ask what distinctive uses of language occur in the text you are reading, you are also asking: What are the particular ideological values associated with the language? Both textual details *and* ideological values are implied by a question like: "What are the words you use and encounter in your daily lives trying to get you to do?" Language is not just a value-neutral text feature: *language is power*. Your knowledge (and questioning) of the languages that surround you constitutes your access to power.

Likewise with *history*. People are deeply influenced by that which comes to them from the past. Readers impoverish themselves if they don't investigate at least parts of that past and become aware of how concepts about love, politics, freedom, fulfillment, or belief have changed through history. But such study is not just to locate and label features of the text. When readers read any text that comes to them from a distant time, they can then develop their own sense of the past, not for its own sake but for the sake of understanding themselves in the present—in short, to relate their own repertoire to that of the text.

And when you think of *culture*, try to make connections from the text you are reading to the wider, complex world you are living in, thereby enlarging your general repertoire. Reading a book, watching a movie, looking at television, listening to *American Top Forty*—all have implications for the way you live your lives, interpret your society, adapt to or try to change it. Your reading habits don't just give you access to a "timeless," escapist world of the imagination; they have significant implications for your understanding of the complex conjunction of forces making up your culture.

Above all, we want you to become strong readers and writers, able and enthusiastic, and we urge you to ask demanding and interesting questions of literary and larger cultural texts. To read a story or a poem, or to listen analytically to a rock album, can help you to expand your experience and your understanding and—perhaps even more important—to explore your own normally unexamined or accepted assumptions and ideological conditioning. To read with a conscious awareness of the influences of language, history, and culture is to engage in a quest for a little more knowledge about the way you have been produced by your history, the way you can speak and write within the language you have been given by your society, and the ways in which you can act within our rich, complex, and fascinating culture.

Checkpoints for Chapter 2

1. Reading always takes place in the context of language, history, and culture.
2. We are "written by" language, just as we write it.
3. Language is always value-laden.
4. We are beings-in-history and interpret the past from the present.
5. We can expand our repertoires by acquiring knowledge of the past.
6. Contemporary literary texts are part of the textual practices of our culture.
7. To read the texts of our culture is to gain insight into who we are.

Part 2
Understanding the Writing Situation

𝓗𝓡 Chapter 3
Reading to Write
Response Statements

Reading Situations
and Task Representations

The way you read a text frequently depends on what you have to *do* with it. You read a novel differently if you're reading it for pleasure on the beach from the way you would if you were reading it to write a term paper for your English class. It's important to be able to spell out the differences between those two kinds of reading. Most readers suggest vaguely that they would "pay more attention" and would be more likely to underline or take notes on the book for school while they would be more likely to skim the bits that they didn't like if they were reading just for pleasure.

Whenever people have a task to accomplish or a problem to solve, the first thing they must do is to represent that task to themselves. That is, they must construct their own image of what that task requires. They ask: What are the **goals** in this situation? What **strategies** are appropriate? People solve the problems they give themselves, but they may not be aware that their image of a problem is an image they have *created* until they see someone else's.

For example, imagine two people thinking about the task of planting beans. The first person has a relatively simple image of the task. Her *goals* are straightforward: get 'em in the ground, pick 'em, and eat 'em. Her *strategies* are equally simple and direct: you make a row, sprinkle the beans, stomp 'em in, and pray for rain.

Now let us compare this image of the task to that of a second bean planter, specifically that of the nineteenth-century American writer Henry David Thoreau, who wrote a whole chapter on "Planting Beans" in his book *Walden*. His strategies were much more elaborate than the other bean planter's. "Daily the beans saw me come to their rescue armed with a hoe," he writes, "and thin the ranks of their enemies, filling up the trenches with weedy dead." Not everyone looks at weeding in quite this way. His goals also suggest that he had a very different image of what it meant to plant a field of beans. Thoreau's agenda was "to live deliberately." "I was," he said, "determined to know beans." It mattered little to him if woodchucks ate some of his beans; he was not trying to feed his family or fill the barn with beans. The goal of the True Husbandman, in Thoreau's vision of the task, was nothing less than to "cease from anxiety."

The point of this comparison is that people construct their own tasks differently—in particular, they determine the goals and the strategies that define the problem they are trying to solve or the task they will undertake. And we can see that the representations of the tasks people give themselves vary a great deal in their complexity. To "cease from anxiety" can be a pretty tall order!

Now if this can happen with beans, what happens when people represent the task of academic reading and writing to themselves? Do the other students in your class construct the same image of a writing task as you do when they interpret an assignment? Does their image of the task look like that of the instructor? And if these images do differ—as at some level, of course, they must—do these differences really matter?

Have you ever asked classmates of yours how they thought you were supposed to do an assignment and, upon hearing their answer, got that sinking feeling in the pit of your stomach that you were "doing it all wrong"? What you discovered in that situation, besides feelings of wild panic, was that you and your classmates have different task definitions.

Every kind of writing assignment has certain **conventions** that writers are expected to follow, and the **response statement**—the kind of writing assignment that best suits our approach to reading texts and that we will introduce later in this chapter—is no exception. Learning the conventions of a kind of writing can help you develop appropriate task definitions for it. Frequently college teachers do not explicitly spell out the conventions of a writing assignment—say, the "formal essay" or the "research paper"—because you, the student, are expected to know them already. However, we can't expect that you will automatically know how to write response statements because the approach we are advocating in this book is so new. Thus, in this chapter and the next, we want to familiarize you with the conventions and uses of the response statement. While we will be suggesting plans and strategies for your *process* of reading and writing, it is important for you to recognize that we are not in any way prescribing *what* you say about any given text. We want to open up methods and areas of investigation for you. What you find when you use those methods—whether you like or dislike a text, whether you think it is optimistic, pessimistic, humorous, scandalous, "good literature," propaganda, sacred, profane—is really up to you. We want to teach you ways to analyze your reactions to texts, not to tell you what reactions to have.

In this chapter, therefore, we will explore in detail the kind of reading situations you can create for yourself and the kinds of task definitions that we feel are appropriate for developing self-consciously interactive **responses** to a text. We will introduce you to the conventions of response statements and present you with some general guidelines for writing them. We want also to provide you with a fairly extensive menu of reading strategies and goals that not only can make you good writers of response statements but can help you generally become more aware of the options you have whenever you are reading to write. In the next chapter we will suggest various ways in which you can turn a response statement into a more formal paper.

Writing Suggestion

Make a list of the typical questions, issues, strategies, and goals you have when reading a text for pleasure versus reading a text for class.

A Reading and Writing Assignment: Robert Lowell's "Skunk Hour"

Whether or not you are conscious of it, you have some plan in your mind whenever you read a text, particularly if you know you have to write about it. Your plan or task definition affects the strategies you use to read and the goals you set yourself in your reading and writing tasks.

Read the following poem, "Skunk Hour" by Robert Lowell—you may have to read it a couple of times—and then write a paragraph or two about it. At this point, we are purposely not giving you any explicit instructions for these reasons:

- so you can see how you define your own task if one isn't specifically given to you
- so you can discover some ways in which your task definition differs from that of your classmates
- so you can later analyze the reading strategies and writing goals you adopted to complete this task

ROBERT LOWELL (1917–1977)

Skunk Hour

(For Elizabeth Bishop)

Nautilus Island's hermit
heiress still lives through winter in her Spartan cottage;
her sheep still graze above the sea.
Her son's a bishop. Her farmer
is first selectman in our village,   5
she's in her dotage.

Thirsting for
the hierarchic privacy

of Queen Victoria's century,
she buys up all   10
the eyesores facing her shore,
and lets them fall.

The season's ill—
we've lost our summer millionaire,
who seemed to leap from an L.L. Bean   15
catalogue. His nine-knot yawl
was auctioned off to lobstermen.
A red fox stain covers Blue Hill.

And now our fairy
decorator brightens his shop for fall,   20
his fishnet's filled with orange cork,
orange, his cobbler's bench and awl,
there is no money in his work,
he'd rather marry.

One dark night,   25
my Tudor Ford climbed the hill's skull,
I watched for love-cars. Lights turned down,
they lay together, hull to hull,
where the graveyard shelves on the town. . . .
My mind's not right.   30

A car radio bleats,
"Love, O careless Love. . . ." I hear
my ill-spirit sob in each blood cell,
as if my hand were at its throat. . . .
I myself am hell;   35
nobody's here—

only skunks, that search
in the moonlight for a bite to eat.
They march on their soles up Main Street:
white stripes, moonstruck eyes' red fire   40
under the chalk-dry and spar spire
of the Trinitarian Church.

I stand on top
of our back steps and breathe the rich air—
a mother skunk with her column of kittens swills the garbage pail. 45
She jabs her wedge head in a cup
of sour cream, drops her ostrich tail,
and will not scare.

As you read and reread the poem, jot down a few ideas for what you want
to say in your paragraph. Now take two or three minutes to take some notes and
write for ten to fifteen minutes on the poem. Then return to this page and read
on.

Task Definitions

In this exercise we are initially asking you to create your *own* task definition. Let's look at some typical task definitions for reading and writing about a text. Some may be familiar to you; others, we expect, will be new. You will have used one (or more) in your paragraph on "Skunk Hour."

These task definitions can be loosely divided into two categories:

1. Those that are either text-based or reader-based
2. Those that are interactive, stressing connections between text, reader, and often larger contexts

As you might expect, we will advocate that you adopt an interactive organizing plan. But first we want to review a number of task definitions, only some of which are interactive, and we invite you to compare your response to "Skunk Hour" with those of our students in order to discover how *you* defined your writing task. We will also review for you what we have discovered to be the primary *benefits* and *costs*—the advantages and disadvantages—of adopting each task definition.

Test-Based or Reader-Based Task Definitions

1. *Summarizing* the text
2. *Free-Associating* about the text
3. *Interpreting* the text

Interactive Task Definitions

1. *Self-consciously responding* to the text
2. *Analyzing* your response *cognitively* with the goal of becoming a *strong reader*
3. *Analyzing* your response *culturally* with the goal of becoming a *strong reader*

You may want to refer to the chart on pages 88–91 as you proceed.

Text-Based or Reader-Based Task Definitions

Summarizing

We have found that writing a summary of a text is the most common organizing plan students have—whether the text is a play, poem, short story, or essay. In a summary, you try to reduce the text to its key points, to reproduce those points in a clear orderly way, and to keep out (as much as possible) all additional sources of information, such as other poems you've read, your knowledge about L. L. Bean and skunks, and your personal reaction to the poem.

A typical summary of this poem looks much like what one student wrote:

This poem is about all the people, animals, and things the poet sees and thinks about on Nautilus Island one particular fall. He looks over the neglected houses belonging to a rich old woman. He comments that the local millionaire has gone home after selling his yacht because the summer is over. The town's decorator is redoing his shop for the fall. As the poet is driving around (apparently aimlessly), he sees people ''parking,'' hears their car radio playing a love song, and gets deeply depressed because he's alone. Finally a whole pack of skunks parades right in front of him and starts getting into everybody's garbage.

Reading Strategies and Writing Goals for Summarizing

This student's paragraph, as you can see, tries to be "faithful" to the text. It was, its writer told us, "objective." The reading strategies that this student seems to be using, and that most people use in reading to write a summary, are to get the "gist," to read literally, to avoid ambiguities, and to avoid stating a personal opinion.

Notice that this student focused almost exclusively on the events described rather than on the emotions they evoked. When asked why he did this, he said that to discuss emotions would be to involve himself with opinions and he didn't want to express the "wrong" opinion. He just wanted to stick with "the facts." The major goal most students have in writing a summary is to show their reader, generally the teacher, that they have read the material.

Notice that this goal doesn't encourage you to *learn* anything. One student said that he's more likely to use a summary plan (1) when he's in a hurry and his goal is to get the assignment done quickly, (2) when he's confused by a text and doesn't know what to say, or (3) when he has an opinion but feels that, for one reason or another, his opinion will not be seen as relevant. Have you ever found yourself in the position of this student? At what times are you most likely to use summarizing as your task definition?

Benefits and Costs of Summarizing

Let's examine some of the benefits and costs (or advantages and disadvantages) of using the summary plan. The first benefit is that it's fairly easy to do: you don't have to come up with any original ideas or new organizational structure because you generally mirror what you perceive as the organization of the text. Second, it's not risky—as our student noted, very little that you say will be "wrong." Third, and most important for our purposes, it can help give you a kind of *general* orientation to the text.

But what about the costs? While a summary might be easy to write, it lacks originality, so it is not particularly interesting for someone to read. Second, it is superficial because it forces you to repress controversial or ambiguous issues that would require you to take an opinion. Third, if a summary is all you do, it inhibits your own thinking and learning because you refuse to interact with the text, to discover its opinions and challenge them with your own. Fourth, in fact, it's not really "objective" at all, since inevitably your own opinions and choices enter into your summary.

In assessing the costs of summarizing we have discussed the costs to you as a writer as well as to your readers. You may have been encouraged in high school or even at college to write a summary because it shows that you have read the material and that on some level you understand it. We are not suggesting that summarizing is not a worthwhile endeavor: you need to construct some kind of model of what's going on in a text before you can begin to analyze it more perceptively, but it is fruitless to pretend that you can ever create an "objective" statement of what a text is about. In fact, those of you who defined your writing task as summarizing would probably want to argue with our student about the "factual" nature of his summary. Perhaps you chose to include facts that for some reason he left out, like the decorator's desire to marry or the poet's assertion, "I myself am hell." Such omissions demonstrate, as we said above, that summaries are not really objective at all.

Summarizing a text is a good starting point but a poor stopping point. If you wrote a summary of "Skunk Hour" or if you want to write a summary of a text for yourself, that's fine as a first step, but then go back to it and try to assess what aspects of your opinions and ideas affected the ways in which you summarized the text. Once you focus on your own interaction with the text, you will be beginning to *respond* to the poem; we discuss response statements later in the chapter.

Writing Suggestions

1. After writing a summary of "Skunk Hour," explain what your reading strategies and writing goals were, and what you feel are the benefits and costs of your summary.
2. How does your summary compare and contrast with our student's?
3. Write a summary of the following poem or another poem of your choice.

GARY WALLER (b. 1944)

Culture and Anarchy

In the 1860's the swing of fashion was dictating a revolt against over-large crinolines and preferring narrower, even shorter skirts, in startling colors like mauve and magenta and rich greens. But the essential feminine was not to be neglected, with the netted chignon, and charming egret blooms. Of all the

*decades in our fashionable history, it was the one a young lady would most
desire to be born and dressed in.*

it is the annual sale at Laura Ashley
and I am sitting by the display window
picking my nose, waiting for
the eternal feminine to emerge triumphantly
and suggest the best compensation   5
for not being born and dressed
in the most desirable decade of our history
is to sweep majestically home
with at least four boxes
to be unpacked, their contents hung up, admired   10
and occasionally even, maybe, worn until
next year's Laura Ashley sale selects
another decade to emulate

I sit among the $130 leather shoes, size 4AAA,
trying unsuccessfully to thrust my coarse   15
twentieth-century hand, size 8EEEE or so
into their soft magenta insides, but
despite the lack of immediate consummation
strike up an adequate relationship
for the time available   20
*the working classes tended to wear clothing
that was loose, in dark colors, absorbent and
hardy, for the constant and unremitting wear*
that's about right: to be precise, a pair of jeans
which have absorbed the reminders of last year's   25
repainting of the garage quite nicely by now
hardy enough, a little worn between the legs
but even the servant classes need to scratch
their crotches on occasion, though
the display window at Laura Ashley   30
may not be exactly the most appropriate place
—and with shoelaces that I calculate
I have tied together 3 or 4 times
but frugality was also
a high victorian virtue   35
all of which, says the commanding frown
of the eternal feminine—marching purposefully
from the dressing room parading
half a dozen dresses that remind me
more of the last decade   40
of blonde or raven haired undergraduates
auditioning *Oklahoma!* than the fashionable 1860's,
—is nothing to be proud of, and keep your grubby hands
off that wedding dress in the window
besides I need your credit card   45
I just can't take you anywhere. Really.

the modern spirit said Matthew Arnold in 1869, has
entirely dissolved the habits of subordination and
deference that once characterized the working class.
All this, I say, tends to anarchy.   50
just carry those boxes out to the car
and don't make so much noise, she says
the egret plumes bobbing in the breeze.

Free-Associating

At the other extreme from writing a summary in which you try to be objective is writing a response in which you try to be *subjective*. Now, as you know, it is impossible for you to be either totally objective or totally subjective: these two extremes require you to be able to react "purely," outside of a context, and as we discussed in Chapter 2, you always read and write in the contexts of language, history, and culture. Nonetheless, certain readers simply read a text as an occasion to talk about their own experiences without any connection with the text. Many people think that this free response in which "anything goes" is what response statements are all about. A response statement (as we explain later in this chapter) is *not* merely an analysis of your own experiences or personality. But of course students can misunderstand us when we ask them to analyze their own reactions to a text, and if they do misunderstand, they may define their reading and writing task as simple free-associating. Let's look at an extract from a response that does this:

> ''Skunk Hour'' reminds me of just how boring it can be to go to a
> resort town off-season. When I was a child, my parents always used
> to drag my brother and me to the shore in May and October. They
> said they liked it because there weren't many people around, but I
> think it's also because it was cheaper. None of the amusement
> parks were open: no rides, no cotton candy. And generally it was
> too cold to go swimming or to get a decent tan.

Reading Strategies and Writing
Goals for Free-Associating

Notice that this student is certainly talking about her reactions but not really her reactions to the poem. The fall setting in the resort area was all she appears to have noticed about the poem. The rest of her response is simply her own associations. When we asked her about her response, she said that she had not intended to write a response entirely of free-associations about the poem, though she recognized that is what her response looked like. She suggested that her aim was to offer a reaction that paralleled the poet's—depression in a resort area after the summer season—in order to help link the source of his depression to hers: boredom. Yet, as you can see, this student became so caught up in exploring her own memories that she never got around to dealing with the poem. This kind of free-association may be a useful starting point for exploring your reaction to a text, but, as with summary, it's not a good place to stop.

Perhaps what *you* wrote on "Skunk Hour" fell into the category of free-association. If it did, begin to analyze what kinds of reading strategies and writing goals you had when reading the poem. We find the most common reading strategy our students employ when they read to free-associate is the springboard strategy, that is, they read as a springboard for thinking about their own experiences. While many types of reading employ this strategy combined with other strategies, free-association uses this strategy exclusively and also focuses entirely on the reader. A related reading strategy that may to some extent broaden the free-association is to skim to interesting points and respond. This second strategy acknowledges the role of the text in leading the reader to a reaction, but the focus again is primarily on the reader.

Our students reported that their primary goal in writing free-association responses was to explore some aspect of their own experiences, but their focus was on the personal aspects of their experiences, not the reading situation that triggered them. This writing goal reflects another common reading strategy of free-association—to avoid any self-conscious analysis of the relationship between the text and personal experiences. Generally writers who represent their task as free-association do not have in mind any specific goals for their readers.

Benefits and Costs of Free-Associating

Having looked at these strategies and goals and perhaps added some of your own, what do you think are some of the benefits and costs of doing a free-association?

We think that one of the benefits of using free-association as your task definition is that, like a summary, it is fairly easy to write: you talk about the first thing that pops into your head upon reading the text. Second, it can be enjoyable to write because it's often fun to let your mind wander and try to link various of your experiences together. Third, it can be an important way to begin to analyze how your general or literary repertoires intersect with those of the text. We suggest that you think about your associations from reading and certainly jot them down, but that the focus of your response should always be to *analyze* those associations, not just to present them.

There are definitely costs to free-association. Although your pattern of associations may be interesting, unless you explicitly link them with an analysis of the text or with a broader cultural context, they may seem rather arbitrary and irrelevant to your readers. Second, when you just free-associate while reading, you will most likely miss much of what is going on in the text—its strategies, images, conflicts, metaphors, and so forth. Third, unless you analyze your own response, you may fail to recognize your culture's influence on your response.

Writing Suggestions

1. If you wrote a free-association response to "Skunk Hour," explain what your reading strategies and writing goals were, and describe what you feel are the benefits and costs of your free-association.
2. How does your free-association compare and contrast with our student's?
3. If you did not write a free-association response to "Skunk Hour," do so with the following poem or with another text you are reading:

SIR ROBERT SIDNEY (1554–1626)

Song 17

The sun is set, and maskèd night
Veils heaven's fair eyes:
Ah what trust is there to a light
That so swift flies.

A new world doth his flames enjoy,   5
New hearts rejoice:
In other eyes is now his joy,
In other choice.

Interpreting

Interpreting the text is a much more sophisticated task definition than either of the two discussed above. Generally interpreting is what you try to do in formal papers, and this is the task definition that students have learned to expect in high school and college.

Reading Strategies and Writing Goals for Interpreting

While on the one hand interpreting encourages its writers to develop an original position, on the other its major goal is that the reader's originality should be disguised as a discovery of something *in* the text rather than as a creation of a reader interacting with a text. In the reading situation, each reader brings his or her own general and literary repertoire to bear on a text that has, in its turn, been written out of a general and literary repertoire. The traditional notion of interpreting as finding something "in" the text also encourages readers to adopt the strategy of downplaying multiple meanings and unresolved ambiguities in favor of presenting an authoritative voice that appears to understand the text "objectively." Finally, interpreting encourages readers to assume that the only reason they read a text is to find out "what it means." We suggest that you can and should read a text for much more than its "main ideas." You can look for cultural differences, pleasure, the matching of repertoires, or the development of new reading strategies. If you find yourself choosing the traditional mode of interpreting, we suggest not that you abandon all your interpretive reading strategies but that you expand them.

For most student readers, writing a text-based traditional interpretation is a very familiar task definition. Let's look at a traditionally styled interpretation written by a student. When you read this extract, keep in mind the points we made above about interpretation and see if you can apply them to this analysis. Check also to see if the two or three paragraphs you wrote on "Skunk Hour" constitute an interpretation. If so, what are *your* reasons for having written an interpretation of the poem?

"Skunk Hour" by Robert Lowell suggests the absurdity, "illness," and hellish nature of existence for a sensitive, self-conscious person in a world populated by "skunks." All of the people the poet describes—the heiress, the summer millionaire, the decorator—lead absurd lives, yet they are unaware of it. The heiress buys up homes, preventing other people from living in what's probably a nice area just so she doesn't have to put up with neighbors. The millionaire dresses absurdly like people in a catalogue just so he'll look "right." The decorator, with no interest in his job, would like to marry a woman with money so he won't have to work. These people are, in a way, mad, like the skunks marching up Main Street with "moonstruck eyes." The self-absorbed people on Nautilus Island walk around the town and act just as selfishly as the mother skunk who wants to eat that sour cream so much that she "will not scare." But the people are worse than skunks because they could choose to be different. The skunks have to live their way to survive.

This student offers an interesting interpretation of the poem: the people on Nautilus Island can be equated with skunks in their madness, selfishness, and absurdity. But however objective it looks and authoritative it sounds, this student *created* this reading of the poem. It is certainly not the only interpretation possible, and your interpretation will probably differ from hers in many ways. Yet note that she presents it as if it were the only interpretation.

Benefits and Costs of Interpreting

Writing a traditional interpretation certainly has advantages: it is a powerful tool that can suggest to the reader that the writer is authoritative and correct, and (if a student) should get a good grade. In fact, writing interpretations in this way has been the dominant style of literary criticism since the 1940s. But once you realize that there can be alternative interpretations—for example, that the skunks could symbolize something natural and good, and instead of being equated with the people on the island, the skunks could be opposed to them—then it appears that this authoritative style of writing can become very constraining and, finally, can lose much of its authority. You might instead want to talk about the difficulty of assigning any particular meaning at all to the skunks; perhaps you feel only intermittently sympathetic to the poet's voice and at other times feel it expresses too much self-indulgence. Where is there room in a traditional interpretation for these kinds of tentative reactions and ambiguous responses? Where is there room for discussing the process of discovery?

The advantages of writing an interpretation are that it can be very persuasive. It also is a type of writing that requires you to have one main point; notice the way in which our student subordinated her summary of the poem to her major idea. Finally, because it does require you to take a particular position, an interpretation can often be interesting for your reader to read.

But traditional interpretations, we suggest, have their costs as well. Interpretations require readers to suppress their own voice; hence we have little sense of the reader's level of engagement with the poem. Did she like it? Did she find it difficult to read? How did she decide to read the skunks as a metaphor in the first place? Interpretations, as opposed to response statements, focus on the final reading product rather than on your reading process. Traditional interpretation tasks assume that the only legitimate topic to write about is the meaning of a text and therefore fail to analyze the complex cognitive and cultural factors that influence the creation of meaning. The only "evidence" readers generally give for a particular interpretation is to quote passages from the text. Finally, interpretation tasks require you to suppress multiple meanings.

Writing Suggestions

1. If you chose to develop an interpretation of "Skunk Hour," use it to open your response, not close it off. Go back to your paragraph and to the poem. Reread both, examining the different interpretive options you saw yourself as having while you were first reading:

   (a) Why do you think you chose to interpret this poem rather than write about it in some other way?

(b) What were your reading strategies and writing goals?

(c) What questions did you ask of yourself and of the poem?

(d) What questions, perhaps more importantly, did you not ask?

2. (a) If you did *not* write an interpretation in your paragraph, write one on the following poem (or another text you are studying):

WILLIAM WORDSWORTH (1770–1850)

I Wandered Lonely as a Cloud

I wandered lonely as a cloud
That floats on high o'er vales and hills,
When all at once I saw a crowd,
A host of golden daffodils;
Beside the lake, beneath the trees,   5
Fluttering and dancing in the breeze.

Continuous as the stars that shine
And twinkle on the milky way,
They stretched in never-ending line
Along the margin of a bay: 10
Ten thousand saw I at a glance,
Tossing their heads in sprightly dance.

The waves beside them danced, but they
Outdid the sparkling waves in glee:—
A poet could not but be gay   15
In such a jocund company:
I gazed—and gazed—but little thought
What wealth the show to me had brought.

For oft when on my couch I lie
In vacant or in pensive mood,   20
They flash upon that inward eye
Which is the bliss of solitude,
And then my heart with pleasure fills,
And dances with the daffodils.

(b) Now answer parts a, b, c, and d of question 1.

Moving Beyond These Preliminary Task Definitions

After we present you with some guidelines for writing response statements, we will ask you to write another two to three paragraphs on "Skunk Hour." Some questions and issues follow that may help you develop alternative reading strategies and goals that can prepare you to write response statements.

1. Did you like the poem?
2. Did you find it difficult to understand?
3. How do other poems that you have read inform your reading of this poem?
4. Examine your reading strategies and assumptions. Why did you, for example, focus on the skunks rather than the "I" of the poem?
5. Did you write something about the poem that pretended it was easy to understand? Would you have done this if you knew your writing was *not* being graded?
6. Try to see your reading habits in a larger cultural context, exploring the values of the poem and the ways in which they relate to your and your society's values.

Questions such as these begin to introduce you to task definitions that may be quite different from ones you may be accustomed to, or certainly different from those discussed above. But they can help you to move away from task definitions that are either purely reader- or text-centered to those that are interactive.

The Interactive Response Statement

The kind of writing about literature traditionally taught in college literature classes usually focuses on developing an interpretation of a text, though it may ask you simply to summarize. The literary text is examined for its formal, structural, or thematic characteristics; and the quality of a student's work is usually judged by whether the points made can be verified from the text, whether all the evidence afforded has been considered, whether the interpretation is in accordance with the author's apparent intention. Sometimes such an approach will focus on "themes" or "issues" found "in" the text and about which the text (or its author) is supposedly concerned.

Clearly such an approach tends to treat the text as a stable object and to subordinate the reader's contributions to the making of meaning to the demands of the text. Such writing is not always appropriate for the approach to reading texts we advocate in this book, the major emphasis of which is that meanings are not to be found "in" texts but rather that reading is an interactive process.

Another major emphasis of our approach is that texts and readers, writing and reading, are the products of wider ideological forces than are seemingly highlighted in the text. The traditional teaching of literature has often required students to investigate social or cultural backgrounds of texts, to bring information from, say, Elizabethan politics to bear on Shakespeare's plays. But it is only recently that readers have been asked to account for their relations to their own age—to make the *reader*'s social and cultural views part of the investigation.

The best kind of writing for the approach to reading texts we are advocating is the **response statement.** A response statement is interactive: it deliberately asks readers to focus not on what is seemingly "in" a text but on their own experience of reading a text. It starts not as a summary but as an informal record of your reactions to the text; it asks you for an analysis of the assumptions underlying these reactions; and, finally, it asks you to attempt to situate your reactions and analysis in a broader cultural context. In a response statement, you explore the factors that influence your reading from both *your own* and the *text*'s general and literary repertoire. You then try to explore the *implications* of the assumptions you bring to your reading, both for reading texts and for analyzing other areas of interpretation and action in your daily lives.

Response statements, as we use them, are not merely "subjective" reactions; but they take seriously the personal involvement of the reader in the experience of reading. By analyzing the cultural situation of both text and reader, you can avoid the merely personal and anecdotal, even while your personal repertoires— both literary and general—are involved. We will ask you to explore how various of your opinions, experiences, and ideas influence your reading, but we will always expect that you situate this analysis in a larger cultural context.

So response statements should not be merely exercises in free-association. At the other extreme, some readers have used response statements as a means of returning to interpretation and to a more text-centered approach to reading, rather like the traditional notion of interpretation discussed above. From this perspective, the response statement is regarded as a rough first draft of a paper that will eventually explain what a text means by means of an interpretation. This type of response statement is seen as a means to an end rather than as an end in itself—and that end is a rather traditional one. Although the response statement in this method becomes an important stage in the writing process, it is never used to explore the student's own reading process.

Our use of response statements, therefore, is contextual: it acknowledges the importance of both reader and text; it focuses on the interactive nature of reading without necessarily privileging either side; and it helps to account for the fact that both text and reader are situated in language, history, and culture.

The types of response statements we use not only ask our students to react to texts but ask them explicitly to *analyze* their reactions. They do this by exploring their own and the text's general and literary repertoires. Sometimes our students write short, informal assignments; sometimes they produce more elaborately structured ones. But in all cases we insist that they try (1) to understand their reading experiences in terms of the assumptions they bring to reading; (2) to analyze the cultural sources of those assumptions and the cognitive processes by which they construct meaning; and (3) to focus on the implications of the readings they construct. The result is that they become much more aware of themselves as interpreting beings, aware that humans are always in situations (and not only with literary texts) where they have to interpret signs, symbols, codes, languages, and one another's actions. Reading, in short, becomes seen as a basic human activity. Becoming more self-conscious and analytical about what you do when you "read" is thus a vital part not merely of your experience of reading texts but also of your growth as individuals and members of society.

General Guidelines for Writing Response Statements

It is useful to start any reading experience—and especially if you want to become more self-conscious about what is going on in your reading—with a set of general guidelines in mind that can be used in most reading situations. In what follows we outline the most general stages of developing a response to a text. Although response-statement assignments for particular texts will be much more specific and directed than the general questions that follow, these general questions underlie specific assignments. Note that these questions draw attention to the experience of reading itself, not merely to the text.

The first matter on which we will focus is the *initial reaction to reading a text*. First impressions are rarely where your understanding of a reading experience should stop, since they may simply become exercises in free-association, but articulating them is a crucial initial step. So we always ask our students a starting question:

What Are Your Initial Reactions to Reading the Text?   With this question, you focus on the *affective* (or emotional) part of the reading experience, acknowledging that reading a text always evokes some response. The initial response may be deepened or qualified very quickly, but it remains a central factor in developing some understanding of reading. Typical affective responses are interest, excitement, confusion, suspense, identification with characters, terror, anger—even boredom. We ask our students to elaborate on their responses as much as possible. Here is a typical opening for an informal response statement:

```
My initial response to Wordsworth's ''I Wandered Lonely as a
Cloud'' was embarrassment. I felt annoyed that someone should be
so sentimental about watching flowers. The speaker seems very
self-concerned, very egocentric, and I imagined him as a real
flake out there in the hills and dales.
```

Note how this writer has avoided both free-association and "objective" interpretation and instead turned, in a preliminary way, both to his own repertoire of experiences or values *and* to that of the text. Our second general question is, therefore, as follows.

Why Did the Text Have That Effect on You?   This question is designed to probe the interactive nature of the reading process—to examine the *matching* of repertoires of the reader and the text. To answer it adequately, *two* aspects of the question should be examined: *the contribution of the text* and *the contribution of the reader* to the reading experience.

What Effect Does the Text Have on Reading? Here you are looking at the text's *literary* and *general repertoires*—various formal, conventional text strategies (see pp. 19–27). But look at the features of the text not as independent characteristics but for their effect on your reading. These characteristics may raise specifically "literary" or more general ideological issues. For instance, you might find the subject matter, the "theme" of the text, particularly striking. You might also focus on the distinctive features of language in the text—powerful metaphors, striking images, recurring motifs or references, unusual idioms, witty dialogue—all the familiar "formal" features of a text, all the product of its literary repertoire. Or you might focus here on the text's use of conventions, its organization and structure, its characterization, its gaps or blanks (that you as a reader must fill in). For example, one student wrote on Beckett's *Waiting for Godot:*

> One of the aspects I responded to most in this play is the strategy
> of discontinuity. Vladimir says something and Estragon responds
> with something that may relate to what they were talking about
> three minutes ago, but that has no relationship to what Vladimir
> has just said. But oddly enough, neither of them seems to notice.
> This makes me question how clearly any of us really communicates,
> even when we think we're making sense.

Whatever text features, strategies, and conventions you focus on, always look at them in terms of your reaction to them.

What Effect Does the Reader Have on Reading? Here is where you start to become particularly analytical and self-conscious about your own literary and general repertoires. In analyzing your reaction to a text, you must take account of your literary repertoire—your literary assumptions and reading strategies. Some of your reading strategies may be to look for a consistent theme, to use the dictionary to develop multiple meanings of words, to create a clear, well-developed plot or rounded characters, to make literal versus figurative distinctions. Your literary assumptions grow out of your past reading experiences of novels, or poems, or plays. You, for example, may expect poems to rhyme, narrators in stories to be reliable, and plays to have "realistic" dialogue. You also have to take into account your general repertoire—your attitudes toward marriage, love, competition, racial relations, attitudes that will be challenged or confirmed by the texts you read. Part of the way you respond to texts, therefore, depends on your reading strategies and repertoires, whether literary or general. Look, for example, at these two divergent responses to a particular text strategy, the multiple use of "I" in Dave Smith's poem, "Messenger" (p. 78).

> In this poem the narrator switches from a little boy to a man and
> then to other voices. I expect the "I" of a poem to be consistent
> through the whole poem and to tell me what he or she thinks. What—

ever the "message" was of this poem, I think I didn't get it because I couldn't figure out who was talking.

In contrast, here is another response:

To me, the shifts in time and voice of the "I" of "Messenger"
suggest the way memory works. You constantly go back and forth in
time in your mind. It was a bit confusing at first, but I found
that my confusion over who was speaking mirrored the poet's confusion about who he really is or was.

These two students reacted very differently to the same text strategy because
they employed different reading strategies. Both of them have in their literary
repertoires an expectation that the "I" of a poem will be consistent, but the
second student, unlike the first, has alternative reading strategies to call forth if
this does not prove to be the case. The first student essentially gives up on trying
to develop a reading of the poem because her reading strategy—to find the main
point asserted by the "I" and believe it—is thwarted by the text strategy of a
multi-perspective "I."

The second student, in contrast, does not rely on the text to tell her "its
point." Rather, she chooses to integrate her experience of reading the text with
the experiences described by the "I" in the poem. She uses her confusion as an
aid to interpretation rather than a hindrance. Her predominant reading strategy
seems to be to relate aspects of her own personal experiences to those described
in the poem and then to create a "point" for the poem.

The repertoire of the reader, therefore, influences the effect a particular text
will have. It is impossible to say that "Messenger" does or does not make sense
in itself. We can only talk of certain strategies, certain assumptions, certain
expectations that readers have for making sense of it. Where do those strategies,
assumptions, and expectations come from? The next question helps you address
this issue.

What Does Your Response Tell You About Yourself as a Reader? It would
be possible to turn such a question into a self-analysis or a personality profile,
as if what you read was totally dependent on the kind of person you are. But
individuals are, as we explained in Chapter 2, created as "subjects" by a host
of different social and cultural forces, so that to ask this question is really to
focus on readers' general repertoires. To answer this question, therefore, you
must begin to explore the cultural factors underlying your cognitive acts. This
kind of analysis marks an essential difference from exercises in free-association
or self-analysis.

In relation to the two response statements on Dave Smith's "Messenger,"
you might ask yourself: What reading strategies have these readers been taught
that encourage them to look for "messages" in literary texts? What attitudes
towards the self, individual identity, the "I" (especially as filtered through

memory) have they acquired from their society? Do *you* share their reading strategies and attitudes? Such questions help you to begin to situate your reading experiences both cognitively and culturally.

Writing Suggestions

1. Using this new information about response statements, write *another* two- to three-paragraph response to "Skunk Hour," based in part on this information and in part on the questions on pp. 73–75; in this response focus not just on the text and not just on yourself as reader but explore your *interaction* with the text.
2. As we move on to discuss three different, interactive ways to respond and analyze your response to a text, try to find where your response fits in and try also to develop your response to overlap with or fit into various of these categories.

Interactive Task Definitions

Self-Consciously Responding to the Text

The simplest kind of response statement is one in which you self-consciously explore your reactions to a text but in which you are not certain of your focus or direction. This type of response statement is more focused on the reading experience than a free-association. It is also a much more useful starting point than a summary for discovering ways in which to expand and deepen your reactions to a text and eventually to produce a strong reading.

Here is an extract of a student's initial response statement to "Skunk Hour."

I found this poem to be very confusing. I was doing all right with the first four stanzas, but when the poet started talking about himself and then those skunks, I was lost. It's obvious that he's in some kind of state of despair, feeling lonely and left out of everything, but it doesn't seem that he'd actually want to be part of the town he described. But those skunks are what really caused me problems. Why skunks? The author has provided almost straight description up to this point, but am I supposed to believe there's a pack of skunks walking up Main Street? The whole skunk pack seems like it has to be symbolic—they even walk past a church! But I can't figure out how to read them as a symbol. Generally I think I know whether something should be read literally or as a symbol, but here I'm not sure.

Reading Strategies and Writing Goals
for Responding to the Text

Notice that this student is not doing an interpretation of the poem, nor is he merely free-associating. His major strategies are to *observe his process of reading,* that is, to become self-conscious about the particular reading strategies he is using, and to pay attention to the text's effects on him as he is reading it. His analysis at this point is still quite vague, as it generally is at this first stage of a response statement. We can already see, though, that his focus is more literary than cultural—on trying to decide how and when to read symbolically. So in a conference and in class, we focused on his literary repertoire. We asked him to try to be more explicit about the literary expectations he had when coming to this poem and about the particular expectations this poem sets up in him. Obviously, he's concerned about his reading strategies, particularly whether he should read the skunks literally or figuratively. He seems to assume that there is *one* correct way to read this poem, and if he could only figure this out, he would be more comfortable with it. But this is our analysis rather than his. We asked him to write another response statement in which he tried to analyze his response cognitively, that is, to explore in more depth his expectations, his reading strategies, and his process of interacting with this particular text.

But before we look at his second response, let's think about some of the goals of doing this kind of basic response to the text. First, you try to go beyond a simple free-association—you record your reactions—literary and cultural—to the text. Note that in recording his reaction, our student commented that he found the text as a whole confusing because he couldn't decide how to interpret the skunks. Simultaneously, you record as much as possible of your *process of reading.* Our student focused on his reading process as well as his general reactions to the text: he feels comfortable and confident when he thinks he can read literally—the way he experienced the first four stanzas of the poem—and we can pinpoint where the poem became difficult for him.

Focusing on the process of reading often leads readers, as it did this student, to generalize about their reading process and to discover some assumptions in their general or literary repertoire that could be expanded into a strong reading. In this particular response, our student is beginning to recognize his strategy of labeling a whole text as either literal or metaphorical. His focus, therefore, in his next response statement was to analyze his response *cognitively.* Other students, however, might choose to look at the poem as a statement about our society, and they would therefore be encouraged to explore their cultural assumptions.

Benefits and Costs
of Responding Self-Consciously to the Text

The benefits of writing response statements are many. First, the focus of this and all the types of response statements we'll be discussing is more on learning than on showing that you've read the text. Discovering that you have certain cultural assumptions, certain habits of reading, certain theoretical orientations can be exciting and fun and, for many readers, makes writing about texts much more enjoyable. Second, you as the reader decide what issues are important in your reading of a text; consequently, there can be no "wrong" responses, only ones that are insufficiently developed and analyzed. This can help you gain confidence in your abilities as a reader because you will discover that you have specific opinions. This exploratory response statement, therefore, can lay the groundwork for you to develop a deeper cognitive or cultural analysis of your response to a text.

There are, of course, some costs to writing exploratory response statements. Although there are no "wrong" responses, a response statement can, nonetheless, be more *challenging* to write than a simple summary or free-association. As you become more attuned to writing response statements, your teacher will expect you to analyze more and more deeply the factors influencing your responses to texts. This will require you to become increasingly aware of the cognitive and cultural forces that influence not only the way you read a given poem but the way you perceive yourself and your world.

Second, unlike an interpretation, response statements do not put closure on a text. While some students feel quite liberated that they no longer have to write essays that pretend to present definitive meanings, others feel upset or threatened by the fact that their interpretations of a text can never be regarded as the "correct" interpretation. Once you recognize that dominant interpretations can and do change over time because they are culture-centered, you realize that text analysis can theoretically go on forever.

Finally, although you can discuss what you feel is the meaning of a text in a response statement, the notion of interpreting the text is definitely subordinated to analyzing your process of reading it and to analyzing the cultural factors that influence that process. Again, for many students, this characteristic of response statements is not a cost; other students, however, who have been traditionally trained, may find greater difficulty in adjusting their writing goals.

Writing Suggestion

Using some of the issues discussed above, write a response statement on the following poem:

DAVE SMITH (b. 1942)

Messenger

It was not kindness, but I was only buckle-high in the door.
I let him in because the knock had come, the rain
clawed each window and wall. I was afraid.
Climbing down the stairs I did not know
how my country, cunningly, had rotted,
but hear, now, my steps creak in memory

5

and the rocks let go in the blind nightglass
where you get up, frightened, to reenact
the irrational logic of flesh.

Even now I can't see why it happens, the moment of change,   10
but must try to witness each particular index
of landscape and irony of promise. I know
I was a child when the banging began, sleepless
with every light in the house blazing. Then
the man whose speech entangled me came in   15
from the mud-world. He could not
put together the clear words of hope
we dream, only the surge of a river.
He, who said it wasn't a fit thing

for anyone, half-grown, to have to imagine in this godforsaken   20
life, said there was a message, the river high,
no chance. I remember the wind at that door
breaking like a father's hand on my face.
Such hurting does not cease and maybe
that is why the man went on fumbling   25
for love, for the loving words
that might be knowledge. He gave me

this message. I took it, and took, without warning, grief's
language that piece-by-piece has showed me how
to connect dreamed moments skidding like rocks   30
in the silence of a Wyoming midnight.
Each of his rainy words, fragments
of the old sickness, passed into me,
then he was gone, miserable and emptied,
and I had no home but the heart's hut,   35
the blistering walls of loneliness,
the world's blue skymiles of longing.

Common with drowned fir and uncoiling crocus, then, I
walked in ignorance and entered this terrible life
that was always a dream of the future   40
in the relentless unsleep of those
who cannot remember the last thing they wanted
to say: that love exists. And in darkness
you have dreamed me into your world
with their message, their words   45
whispering an hour before black, sudden knocking

that, even as I recall it, begins in your heart's meat
to reverberate, oh, its noise is going
to wake you like a dove's desire.
This is the dream of the soft buckling   50
of flesh, the beautiful last erosions,
and I swear I would give up these words

if I could, I would stop the code
of that streetlight just beyond your bed—

but it is too late, for the secret of hope swells in you   55
and who can stop the news that already screams
like the roof's edge leaving its nails
over your child's bed that is, now,
splintered and empty as every moment
skidding at the back of your neck? Leaves   60
not a month old hurl out of the storm
and steady splatter of time, and tomorrow
will lie still ripening, but only long enough
for you to catalog, in dream, what was possible

before the rake must drag its scritch-scratch over ground.   65
All I ask is that you turn to the child
inside, those words dreaming and changeless
as love's last chance—let them be said
against whatever, crying in the night,
we still think may be stopped, the black   70
historical fact of life's event
crashing, like a wall of water,
over the actuary's lawn and yours.

You have seen me before and would not hear, stung by your
wife's fierce beauty, when I called your name,   75
and the day your mother died I begged
your attention and got your dollar.
I followed you once, in New York, like truth,
always to give you the message, and now
on your porch, mud-spattered, I am   80
knocking to make you see what love is.
Call your wife, the police, anyone you like,

for everyone is waiting. We don't mean to be unkind but are
compelled to deliver, faithfully, the words
that have been fluttering in your ear   85
like a scream. It is not the wind
waking you, but the low roar of years
fumbling to tell you what has happened,
or will, when the door flies open
and the naked message of love   90
stands there stuttering in your face,
alive, crying, leaving nothing out.

Now let's return to "Skunk Hour" and look at more detailed responses to
the poem that can help you get a better sense of the diverse types of task definitions
you can have while writing response statements. First, let's examine how our
student (quoted above) revised part of his response statement to analyze it
cognitively.

Analyzing Your Response Cognitively

. . . . I assume when a poet starts to speak in his own voice that the point is coming, but in ''Skunk Hour'' that doesn't seem to be the case. I'm starting to realize that maybe this is the major assumption confusing my reading. I expect the skunks to be, somehow, significant because the poet is talking about them in the first person. Actually, the whole poem, including the skunks, is descriptive, but the text strategy of the voice speaking in the first person suggests to me that the description should mean something more. For that reason I think I tried in my first response to read the skunks as symbols for something—there's really nothing in the poem to suggest they aren't actual skunks. One of the things I'm discovering is that it isn't the text alone that dictates how I read, but my own assumptions about the text strategies and my own reading strategies. I'm beginning to recognize that I could choose to read any part of ''Skunk Hour'' either literally or metaphorically, and that choice would determine the way I interpreted the poem.

Reading Strategies and Writing Goals for Analyzing Your Response Cognitively

Notice how our student has begun to move away from suggesting that the poem is dictating its meaning to him toward an understanding of the various ways in which his assumptions and reading strategies influence his reading. In other words, he's beginning to show how his repertoire interacts with the poem's. He recognizes the force of the first-person text strategy upon his own reading strategies. He assumes that the "I" is going to give him the message of the poem, and he changes his reading strategies—he begins to read for symbols—in an attempt to discover this message. But he comes to realize that because he's chosen to adopt this symbolic reading strategy, he can also choose to adopt other strategies that can help him read the poem in diverse ways.

Can you look at *your* response to the poem and begin to analyze one or more of your reading strategies? Did you, like our student, play with literal/ figurative distinctions? Did you react in some way to the use of first person? What other kinds of reading strategies did you use that you might want to explore further?

Let's list a variety of reading strategies that you might use in any number of reading contexts, but which you would want to refine and explore if you were analyzing your response cognitively. Did you, for example, read playfully for multiple meanings of individual words or phrases? Many of our students have found that using the dictionary is a great way to enhance this strategy. You have probably been frequently told to look a word up in the dictionary when you don't know its meaning, and upon doing so, you have discovered that it has many divergent meanings. This can be a source of pleasure for you rather than one of frustration if you adopt the strategy of reading playfully for multiple meanings. Did you relate "Skunk Hour" to other poems you've read? Did you relate it in some way to a personal experience? Did you read it primarily to build consistency, that is, to find a single meaning?

After you have discovered what your reading strategies were, your goal then becomes to determine what particular assumptions about certain text strategies, about poetry in general, about the text's subject matter, and so forth, influenced your using certain reading strategies. Recall that our student (quoted above) discovered that he began to read symbolically after the poet started speaking in the first person because he expected that "the message" of the poem would occur there.

Benefits and Costs
of Analyzing Your Response Cognitively

Becoming self-conscious about your own cognitive processes can help increase your pleasure in reading because it will enhance your interpretive options. Once you realize how and why you've read a text in a particular way, you can then choose to read it in alternative ways. You can also generalize your discoveries about your reading strategies to your reading of other texts. An awareness of your cognitive processes can also help you to become a stronger reader of texts because you will be able to explore factors underlying your responses instead of just the responses themselves. The only cost that we would warn you against in analyzing your responses cognitively is that you do not ignore the *cultural imperatives* that underlie cognitive assumptions.

Writing Suggestions

1. If you analyzed your response to "Skunk Hour" cognitively, explain what reading strategies of yours you focused on and what you feel are the benefits and costs of your analysis.
2. In what ways could you develop your analysis further?
3. Analyze cognitively your response to the following poem or to another text you are reading.

ANDREW MARVELL (1621–1678)

To His Coy Mistress

Had we but world enough, and time,
This coyness, Lady, were no crime.

We would sit down and think which way
To walk and pass our long love's day.
Thou by the Indian Ganges' side
Shouldst rubies find; I by the tide
Of Humber would complain. I would
Love you ten years before the Flood,
And you should, if you please, refuse
Till the conversion of the Jews.
My vegetable love should grow
Vaster than empires, and more slow;
An hundred years should go to praise
Thine eyes and on thy forehead gaze;
Two hundred to adore each breast,
But thirty thousand to the rest;
An age at least to every part,
And the last age should show your heart.
For, Lady, you deserve this state,
Nor would I love at lower rate.

But at my back I always hear
Time's wingèd chariot hurrying near;
And yonder all before us lie
Deserts of vast eternity.
Thy beauty shall no more be found,
Nor, in thy marble vault, shall sound
My echoing song; then worms shall try
That long preserved virginity.
And your quaint honor turn to dust,
And into ashes all my lust:
The grave's a fine and private place,
But none, I think, do there embrace.

Now therefore, while the youthful hue
Sits on thy skin like morning glew[1]
And while thy willing soul transpires
At every pore with instant fires,
Now let us sport us while we may,
And now, like amorous birds of prey,
Rather at once our time devour
Than languish in his slow-chapt power.
Let us roll all our strength and all
Our sweetness up into one ball,
And tear our pleasures with rough strife
Thorough[2] the iron gates of life:
Thus, though we cannot make our sun
Stand still, yet we will make him run.

5

10

15

20

25

30

35

40

45

---

[1] glew: glow

Analyzing Your Response Culturally

Analyzing your reading strategies helps you situate yourself cognitively in relation to the text to see how its strategies and yours intersect. But reading is not just a mental act. You still need to situate yourself and the text in a broader cultural context. Writing and reading always take place within cultural contexts: they are produced by the ideology of the societies in which they occur. For example, our student quoted above placed a tremendous amount of importance on the "I" of the poem, perhaps because our culture places such value on the notion of the individual. Thus our student was not just responding to a text strategy when he chose to look for the "message" of the poem in those places where the poet spoke in first person; he was responding to a whole host of cultural values that regard the individual as a unique being, as a source of subjectivity. It was only after a fair bit of research into the use of the first person in poetry and into the evolution of the concept of the individual from such sources as Raymond Williams's *Keywords* that our student began to recognize the cultural assumptions that were motivating his cognitive acts. Although you certainly cannot do research for every text you read, talking to your peers and your teachers and discovering differences as well as similarities in your responses can help you become attuned to many cultural assumptions—that often seem "true" and "natural" rather than cultural—underlying your cognitive responses to texts.

At times, however, you will find yourself immediately moving into a cultural analysis. You will discover that the general repertoire of the text interacts or clashes with yours in such a way that you want immediately to explore the ideological forces underlying your response. Look, for example, at this student's response:

Generally people are attracted to rich people and repelled by
skunks. This poem was interesting to me because it had the opposite effect. I was brought up by parents who, I think, would have
both admired and felt suspicious of the people described in this
poem. Yet the poem undermines their place on the social ladder by
suggesting that they are all poor—despite their pretenses. In a
way it's still hard for me to know how to react to them: should I
despise or resent them because they're phoneys or admire or be
jealous of them because they have things I don't? It seems that
our society is very divided in how it treats its well-to-do, and I
think this poem and my reaction to it reflect that. On the one hand
all those TV shows like *Dynasty* make everyone sad because they
aren't rich, but on the other hand the rich are actually portrayed
on these shows as mean and nasty! So we're divided as a culture: do
we admire them because they have money or hate them because
they're vicious and deceptive?

Actually this poem has suggested to me a third attitude one can have toward the rich: pity because they're placed in a role by society where they feel they have to maintain some kind of front. I think that the ''I'' of the poem feels all these emotions. He's obviously alienated from these people, yet he seems to wish he had somebody to love—but he doesn't. He says, ''nobody's here.'' The presence of the skunks and the poet's reaction to them are actually what made me think of the third way of looking at the rich. The skunks, according to the poem, ''will not scare,'' and they're the only ones who won't. Everyone else in this poem is afraid. When you think about it, it's not just the rich that feel they have roles to play; we all do. We all have our pretenses, and because our society gives us such contradictory messages, for example, about the rich on *Dynasty,* we're never sure we are playing ''the appropriate role.'' This is actually a troubling thing to think about because you're often told to ''be yourself,'' yet what does that even mean. If you were ''marching up Main Street'' in your town, could you really be as unself-conscious as the family of skunks?

Reading Strategies and Writing Goals
for Analyzing Your Response Culturally

What do you think of this student's response? Regardless of whether you agree with it or not, can you see some of the ways in which the reading strategies she uses are different from and similar to other types of writing we've discussed? Notice that, like the free-association, she does present some personal information, but her strategies in using it are different. Her personal information is set in a context in which it relates, first, to her response to the text and, second, to her larger cultural analysis.

This response also offers, to some extent, an interpretation of the poem: it suggests that we should have more compassion for one another because we are all struggling to play contradictory roles. Yet her strategies for developing an interpretation differ in a number of ways from those of the traditional interpretation discussed earlier. First, she assumes that her reading is not derived solely from "the text" but is the result of a complex interaction of personal, cognitive, and cultural as well as text variables. Second, her position is much more tentative throughout than the traditional text-centered interpretation discussed above; consequently, she develops her position and then moves in a new direction near the end of her response, extending the notion of role-playing from the rich to society in general. Because she implicitly acknowledges that there are many ways to read this poem, she can leave more interpretive options open to herself. Third, she is reading not only to discover "what the poem means" but to look at how it and her responses to it are constituted by larger cultural forces.

Notice how in this response statement our student moves casually from one idea to another. First, she establishes a parallel between her attitude toward the rich in this poem and society's general attitude—that it is difficult to decide whether to admire or resent the rich. Second, she suggests another possible reaction to the rich: to pity them because they are forced by society to play roles. Third, she suggests that we all have to play roles.

One of the clear differences between a response statement and a formal paper is that in the response statement the writer is allowed—and encouraged—to move freely from one idea to another. This student has in her response the potential for developing at least three quite different strong readings of the poem, all of which would explore the interactive nature of reading and would situate her response in her cultural context. We will address how you move from response statements to formal papers in the following chapter, but for now recognize that while response statements must be comprehensible, certain rules of coherence—the need for a unified and developed single idea does not have to apply to response statements. Such rules, we believe, may sometimes constrain your ability to explore your reactions to a text, particularly when your goal is the complex one of situating your response culturally.

Benefits and Costs
of Analyzing Responses Culturally

One of the benefits of writing response statements in which you analyze your response culturally is that you develop links between literary and non-literary texts, particularly those of popular culture. You thus can begin to see that all acts of perception are a kind of reading—from watching television to going to the movies to staring at billboards to reading Shakespeare. This recognition can help you begin to "read" your wider culture with the closeness and attention you give to a poem: this new kind of reading can make you much more critically aware of the ways in which your culture influences you and can give you the tools to, if you so choose, resist or embrace dominant trends in a given aspect of your culture. Finally, in terms of your particular English course, writing cultural analyses of your responses can help you develop strong readings of texts that can be expanded into a formal paper.

Also notice that this response does not focus, as did the previous one, on reading strategies. All response statements are not the same, and you will often discover that you feel compelled to analyze your reading strategies primarily when you are confused by a text. What you have to keep in mind is that although cultural analyses are the most expansive kinds of response statements, they are not comprehensive. No analysis is, even though some pretend to be. A good culture-centered response statement will open up to you more possibilities than you can develop in a paper. Such a sense of multiplicity should not frustrate you but should, rather, help you recognize the powerful and exciting options you have as a reader and a writer.

Writing Suggestions

1. If you did not analyze your response to "Skunk Hour" culturally, try to do so now.
2. Analyze culturally your response to the following poem or to another text you are studying:

WILLIAM WORDSWORTH (1770–1850)

She Dwelt Among the Untrodden Ways

She dwelt among the untrodden ways
   Beside the springs of Dove,
A Maid whom there were none to praise
   And very few to love:

A violet by a mossy stone   5
   Half hidden from the eye!
Fair as a star, when only one
   Is shining in the sky.

She lived unknown, and few could know
   When Lucy ceased to be;   10
But she is in her grave, and oh,
   The difference to me!

In the chart that follows, we will recapitulate the different task representations we've described, some common reading strategies and writing goals that underlie them, and some of their costs and benefits.

Reading Strategies	Writing Goals

SUMMARIZING

- get the gist
- read literally
- avoid ambiguities
- avoid personal opinions

- do the minimum and do it quickly
- demonstrate that you have read the material

FREE-ASSOCIATING

- read as a springboard for thinking
- skim to recognizable points and respond
- avoid analyzing the relationship between the text and your personal experience

- say something about yourself
- no goals for your readers

INTERPRETING TRADITIONALLY

- find or invent an organizing idea
- resolve, downplay, or ignore multiple meanings, ambiguities

- discover "what the text means"
- present an authoritative voice
- disguise a created interpretation as something discovered in the text

SELF-CONSCIOUSLY RESPONDING

- begin to observe your process of reading: begin to become self-conscious about the particular reading strategies you are using
- pay attention to your reactions to the text as you are reading it

- record your reactions—literary and cultural—to the text
- record your process of reading the text
- discover some assumption(s) in your general and/or literary repertoires that can be expanded into a strong reading

Benefits	Costs
• easy to do • not risky • gives a general orientation to the text	• lacks originality • superficial • inhibits thinking • not really "objective"
• easy to do • enjoyable to write • begin analysis of intersection of reader's repertoire with text's repertoire	• may seem arbitrary or irrelevant to your reader • ignores much of the text • may fail to recognize your culture's influence on your response
• can be persuasive • requires clear organization: one main point • can be interesting to read	• requires you to suppress your own voice • focuses on the final reading product, not reading process • fails to analyze cultural contexts influencing reading • suppresses multiple meanings
• focus of writing is on learning, not on showing what you've learned • can make writing on texts more enjoyable • the reader decides what issues are important: there are no "wrong" responses • can lay the groundwork for a deeper cognitive or cultural analysis	• challenging to write • does not put closure on a text: no single "correct" interpretation exists • interpretation is subordinate to analysis of reading process

| *Reading Strategies* | *Writing Goals* |

ANALYZING YOUR RESPONSE COGNITIVELY

- read self-consciously to discover your reading strategies
Menu of reading strategies
- decide to read literally or figuratively
- fill in gaps
- focus on key words in the text
- read playfully for multiple meanings
- develop contradictory readings of the text
- relate text to other texts
- relate to personal experiences
- build consistency
- respond to certain text strategies (person, tone, mood, meter etc.)

- analyze the assumptions in your literary and general repertoires that influenced your choice of certain reading strategies

ANALYZING YOUR RESPONSE CULTURALLY

- relate your "personal" response to the text and to larger aspects of your culture
- recognize that interpretations derive from complex personal, cognitive, cultural, and textual interactions
- do research, particularly with an older text, to enhance your understanding of its repertoire
- compare your general and literary repertoires to those of the text
- be tentative when you feel unsure
- leave yourself multiple interpretive options
- allow yourself to change or develop your interpretation

- analyze the roles your culture plays in forming your general and literary repertoires
- determine how your repertoires and those of the text intersect to influence your responses and interpretations

Benefits	Costs

- increases your interpretive options and your pleasure in reading
- can generalize your discoveries about your reading strategies to other texts
- can help you become a strong reader

- can ignore the cultural imperatives that underlie cognitive assumptions

- develops links between literary and non-literary texts, particularly those of popular culture
- you discover that all acts of perception are a kind of "reading"
- makes you a critical reader of your culture

- challenging and time-consuming
- you can't do everything

ℋ Chapter 4
From Response Statements to Formal Papers

Dispelling Common Assumptions About Formal Papers

Most literature courses ask you to write a formal paper, often involving research into relevant scholarship and criticism. In Chapter 3, we introduced you to a number of strategies for writing cognitively and culturally aware response statements. In this chapter we will raise the question of how formal papers differ from response statements and show you how writing response statements can change the ways in which you write formal papers.

One of the strengths of the response statement is that it is tentative and explorative. It is generally thought that a formal paper, however, unlike a response statement, must sound authoritative and objective, much like the text-based interpretation discussed in Chapter 3. According to this view, it ought to review current criticism, show an awareness of historical background, and come to a definitive conclusion that somehow transcends its own cultural situation. But with all that you have learned about how meanings of a text change over time, how your readings of a text are a result of a complex conjunction of cultural and cognitive forces, can (or should) you now return to writing formal papers, many of whose traditional conventions go against the principles of writing response statements? It is tempting to want to write a paper that sounds "objective" and so appear authoritative, knowledgeable, and "correct." This is probably the kind of writing for which you have been most rewarded in English courses. A well-written traditional formal paper has conventionally been a sign that you have "mastered" your subject.

Is there a way to write a paper that presents an interesting and persuasive strong reading of a text without returning to an objective text-based interpretation?

Without specific guidelines for writing an alternative kind of formal paper, you may well find yourself attempting only an objective mode of writing, arguing (perhaps without meaning to) that meaning is objectively contained in texts and ignoring the cognitive and cultural factors that influence both the writing of a text and your reading of it.

In this chapter we present you with some strategies and goals for writing formal papers that build on cognitively and culturally aware response statements. We will give you some samples of student papers that effectively translate some of the benefits of writing response statements to the writing of formal papers.

Four Major Goals for Formal Papers

We want first to stress four points about writing a formal paper.

1. A formal paper should differ from a response statement *only* in its greater coherence, more formal organization, greater detail, and persuasiveness—not in its methods of approaching the text. The theories and assumptions that underlie your response statements apply equally to your more formal papers.

2. The goals and strategies for response statements not only are acceptable but also are, we believe, equally important for writing a formal paper. In other words, in writing your formal paper, you do not have to determine *what* the meaning of a text is (which is, of course, one of the only acceptable goals for writing a traditional text-based paper). Rather, you can pursue the goal of analyzing *how* a text is able to have a certain meaning (or meanings). You may also choose to write on such issues as: the ways in which your reading strategies intersect with the text's strategies; how your assumptions about literature influence you to read a text in a particular way; how some aspect of your general repertoire clashes with the text's; how the text opens up multiple interpretive options; or you may also develop a strong reading of the text. Your response statements should remain the basis of your inquiry as you move toward a formal paper.

3. If you choose to do a strong reading for your formal paper, you should not let it become a traditional interpretation. Recall what a strong reading is and how it differs from a traditional interpretation. Both can be argued forcefully and persuasively, but there the similarity ends. A traditional interpretation asserts that it is "faithful" to the text; a strong reading actively seeks to take a distinctive position in relation to the text, even reading it "against the grain." In order to be persuasive, remember a traditional interpretation frequently asserts that it represents the only correct reading of a text; a strong reading always acknowledges that it is only one of many possible readings from different perspectives. A strong reading can nonetheless be persuasive. It derives its power from analyzing in detail how particular aspects of the reader's and the text's repertoires intersect. A strong reading explores the cognitive and cultural underpinnings of the reading experience; a traditional interpretation hides them. While offering a particular analysis of a text, therefore, a strong reading focuses on the *process*

of reading, that is, on the strategies and assumptions necessary to form a certain reading; an interpretation focuses on what is seemingly "in" the text.

4. You should read critical and scholarly material (and indeed any nonfiction prose) with the same cultural and cognitive awareness with which you read works of literature. One kind of formal paper often required, especially at the end of a course, is the *research paper*. Like the methods of the traditional interpretation, the methods of the traditional research paper (such as merely summarizing and synthesizing critical approaches and then selecting one as the basis of your own analysis) work against the new model we advocate.

The traditional way of interpreting requires that you evaluate critical texts as right or wrong rather than as explicable in terms of their particular literary and general repertoires. Critics, like all writers and readers, reflect their own cultural context. If you read critical arguments with the same strategies that you use with literary texts, you can establish contexts—whether historical, cultural, political, or psychological—to explain them. You may analyze the cultural and cognitive factors that influenced the critics' readings and compare them with the factors that influenced your own reading; you may investigate the time in which the essays were written; or you may explore the biases of the magazines, journals, or books in which they were published. In short, you need to examine how your repertoire intersects with that of a critical or scholarly essay just as much as how it intersects with a literary text's. Your goal for reading criticism changes, therefore, from one in which you read passively to discover what the literary text "really" means to one in which you read actively to investigate how the critic's repertoire intersects with the literary text's—and how your repertoire intersects with the critic's. Reading criticism in this way helps to increase your interpretive options because you no longer regard critical texts as telling you facts or truths, but rather you study critics' repertoires of assumptions and strategies as a possible way to expand your own.

Using our first three principles, we will next illustrate various strategies and goals our students adopted when they moved from writing a response statement to writing a formal paper. We will then turn to the fourth of these principles, reading critical essays with cultural and cognitive awareness, and examine how our students wrote response statements on *Hamlet* using critical essays on the play. Finally, to review all four principles of adapting response statements to writing formal papers, we will look at a student's formal research paper, which investigates the critical reception of Doris Lessing's novel *Summer Before the Dark*.

Reading and Writing Are Always Processes

Building a reading—whether it is an initial response statement or a formal research paper—is always a process. An initial response statement can focus on the immediate effects that the text produces on you. Subsequent readings can build on that initial response but need not be restricted to it, especially as your interpretive strategies will change in the act of reading and rereading, as you develop more cognitively and culturally aware responses. (In one very important sense, there is never any final reading. To some extent, readers will always change the questions they ask and the issues they pursue, and so their readings will always be under revision.)

Consequently, when you come to write a formal paper, you can build on the discoveries you have made while writing your response statements. You will want to deepen your analysis of the issues involved—by rereading the text, carrying out research, reading criticism, developing your thinking on parts of your own as well as the text's general and literary repertoires—but you should not abandon the explorative nature of the response statement. You should retain the emphasis on the interactive quality of reading and the cognitive and cultural awareness that your responses gradually develop. In fact, in our experience, students can easily extend a culturally and cognitively aware response statement into a formal paper. The main difference is that the issues discovered and raised in the response statement are analyzed in more depth and at greater length. Although additional research findings and material may be included, the self-aware, explorative nature of the response statement remains the foundation of your formal paper. Response statements are not pre-writing exercises to be abandoned when something more "objective" is needed.

From Response Statements to Formal Paper: Kafka's "The Metamorphosis" and Calvino's "The Canary Prince"

All readers have in their literary repertoires a set of assumptions based on the texts they have previously read. Readers accumulate expectations about texts, and when reading a new text, they bring previous expectations to bear to explain their reading experience. Part of the effect of rereading is to increase and deepen those assumptions, and thus to enlarge their literary repertoires. We want to review with you, first, how response statement assignments that focus on your literary repertoires can reveal how your cognitive and cultural knowledge interacts with the text to shape your reading. Second, we will show how your increased awareness can be translated into a more formal paper. To do this, we will give you the initial response statement assignments we give our students on Italo Calvino's "The Canary Prince" and Franz Kafka's "The Metamorphosis," and the subsequent more formal paper topic. We will analyze some of the ways in which our students developed their responses into more formal papers. We suggest you do these assignments as well, and compare your readings of the texts and your writing styles with those of our students.

One very common assumption many readers have is that they can objectively describe the strategies and conventional features of a text. Our work shows that the formal features of texts cannot be studied in isolation from the experience of reading. We want you to explore the relationship between the seemingly systematic structure of the text's repertoire and your own literary repertoire. We will ask you to compare and contrast your reactions to "The Canary Prince" and "The Metamorphosis," two stories that have distinctive literary repertoires.

Response Statement Assignment on "The Canary Prince": Exploring Your Repertoire

ITALO CALVINO (1923–1985)

The Canary Prince

There was a king who had a daughter. Her mother was dead, and the stepmother was jealous of the girl and always spoke badly of her to the king. The maiden defended herself as best she could, but the stepmother was so contrary and insistent that the king, though he loved his daughter, finally gave in. He told the queen to send the girl away, but to some place where she would be comfortable, for he would never allow her to be mistreated. "Have no fear of that," said the stepmother, who then had the girl shut up in a castle in the heart of the forest. To keep her company, the queen selected a group of ladies-in-waiting, ordering them never to let the girl go out of the house or even to look out the windows. Naturally they received a salary worthy of a royal household. The girl was given a beautiful room and all she wanted to eat and drink. The only thing she couldn't do was go outdoors. But the ladies, enjoying so much leisure time and money, thought only of themselves and paid no attention to her.

Every now and then the king would ask his wife, "And how is our daughter? What is she doing with herself these days?" To prove that she did take an interest in the girl, the queen called on her. The minute she stepped from her carriage, the ladies-in-waiting all rushed out and told her not to worry, the girl was well and happy. The queen went up to the girl's room for a moment. "So you're comfortable, are you? You need nothing, do you? You're looking well, I see; the country air is doing you good. Stay happy, now. Bye-bye, dear!" And off she went. She informed the king she had never seen his daughter so content.

On the contrary, always alone in that room, with ladies-in-waiting who didn't so much as look at her, the princess spent her days wistfully at the window. She sat there leaning on the windowsill, and had she not thought to put a pillow under them, she would have got calluses on her elbows. The window looked out on the forest, and all day long the princess saw nothing but treetops, clouds and, down below, the hunters' trail. Over that trail one day came the son of a king in pursuit of a wild boar. Nearing the castle known to have been unoccupied for no telling how many years, he was amazed to see washing spread out on the battlements, smoke rising from the chimneys, and open casements. As he looked about him, he noticed a beautiful maiden at one of the upper windows and smiled at her. The maiden saw the prince too, dressed in yellow, with hunter's leggings and gun, and smiling at her, so she smiled back at him. For a whole hour, they smiled, bowed, and curtsied, being too far apart to communicate in any other way.

The next day, under the pretext of going hunting, the king's son returned, dressed in yellow, and they stared at each other this time for two hours; in addition to smiles, bows, and curtsies, they put a hand over their hearts and waved handkerchiefs at great length. The third day the prince stopped for three hours, and they blew each other kisses. The fourth day he was there as usual, when from behind a tree a witch peeped and began to guffaw: "Ho, ho, ho, ho!"

"Who are you? What's so funny?" snapped the prince.

"What's so funny? Two lovers silly enough to stay so far apart!"

"Would you know how to get any closer to her, ninny?" asked the prince.

"I like you both," said the witch, "and I'll help you."

She knocked at the door and handed the ladies-in-waiting a big old book with yellow, smudgy pages, saying it was a gift to the princess so the young lady could pass the time reading. The ladies took it to the girl, who opened it at once and read: "This is a magic book. Turn the pages forward, and the man becomes a bird; turn them back, and the bird becomes a man once more."

The girl ran to the window, placed the book on the sill, and turned the pages in great haste while watching the youth in yellow standing in the path. Moving his arms, he was soon flapping wings and changed into a canary, dressed in yellow as he was. Up he soared above the treetops and headed straight for the window, coming to rest on the cushioned sill. The princess couldn't resist picking up the beautiful canary and kissing him; then remembering he was a young man, she blushed. But on second thought she wasn't ashamed at all and made haste to turn him back into a youth. She picked up the book and thumbed backward through it; the canary ruffled his yellow feathers, flapped his wings, then moved arms and was once more the youth dressed in yellow with the hunter's leggings who knelt before her, declaring, "I love you!"

By the time they finished confessing all their love for one another, it was evening. Slowly, the princess leafed through the book. Looking into her eyes the youth turned back into a canary, perched on the windowsill, then on the eaves, then trusting to the wind, flew down in wide arcs, lighting on the lower limb of a tree. At that, she turned the pages back in the book and the canary was a prince once more who jumped down, whistled for his dogs, threw a kiss toward the window, and continued along the trail out of sight.

So every day the pages were turned forward to bring the prince flying up to the window at the top of the tower, then turned backward to restore his human form, then forward again to enable him to fly away, and finally backward for him to get home. Never in their whole life had the two young people known such happiness.

One day the queen called on her stepdaughter. She walked about the room, saying, "You're all right, aren't you? I see you're a trifle slimmer, but that's certainly no cause for concern, is it? It's true, isn't it, you've never felt better?" As she talked, she checked to see that everything was in place. She opened the window and peered out. Here came the prince in yellow along the trail with his dogs. "If this silly girl thinks she is going to flirt at the window," said the stepmother to herself, "she has another thought coming to her." She sent the girl for a glass of water and some sugar, then hurriedly removed five or six hairpins from her own hair and concealed them in the pillow with the sharp points sticking straight up. "That will teach her to lean on the window!" The girl returned with the water and sugar, but the queen said, "Oh, I'm no longer thirsty; you drink it, my dear! I must be getting back to your father. You don't need anything, do you? Well, goodbye." And she was off.

As soon as the queen's carriage was out of sight, the girl hurriedly flipped over the pages of the book, the prince turned into a canary, flew to the window, and struck the pillow like an arrow. He instantly let out a shrill cry of pain. The yellow feathers were stained with blood; the canary had driven the pins into his breast. He rose with a convulsive flapping, trusted himself to the wind, descended in irregular arcs, and lit on the ground with outstretched wings. The frightened princess, not yet fully aware of what had happened, quickly turned the pages back in the hope there would be no wounds when he regained his human form. Alas, the prince reappeared dripping blood from the deep stabs that had rent the yellow garment on his chest, and lay back surrounded by his dogs.

At the howling of the dogs, the other hunters came to his aid and carried him off on a stretcher of branches, but he didn't so much as glance up at the window of his beloved, who was still overwhelmed with grief and fright.

Back at his palace, the prince showed no promise of recovery, nor did the doctors know what to do for him. The wounds refused to heal over, and constantly hurt. His father the king posted proclamations on every street corner promising a fortune to anyone who could cure him, but not a soul turned up to try.

The princess meanwhile was consumed with longing for her lover. She cut her sheets into thin strips which she tied one to the other in a long, long rope. Then one night she let herself down from the high tower and set on the hunters' trail. But because of the thick darkness and the howls of the wolves, she decided to wait for daylight. Finding an old oak with a hollow trunk, she nestled inside and, in her exhaustion, fell asleep at once. She woke up while it was still pitch-dark, under the impression she had heard a whistle. Listening closely, she heard another whistle, then a third and a fourth, after which she saw four candle flames advancing. They were four witches coming from the four corners of the earth to their appointed meeting under that tree. Through a crack in the trunk the princess, unseen by them, spied on the four crones carrying candles and sneering a welcome to one another: "Ah, ah, ah!"

They lit a bonfire under the tree and sat down to warm themselves and roast a couple of bats for dinner. When they had eaten their fill, they began asking one another what they had seen of interest out in the world.

"I saw the sultan of Turkey, who bought himself twenty new wives."

"I saw the emperor of China, who has let his pigtail grow three yards long."

"I saw the king of the cannibals, who ate his chamberlain by mistake."

"I saw the king of this region, who has the sick son nobody can cure, since I alone know the remedy."

"And what is it?" asked the other witches.

"In the floor of his room is a loose tile. All one need do is lift the tile, and there underneath is a phial containing an ointment that would heal every one of his wounds."

It was all the princess inside the tree could do not to scream for joy. By this time the witches had told one another all they had to say, so each went her own way. The princess jumped from the tree and set out in the dawn for the city. At the first secondhand dealer's she came to, she bought an old doctor's gown and a pair of spectacles, and knocked at the royal palace. Seeing the little doctor with such scant paraphernalia, the servants weren't going to let him in, but the king said, "What harm could he do my son who can't be any worse off than he is now? Let him see what he can do." The sham doctor asked to be left alone with the sick man, and the request was granted.

Finding her lover groaning and unconscious in his sickbed, the princess felt like weeping and smothering him with kisses. But she restrained herself because of the urgency of carrying out the witch's directions. She paced up and down the room until she stepped on a loose tile, which she raised and discovered a phial of ointment. With it she rubbed the prince's wounds, and no sooner had she touched each one with ointment than the wound disappeared completely. Overjoyed she called the king, who came in and saw his son sleeping peacefully, with the color back in his cheeks, and no trace of any of the wounds.

"Ask for whatever you like, doctor," said the king. "All the wealth in the kingdom is yours."

"I wish no money," replied the doctor. "Just give me the prince's shield bearing the family coat-of-arms, his standard, and his yellow vest that was rent and bloodied." Upon receiving the three items, she took her leave.

Three days later, the king's son was again out hunting. He passed the castle in the heart of the forest, but didn't deign to look up at the princess's window. She immediately picked up the book, leafed through it, and the prince had no choice but to change into a canary. He flew into the room, and the princess turned him back into a man. "Let me go," he said. "Isn't it enough to have pierced me with those pins of yours and caused me so much agony?" The prince, in truth, no longer loved the girl, blaming her for his misfortune.

On the verge of fainting, she exclaimed, "But I saved your life! I am the one who cured you!"

"That's not so," said the prince. "My life was saved by a foreign doctor who asked for no recompense except my coat-of-arms, my standard, and my bloodied vest!"

"Here are your coat-of-arms, your standard, and your vest! The doctor was none other than myself! The pins were the cruel doing of my stepmother!"

The prince gazed into her eyes, dumbfounded. Never had she looked so beautiful. He fell at her feet asking her forgiveness and declaring his deep gratitude and love.

That very evening he informed his father he was going to marry the maiden in the castle in the forest.

"You may marry only the daughter of a king or an emperor," replied his father.

"I shall marry the woman who saved my life."

So they made preparations for the wedding, inviting all the kings and queens in the vicinity. Also present was the princess's royal father, who had been informed of nothing. When the bride came out, he looked at her and exclaimed, "My daughter!"

"What!" said the royal host. "My son's bride is your daughter? Why did she not tell us?"

"Because," explained the bride, "I no longer consider myself the daughter of a man who let my stepmother imprison me." And she pointed at the queen.

Learning of all his daughter's misfortune, the father was filled with pity for the girl and with loathing for his wicked wife. Nor did he wait until he was back home to have the woman seized. Thus the marriage was celebrated to the satisfaction and joy of all, with the exception of that wretch.

Response Statement Assignment on "The Canary Prince"

1. What text strategies and conventions tell you that this story is a fairy tale?
2. When in the story do you recognize it is a fairy tale?
3. What expectations do you have about how the story will develop and end?
4. How does your knowledge of the conventions of writing fairy tales affect the conventions you use to read them?
5. What kinds of questions do you *not* ask about the story?

Students typically state that they are able to recognize "The Canary Prince" as a fairy tale by a variety of familiar conventions. As one student wrote:

> The story occurs in an ancient and unknown land; a beautiful princess is imprisoned by a wicked stepmother but is nonetheless able to meet and fall in love with a handsome prince, and after a few mishaps, which are resolved by magic, they live happily ever after.

Within one sentence, this student has noted many familiar conventions that seem obvious, "normal," and acceptable with regard to fairy stories. Bear in mind, however, that these text features might seem quite odd to someone who knew nothing of fairy tales.

While your knowledge of fairy tale conventions, on the one hand, makes them accessible and easy to read, on the other hand, it may inhibit your asking certain questions of the story, questions that you would typically ask of other kinds of fiction. Many students discover that they do *not* ask the following questions of "The Canary Prince": What do the prince and princess symbolize? How will their life together turn out? Are they really compatible? How can a book magically turn a man into a canary?

Are these similar to questions you did not ask of this story? What other "inappropriate" questions can you add to the list? Why do you think certain questions seem unsuitable to ask of a fairy tale? Recognizing that you have certain reading strategies in your repertoire that you unconsciously disregard in certain reading situations can help you to investigate and perhaps alter the assumptions underlying those unconscious reading choices.

In writing a response statement exploring your reactions to "The Canary Prince," you can begin to gain insights about your repertoire on fairy tales. When you begin to write your formal paper, you should expand and clarify these insights, perhaps making much of what was *implicit* in your response *explicit* in your formal paper.

Response Statement Assignment on "The Metamorphosis": Expanding Your Repertoire

Read Kafka's "The Metamorphosis"[1] and answer the following questions:
1. What kinds of questions do you ask of Kafka's story?
2. By what reading strategies do you go about interpreting it?
3. What text strategies (or conventions) and what expectations or assumptions of yours influence the way you respond to this story?
4. Can you categorize this story as a certain "type" in the way you were able to categorize "The Canary Prince"?
5. How does your ability (or inability) to categorize it affect your response to the story?

"The Metamorphosis" concerns a young clerk, Gregor, who has in the past dutifully supported his shiftless family but who wakes one morning to find he has turned into an insect. He treats this occurrence as an inconvenience, tries to hide it from his family and his boss, and eventually settles into a life of adapting to his new nature. Once they discover his metamorphosis, the members of his family are horrified; only his sister will care for him and bring him food. The servants are afraid and leave the household. The family is increasingly distraught, until finally Gregor is killed by a new, callous servant, much to the relief of everyone. Gregor's family now starts to live a life without concern for the inconvenience he has caused them.

Students typically ask what "The Metamorphosis" *means* or what its "themes" are—questions they do not ask (at least not initially) of "The Canary Prince." Did you find yourself doing the same? You might ask yourself what Gregor's becoming a bug could symbolize. Or you might question why Gregor's family virtually ignored him or why he turned into a bug rather than some other form of life.

Many students report in their response statements that they identify with Gregor, but they are puzzled by why they would identify with a character who turned into a bug and not with a prince who turned into a canary. When reading "The Canary Prince," our students neither analyzed characters' motivations nor identified with characters—even though they obviously found such responses appropriate to "The Metamorphosis."

Many students felt that the source of their confusion about what "The Metamorphosis" means was that they were unable to state exactly what kind of story it was. Here, for example, is the opening of the story.

> As Gregor Samsa awoke one morning from uneasy dreams he found himself transformed in his bed into a gigantic insect. He was lying on his hard, as it were armor-plated, back and when he lifted his head a little he could see his dome-like

---

[1] "The Metamorphosis" can be found in Gary Waller, Kathleen McCormick, Lois Fowler, *The Lexington Introduction to Literature* (Lexington, MA: Heath, 1987), and many other anthologies.

brown belly divided into stiff arched segments on top of which the bed quilt could hardly keep in position and was about to slide off completely. His numerous legs, which were pitifully thin compared to the rest of his bulk, waved helplessly before his eyes.

What has happened to me? he thought. It was no dream. His room, a regular human bedroom, only rather too small, lay quiet between the four familiar walls. Above the table on which a collection of cloth samples was unpacked and spread out—Samsa was a commercial traveler—hung the picture which he had recently cut out of an illustrated magazine and put into a pretty gilt frame. It showed a lady, with a fur cap on and a fur stole, sitting upright and holding out to the spectator a huge fur muff into which the whole of her forearm had vanished!

Can *you* categorize "The Metamorphosis" as a certain type of story? Do its conventions seem similar to those of any other stories you've read? Is your response to this story dramatically different from your response to "The Canary Prince"?

Why would readers have such different responses to the two stories? Is it the texts themselves or the readers' different literary repertoires that enable them to have such divergent responses? In each story a metamorphosis occurs. Most readers, perhaps including you, have no difficulty reading a story about the metamorphosis of a prince into a canary, even if they think it is just a trivial fairy story. They accept it, just as they accepted all other forms of magic in "The Canary Prince," because they expect to encounter some kind of magic in fairy stories. Most readers, however, cannot so easily **naturalize** the metamorphosis of Gregor Samsa into a bug, and consequently they try to find ways to explain away Gregor's metamorphosis.

As you can see, the response statement assignment on "The Metamorphosis" raises many more issues than it answers. And this is as it should be. Students recognize that they respond differently to the stories, but they cannot clearly articulate *why*. As we said above, one of the advantages of response statements is that they can be tentative and explorative. As you begin to write a formal paper, remember that the basis for a strong reading can be in the very tentativeness of your intitial responses, which can provide an opportunity for you to ask yourself further questions and to probe your repertoire for the possible reasons underlying your responses. After rereading the stories a few times in light of your response statements, you will probably be ready to begin your formal paper.

The Formal Paper: Comparing Responses to the Two Metamorphoses

For your formal paper, we suggest you compare and contrast the kinds of responses you had to these two stories and the kinds of interpretations of them you developed. The major question we want you to discuss in your paper is this: Why did you react to the two metamorphoses in such different ways in your response statements? Such a question requires you to analyze the effect on your reading of your own prior knowledge and expectations about literary genres (such as fairy tales), your reading strategies (see table, p. 88, for menu of reading strategies), and the settings or institutions in which you learned to read.

In asking you to move from a response statement to a more formal paper, we are asking you to analyze and deepen your first responses by reexamining them in more explicitly defined cultural and cognitive contexts. In a real sense, your formal papers will be more fully developed responses to and explanations of your original tentative response statements.

Readers' different assumptions about the two stories are derived from their social and educational backgrounds, and are the product of their culture's general and literary ideologies. Education and earlier reading experiences have given you a repertoire of literary expectations that you apply to these stories. So it is your knowledge of different reading conventions as much as the texts themselves that explains your different reading strategies. As one student remarked: "Simply being able to categorize a text as a fairy tale implies that readers have certain assumptions about how they will read it." Many of our students determined that their ability to accept so readily the fairy world of "The Canary Prince" stems from the time and place in which such stories were introduced to them—in early childhood when the distinction between the real and the imaginary is blurred, and "at home" where "there is no pressure to look for serious meanings."

The Kafka story generally presents more difficulty to readers. Because the tone and setting seemed "realistic," students reported that it was difficult for them to categorize the story either as a fairy tale or as science fiction, two familiar forms that would have allowed them to naturalize Gregor's metamorphosis in the way they naturalized the canary prince's. One student argued: "Kafka's story is more like something taught in English classes where you're expected to find deep meaning: it sounds realistic but, since it doesn't literally make sense, I feel I must read it metaphorically." Here is another extract from "The Metamorphosis." Read it over and see if your reaction is similar to or different from that of our student.

He thought that he might get out of bed with the lower part of his body first, but this lower part, which he had not yet seen and of which he could form no clear conception, proved too difficult to move; it shifted so slowly; and when finally, almost wild with annoyance, he gathered his forces together and thrust out recklessly, he had miscalculated the direction and bumped heavily against the lower end of the bed, and the stinging pain he felt informed him that precisely this lower part of his body was at the moment probably the most sensitive.

So he tried to get the top part of himself out first, and cautiously moved his head towards the edge of the bed. That proved easy enough, and despite its breadth and mass the bulk of his body at last slowly followed the movement of his head. Still, when he finally got his head free over the edge of the bed he felt too scared to go on advancing, for after all if he let himself fall in this way it would take a miracle to keep his head from being injured. And at all costs he must not lose consciousness now, precisely now; he would rather stay in bed.

Having learned in school that if a text does not make literal sense, it might make sense if read figuratively, our students drew on their knowledge of literary symbolism, their knowledge of psychology, and their personal experiences of rejection to analyze Gregor's metamorphosis symbolically.

Interestingly, this particular strategy for naturalizing a text—that is, reading it figuratively—was in our students' repertoires when reading both stories but was activated only when they read Kafka's story because students' assumptions about fairy tales precluded such forms of analysis. Once you recognize that you have accumulated a set of assumptions about the appropriateness of certain reading strategies, you can discover how you "naturally" try to apply them to new texts. Some of our students, therefore, were able to analyze their reactions to "The Metamorphosis" only after they discovered that they had used "symbolic" or "metaphorical" strategies to read it, strategies that allowed them to develop more creative psychological and personal responses to the story. As one student wrote, after developing a psychological analysis of "The Metamorphosis":

> Such a psychological analysis as this can be done to a work which is *perceived to contain* a possible psychological interpretation. To attempt such an analysis on a fairy tale like "The Canary Prince" would be sheer folly. It may seem like a contradiction, on the one hand, to say that no definitive meaning lies in texts but rather in individual interpretations of them while, on the other hand, to assert that to analyze a fairy tale psychologically is ridiculous. This paradox is cleared up when one recognizes that by identifying something as a fairy tale, one is also identifying the various expectations one has of a fairy tale. I do not expect to find symbolism or deep psychological meaning in a fairy tale; hence I do not find it. If the work in question could be perceived as something other than a fairy tale, however, then a new set of expectations might conceivably warrant a psychological analysis.

Other students thought that the story should be read biographically—that is, as a revelation of the personal insecurities of its author. One of our students considered the story to be a "classic case of persecution complex," the story of someone suffering from paranoia and expressing his troubles in fictional form. When asked whether he would think of using the same reading strategies with the Calvino story, however, he laughed and said "fairy stories are not like that." He had learned both from his previous reading experiences and, presumably, in English courses that "serious" fiction was supposed to reveal hidden meanings and that (like a metaphorical or figurative reading) a biographical reading was an appropriate strategy to use with a "serious" story, but not with a fairy tale.

From such an assignment, students realized that from their cultural and educational experiences—at home and in English classes—they had developed certain reading strategies and expectations that played a major role in determining the kinds of meanings they "found" or "created" in texts. They recognized, however, that the more aware they became of the cultural situations in which they had learned their reading strategies and expectations, the more freedom they had to choose when to use them and when to develop new ones.

In preparing to write their formal papers, our students explored and expanded issues raised in their response statements. The issues they addressed did not change but instead were significantly developed. For their more formal papers, our students set out to explain some of the cognitive and cultural factors that influenced their responses. As we saw in the Kafka story, an important cognitive factor was whether they felt compelled to read symbolically or biographically, or, as in the Calvino, found themselves able to suspend disbelief and unquestioningly accept the events of the story. They also began to explore the cultural imperatives underlying those cognitive acts, suggesting that they accepted the events in "The Canary Prince" but not those in "The Metamorphosis" because of the different cultural settings in which they learned to read these kinds of stories.

Sample Student Paper

What follows is a formal student paper comparing "The Canary Prince" and "The Metamorphosis" with marginal and final comments from the teacher on the opposite page. Note that this paper did not require the student to read criticism; we will deal with the type of paper that requires research in the next section.

Teacher's Comments

Western ideology? Remember nothing is "innate." ———————
What seems most natural or "automatic" is often what
is most ideologically influenced.

Good characterization of passive reading. ———————

Be careful about "unique": reading is not a "subjective" matter. Remember ———————
we're all culturally influenced by general ideology.

Good introduction to the no- ———————
tion of reading as an interactive process.

Stephen Vanderhoof
Professor Waller
76–240
April 16, 1987

Changing Conventions and Changing Interpretations

We seek to give everything we read or hear some meaning to make sense of it. This process of assigning meaning is such an innate and automatic response to the written or spoken word that we are often unaware that we are actually involved in this process. We tend to believe that the words of the text itself have meaning, and we are merely "listening to" or "reading" the meaning that is just sitting there waiting for us. This idea does not hold up, however, when one considers the multiple array of meanings that one text, one sentence, indeed one word, can convey to different readers. We are forced to conclude that the text itself does not innately contain any single or fixed meaning at all. Rather, the text serves as a vehicle for creating meaning. When the text's repertoire combines with the reader's, the text assumes a meaning that seems unique for that particular reader, although we can recognize similarities among the interpretations of readers with similar repertoires.

This does not imply that a piece of literature has no particular meaning at all, but that the meaning depends in part on the reader. The text remains the source of potential meaning. Depending on its style, it may project a meaning that is extremely concrete and <u>common to nearly anyone reading it</u>. Or, in contrast, the text may contain many gaps that need to be filled in by the reader to create meaning. This activity requires the active participation of the reader because, in this circumstance, the text encourages a wide range of varied interpretations.

Nice analogy! ————————|

Good emphasis on interactive nature of reading. ————————|

Perhaps talk about the *comfort* of these expectations? ————————|
What psychological functions do these conventions of
fairy tales have?

Nice discussion of fairy tale conventions, but what ————————|
effect do they have on the reader?

A text can be likened to a bag of flour. Alone, flour could hardly be used as food; any attempt at eating it would be met with immediate nausea. However, combined with the cook's additions from his or her own kitchen, it can be made into something quite edible, and could become part of such varied foods as turkey gravy or apple strudel.

In both Franz Kafka's ''The Metamorphosis'' and Italo Calvino's ''The Canary Prince,'' a central part of the story involves a metamorphosis, a total alteration of form and appearance on the part of a character. How we treat the metamorphosis and give it meaning, however, depends on both our past experience with and our attitude toward what we are reading, as well as on the text itself.

Reading ''The Canary Prince'' was very easy: I immediately recognized the fairy tale form, and my interpretations of the story were very much influenced by what I expected from it. The title and the first sentence were quite sufficient signals, and I expected a simple tale set in some unspecified place and time, although the setting would usually be in the romantic and easily imagined medieval period. There would be clear-cut and undeniable ''good guys'' and an evil character, who would be involved in some conflict due to no fault of the good characters and usually involving jealousy. The evil character would cause trouble for a while, then eventually be vanquished by the good, usually with the aid of magic. Not only is the evil queen physically ugly but also she is not the princess's true mother; she is a kind of alien force intruding on a happy family. Thus we as readers feel little or no ambiguity toward her. The princess, who is of course physically beautiful, does nothing to provoke the harsh treatment she experiences and is thus quite innocent. Through magic and love, she is simultaneously married to a handsome prince, reunited with

You might think about how ideology un- ———————
derlies what you call "convention."

Does this mean that fairy tales are defined by how ———————
they are *read*, not just by text strategies alone?

Good discussion of text's lit- ———————
erary repertoire—and your
own.

But as you explain above, it's your *awareness* of the *reading strategies* for fairy ———————
tales that makes the conventions acceptable, not just the conventions themselves.
Don't lose the stress on interaction.

Clear discussion of your expectations and reading strategies. ———————

her father, and rid of her evil stepmother—"to the satisfaction and joy of all, with the exception of that wretch."

Like any literary convention, the fairy tale form is difficult to define absolutely, but it is quite recognizable to readers with a fair experience of fairy tales in their repertoire. There are a great many questions that we ask of other kinds of stories, but the fairy tale form seems to preclude most of such questions from ever being seriously posed. Would it remain a fairy tale if the reader were to ponder over whether the princess and the prince are truly compatible or how they could have fallen so deeply in love from just a view from a tower? Could anything be gained by scoffing at the improbability of a miracle ointment being super-naturally projected to the prince's room, just beyond his view, or of a book having the power to turn a man into a bird? To question these matters would detract from the fairy tale ideal of absolute good triumphing over absolute evil. How good triumphs makes an entertaining story but is not as important as the fact that it always does: good always defeats evil in fairy tales.

My reaction to the prince's metamorphosis is one of so-called willing suspension of disbelief. A metamorphosis of this type occurring in a fairy tale is well accepted, almost expected. Here in the midst of the vague and distant past, such events are simply explained as "magic," something that no fairy tale would be complete without; the convention itself explains it. This quite incredible occurrence is presented in a setting that I can easily naturalize, again making it seem normal, even though it is not "realistic." Were a prince to turn into a bird in my own day and age, in the middle of someone's suburban living room, that is, in a "normal" setting, the metamorphosis would not seem normal at all. Basically this metamorphosis belongs in this story. It

Clear initial analysis of interaction of text strategies and
reader expectations.

You appear to be arguing that this story demands a *mixture* of strategies, yet
you are vague about the actual reading strategies you employed.

Do you know the term "magic realism," applied to stories with a mixture of
realistic and nonrealistic strategies?

Do you know Philip Roth's novel *The*
Breast? It's another (comic) version of the
same kind of thing.

This reads a little too much like a summary here.
Clarify how your repertoire is compelling you to read
the story—as you did in your discussion of "The
Canary Prince."

therefore does not call attention to itself, and I felt no need to analyze or explain it.

Kafka's "The Metamorphosis," on the other hand, struck me in quite a different way. This story's metamorphosis is a turn of events no less bizarre and incredible than that of the fairy tale. Yet the form in which it is written and my expectations of how to interpret and react to that form caused me to interpret the story in another way. The fairy tale is told in a way that announces itself as a fantasy ("There was a king who had a daughter . . ."), yet Kafka's story seems to be told in a conventionally realistic way that suggests that its events are to be taken as plausible occurrences. In effect, it could occur in my living room. Although it is in fact something quite impossible, the apparent metamorphosis is revealed in the <u>very first</u> sentence. I sensed a tone of everyday reality that genuinely affected my interpretation of the text. I felt compelled to carry the realism expressed in the style to my interpretation of the story itself, thereby causing me to perceive a deeper meaning than I had with the fairy tale—to ask serious questions of it.

As the story is clearly told from the point of view of Gregor, I attributed the realism and acceptance of the situation (so odd in a story where a man is transformed into an insect) to Gregor himself. I immediately wanted to ask the question, "Why does he accept so completely the fact that he is suddenly no longer human?" While being turned into a bug is not an everyday experience, Gregor seems to think that it should not require him to take a day off from work. He has been getting up at the same time early every morning to go off and work hard under an overbearing employer and with cold, remote coworkers in order to support his idle and ungrateful family. These are conditions no man could flourish happily in, yet Gregor is quite ready to keep plodding away, even as

This hints at an explanation of your general repertoire, but your analysis needs to go further. ———————

Again, this continues to summarize the story, not analyze your reading process. ———————

Why do you want to develop this symbolic reading? ——————— Examine your own reading strategies and the assumptions behind them.

This is interesting but not sufficiently self-conscious—as you are with "The ——————— Canary Prince." It reads almost like "objective interpretation," not accounting for cognitive and cultural factors. Is this because you're having difficulty figuring them out?

an insect, were he not hampered by the overreactions and hysterics of his family.

People have always associated the most dirty and lowly aspects of the world with insects, and most seem to have a somewhat innate aversion to them. Our natural reaction to an insect is to step on it, to rid ourselves of its disgusting presence in our otherwise tidy world. Yet Gregor, upon becoming one of these creatures himself, seems to feel nothing more than slight surprise. Even more remarkable, he gradually slips more and more into the role of the insect, almost eager to renounce totally the fact that he was ever human. For instance, when his family and coworker express the expected reactions of revulsion and shock upon seeing him in this new form, Gregor is "the only one who had retained any composure" and immediately tries to convince the chief clerk that there is indeed no need for alarm. When the poor man remains unconvinced, it is obvious that "Gregor would have to handle the situation himself." It seems that he considers himself able to function just as he always has and that an insect body is not as bad as one might think. In fact, he feels joy and comfort upon discovering how easily and freely he can move about on his many legs.

This striking attitude led me to develop a symbolic interpretation of Gregor's metamorphosis. I believe that Gregor had ceased being human long before the metamorphosis. He was mainly a functionary who provided support for his family and who had become a lowly traveling salesman looked down upon by everyone he knew. In fact, most aspects of his life were more insectlike than human. So when his physical shape started to reflect the inferior place he had assumed in the world, Gregor was not surprised and expected to keep on assuming the role he had always played. I interpreted most of the events that followed as gradual losses of humanity for Gregor. His loss of the ability to communicate re-

Why is this relevant? Explain more fully. ———————

Why? Don't just present your interpretation as objectively true; you must explain ————————
why you've developed it. This will involve more explicit analysis of how your
general and literary repertoires intersect with the text's.

Is the reader's role only that of following ————————
the suggestions in the text? How do you
develop a strong reading?

This is better—much more explicit about your reading strategies. ————————

You need to be more specific about these ————————
"facets" in discussion of the Kafka story.

minded me of <u>Planet of the Apes</u>, where one of the human characters had been injured in the throat and thus was immediately classified by the apes as incapable of any intelligence and as no possible relation to them. But unlike this man, Gregor willingly loses touch with his former humanity and doesn't fight it. He looks forward to having all the furniture removed from his room, a removal which embodies the last link to his previous life, so that he can crawl mindlessly across the walls and ceiling, a recreation we would definitely associate with a true insect. His eventual death is associated with some uncontrollable and mesmerizing attraction to music, which I interpreted as yet more evidence of his complete assumption of the role of insect.

It became quite evident after considering the differing responses I had to the two stories about a metamorphosis that the same phenomenon expressed in several pieces of literature may elicit widely varying interpretations from the reader. These interpretations come as a result of the literary conventions the text follows, which the reader may recognize. If so, the reader will expect certain meanings from the text, regardless of its superficial content (such as a metamorphosis). Equally important in determining a reader's perception of the text's meaning is the reader's literary repertoire concerning that style of writing or of a particular subject matter.

Intertextuality, such as my connecting Gregor's seeming loss of humanity with a similar situation in a film, can also affect what the reader finds in the text. Thus we find that reading, rather than being merely a passive means through which certain information or a certain story is passed from a text to a reader, is an active process of integration involving many facets of both the text and the individual reader, combining to form a unique interpretation.

Here is the teacher's final comment on this student's paper:

> This paper is excellent in the way you integrate theory and application, and also
> in the ways you show how your repertoire and the text's intersect when reading
> "The Canary Prince," though you might have raised the question of the *adult's*
> (as opposed to the child's) reading of fairy stories.
>
> Your paper, is, however, rather less impressive on "The Metamorphosis." What
> parts of your *literary* repertoire are at work in your reading of "The Metamor-
> phosis"? How do they intersect with your general repertoire? (Recall your mention
> of your living room.) You suggest that you had to mix various kinds of reading
> strategies when reading Kafka's story, but you give no details on this. You might
> also have written in more detail about the sources of your expectations—just as
> you did with the Calvino. Does your culture's general ideology play its part too?
> Or is your reaction primarily a *literary* one?

Writing Suggestion

Use our response-statement and paper assignments (pp. 100–104) to help you
explore the interaction of your literary and general repertoires in your readings
of these or other stories.

Learning to Read Literary Criticism:
Responding to Criticism on Hamlet

Learning to read literary criticism with the same degree of cognitive and cultural
awareness that you use to read literature can at first be difficult. The critics,
after all, are supposed to be experts in the field; they generally know more than
you do about their subject matter, and so you are likely to accept their arguments
as "correct," or perhaps as too authoritative for you to argue with. Further,
most of their essays will be written in just the objective tone we are encouraging
you to avoid because, as we discuss in Chapter 1, it is only recently that critics
have recognized and written about the cultural situatedness of their own responses
to texts.

But rather than either passively accepting critics' arguments or rejecting
them because they are too intimidating, you can use your cognitive and cultural
awareness of your own reading to read *their* arguments critically, asking yourself
questions such as these: What reading strategies did this critic use to read this
play? Are they similar to mine? What repertoire of knowledge does she have
that made her read this text in a way I never would have imagined? What kinds
of text strategies does this critic seem to respond most to? Does this critic's
gender seem to make a difference to the ways in which he reads this character?
From what critical perspective (such as feminist, psychoanalytic, political) is
this critic reading, and should I enlarge my repertoire so that I can also read
from that perspective? If I do, would my reading of the text still differ in some
respects from the critic's?

Reading literary criticism with such questions in mind can help you recognize that while some readings may seem more interesting than others, none provides "the final word" on a text. As long as people read, texts will always be read in diverse ways. And why shouldn't you—recognizing both the strengths and limitations of your own repertoire, as well as its potential to be enlarged—actively engage in this process yourself?

Before we ask you to think about writing a formal research paper, we'd like to give you a "warm up" response statement assignment on a brief selection of criticism on *Hamlet* that we hope will begin to dispel your belief that literary critics—or any writers on any subjects for that matter—have direct access to "the truth."

To study the history of a text's reception, that is, what critics have said about it over the centuries, can help to demonstrate just how fluid a text is, how easily it can be read differently, as well as how transient "dominant" interpretations are. Such an investigation can also raise some interesting theoretical questions about the nature of meaning itself, if meanings of texts are perceived differently throughout history. That a classic like *Hamlet* does not have a definitive agreed-upon meaning is often initially shocking and sometimes disconcerting to many readers. Although a classic, meanings of *Hamlet* have in fact changed radically throughout the play's history—in fact, we suggest, that may be precisely *why* it is a classic.

Writing Suggestion

This assignment has two parts.

1. Read *Hamlet* and write a response to this question: Did you find *Hamlet* to be a particularly ambiguous play? In answering this question, you should (in accord with the general guidelines on response statements, pages 73–76) record both your reactions to the play and the reading strategies you used, asking yourself about such matters as whether you puzzled over and reread any parts of the play, whether you think that Hamlet delayed in killing Claudius, or whether you found the Ghost believable.

2. Consult the brief history of *Hamlet* criticism by John Jump (pages 120–127). Consider in particular the Freudian interpretation by Ernest Jones, in which Hamlet is analyzed as having an Oedipal complex (see page 122). Ask yourself how you can evaluate these different responses. Given that there are serious disagreements, can it be said that expert readers have any more authority than student readers? Specifically, focus on these questions:
   a. Do you agree with any (or many) of the varied, often contradictory interpretations of *Hamlet?* Have any of these interpretations changed your original interpretation of the play?
   b. How do you account for so many interpretations of a single play? What do all these different interpretations suggest about the status of a text?
   c. Are there any meanings or constraints on the production of meaning in the text (if you think there are, give examples), or is meaning determined

solely by the reader's whims?

d. Having read Jump's summary of *Hamlet* criticism, comment on the influences of literary criticism on the interpretation and production of a play.

Did *you* find *Hamlet* to be particularly ambiguous? We have often discovered that most of our students find *Hamlet* difficult but not ambiguous, especially on a first reading. That is, the issue of ambiguity did not seem foremost in their minds, probably because they did not expect to have to read *polyvalently* but were reading initially to *summarize*—to follow the plot, sort out characters, and so forth. Critics base their views on successive rereadings, and (with complex texts) it is only gradually that more open-ended readings result. Becoming aware of the great variety of critical interpretations of *Hamlet,* however, may force you (as it forced many of our students) to ask how the text could support so many different intepretations without seeming incoherent or fragmented. Is it a problem with the text (or the author)? Or are some (or most) of the critics wrong?

What follows is an extract from John Jump's article, a brief review of *Hamlet* criticism.

JOHN JUMP (b. 1925)

Hamlet (Selections)[1]

Hamlet must be the most famous of all European plays. It has been performed again and again in country after country. It has been printed repeatedly and translated into many languages. It has been endlessly discussed. Scholars debate the intricate textual problems with which it confronts them; thoughtful readers and theatre-goers debate the psychological and ethical problems suggested by its characters, and especially by Hamlet himself. Ought it perhaps to be classified as a 'problem play'? E. M. W. Tillyard is not alone in thinking so. But vast numbers of less sophisticated readers and theatre-goers respond to it without concerning themselves consciously with its notorious problems. The sheer bulk of the studies devoted to *Hamlet* has necessitated a policy of ruthless selectivity in the present essay. . . .

The first detailed critical study of the play was apparently *Some Remarks on the Tragedy of Hamlet,* published anonymously in 1736 and believed to be the work of Thomas Hanmer. Before Hanmer, playgoers and readers seem not to have suspected Hamlet of procrastination. In the seventeenth century they saw him as a bitterly eloquent and princely revenger, and, while in the early and middle decades of the eighteenth century they began to ascribe to him a great delicacy and a more melancholy temperament, both of which David Garrick fully realized in his interpretation of the part, they did not

---

[1] From *Shakespeare: Selected Bibliographical Guide,* ed. Stanley Wells (New York: Oxford UP, 1973).

judge him to be lacking in initiative and resolution. Hanmer detected delay, however: 'Had *Hamlet* gone naturally to work, as we could suppose such a Prince to do in parallel Circumstances, there would have been an End of our Play. The Poet therefore was obliged to delay his Hero's Revenge; but then he should have contrived some good Reason for it.'

From the later decades of the eighteenth century, men began to feel sure that Shakespeare could not have failed to contrive 'some good Reason' for Hamlet's delay. They began to look for it. Henry Mackenzie and J. W. von Goethe found it in Hamlet's delicate sensibility. 'Shakespeare meant', writes Goethe, 'to represent the effects of a great action laid upon a soul unfit for the performance of it. . . . A lovely, pure, noble and most moral nature, without the strength of nerve which forms a hero, sinks beneath a burden which it cannot bear and must not cast away.' A. W. von Schlegel and S. T. Coleridge found the reason in an irresolution caused by an excessively reflective or speculative habit of mind. 'Hamlet's character', says Coleridge, 'is the prevalence of the abstracting and generalizing habit over the practical', and a little later he adds, 'I have a smack of Hamlet myself, if I may say so.'

Such comments clearly belong to the period, extending through the nineteenth and into the twentieth century, when character analysis provided the standard critical approach to this as to other plays by Shakespeare. Hartley Coleridge, the poet's son, went as far as to invite his readers to 'put Shakespeare out of the question, and consider Hamlet as a real person, a recently deceased acquaintance.' Critics advanced fresh explanations of Hamlet's delay. One of the more plausible of these was that his conscience restrained him, that he found the wild justice of revenge morally unacceptable. George Bernard Shaw restated this view in terms of his own optimistic evolutionism in the 'Postscript' which he added in 1945 to *Back to Methuselah*. At the opposite extreme, Karl Werder saw Hamlet as an active person hindered in the performance of his duty by difficulties external to himself.

The finest product of the approach to Shakespeare by way of character analysis is undoubtedly A. C. Bradley's *Shakespearean Tragedy* (1904). Bradley rejects all four of the explanations of Hamlet's delay which have been summarized here. In his view, Hamlet has been so deeply shocked by the revelation of his mother's shallowness and sensuality in her hasty remarriage that he has lapsed into 'a boundless weariness and a sick longing for death'. The disclosure of his mother's adultery and of his father's murder overwhelms him while in this state. With the disclosure comes the demand for swift and violent action against his uncle. In his condition of melancholic disgust and apathy he is incapable of this, but he cannot make out why he delays. His various attempts to justify his procrastination are mere rationalizations of an inability to act.

But Bradley does not content himself with analysing the prince. Ophelia, Gertrude, and Claudius also receive his attention; and he detects in *Hamlet*, more than in any other of Shakespeare's tragedies, a 'decided, though always imaginative, intimation of a supreme power concerned in human evil and good'. His discussion of all these matters is remarkable both for its attention to detail and for its balanced view of the work as a whole. Summary inevitably distorts his meaning. Bradley has his limitations; above all, he tends to apply to Shakespeare's characters the kind of analysis that would be more appropriate to those of a nineteenth-century novelist. But his successors, some of whom are highly critical of him, have yet to give us an account of the play as just and as comprehensive as his.

Ernest Jones may be described as a Bradleyite exploiting the new technique of psycho-analysis. As early as 1900, Sigmund Freud had traced Hamlet's irresolution to an Oedipus complex, and Jones, his most eminent British disciple, developed this view in a study of the play that he issued in several versions before publishing it in its finally revised form as *Hamlet and Oedipus* in 1949. He argues that Claudius, by murdering Hamlet's father and entering into an incestuous union with Hamlet's mother, has done something disturbingly similar to what the infant prince must himself have dreamed of doing before the repression of such desires established his Oedipus complex. Now, as he watches his uncle and stepfather, Hamlet's deepest unconscious fantasies threaten to infect his waking mind. There results that paralysing condition of disgust and apathy which Bradley describes so well.

In pointing to these unsuspected hidden depths, Jones writes as a professional psycho-analyst. Students of Shakespeare's play can admit the relevance and the perceptiveness of many of his observations. But in the end they are likely to feel that his Hamlet owes more to Freud's imagination than to Shakespeare's.

Although H. B. Charlton in *Shakespearian Tragedy* emphatically rejects the Freudian interpretation of *Hamlet*, he and Jones start from similar assumptions as dramatic critics. Charlton describes himself as a 'devout Bradleyite'. Seeking to explain Hamlet's delay, he follows Coleridge in ascribing to the prince a 'supreme gift for philosophic thought'. But he gives his own explanation of how this gift inhibits action. It does so by enabling Hamlet to create an ideal world 'and then to mistake it for a true intellectual projection of the real one'. As a result of his error he cannot act properly within the real world; 'or rather, towards those parts of it which the stress of his feeling and the heat of his imagination have made especially liable to intellectual distortion, he cannot oppose the right response. He can kill a Rosencrantz, but not his villainous uncle.' This account rightly stresses Hamlet's exaggerative and generalizing habit of mind, as exemplified by 'Frailty, thy name is woman.' But does it perhaps take 'the stress of his feeling and the heat of his imagination' too much for granted? Are not Jones and Bradley right in thinking that these are precisely what most require explanation?

T. S. Eliot would certainly have said that they are. In his brief essay of 1919 he challenges the collective opinion of mankind formed over a period of three centuries when he pronounces that *Hamlet* is a failure. He objects that, while Hamlet's disgust is occasioned by his mother, it is in excess of the facts as they appear. What is true of him in relation to her is true of Shakespeare in relation to the play as a whole. Like Hamlet, Shakespeare is dominated by an emotion which has no adequate equivalent and which is therefore inexpressible. In all this, the Freudian influence is clear. What notably weakens the essay is Eliot's reliance in it upon the textual fantasies of the Shakespeare-disintegrator, J. M. Robertson. There is a reply to it in Francis Fergusson's *The Idea of a Theater*.

Critics of Bradley sometimes complain that he takes too little account of the facts that Shakespeare intended his plays for stage performance and that they naturally embody a good deal of Elizabethan thought. Without repudiating Bradley, Harley Granville-Barker and John Dover Wilson have sought to repair these omissions.

Granville-Barker had had a distinguished career in the theatre as actor, dramatist, and producer before he started to write his *Prefaces to Shakespeare,* of which the Third Series consists of a single book-length study of *Hamlet.* This is remarkable not for any novel interpretation of the play as a whole but for the constant illumination of detail that proceeds from its author's lively sense of theatrical values. Many of his particular suggestions have been taken up and developed by his successors.

In *What Happens in Hamlet,* the last of his three important publications on the play, Dover Wilson attempts to describe a genuinely Elizabethan *Hamlet.* He argues that the Ghost is an ambiguous figure and that Hamlet has good reason to doubt whether it is his father's spirit or a devil taking that shape to tempt him to murder; that, in ordering him to kill Claudius without compromising Gertrude, it sets him an extraordinarily difficult task; that Hamlet in II.ii overhears Polonius's scheme to 'loose' Ophelia to him; and that Shakespeare intended the audience, but not Claudius, to heed the dumb-show preceding *The Mousetrap.* The effect of some of these views, and especially of the insistence upon the ambiguity of the Ghost, is to focus attention upon the objective difficulties confronting Hamlet and to suggest that up to a point his inaction is prudent. Even so, Dover Wilson continues to think sheer procrastination an important factor, though not as important as Coleridge and his successors maintained.

So Granville-Barker's determination to see the play in relation to the theatre and Dover Wilson's determination to see it in relation to the Elizabethan age stop short of a rejection of Bradley. Other realists take that further step, however. A. J. A. Waldock in *Hamlet: A Study in Critical Method* appeals to our experience of the play in performance in order to challenge the basic assumption of Bradleyite criticism of it. He maintains that in the theatre Hamlet's procrastination is barely noticeable.

> It is not enough to say that Hamlet procrastinates because, as a matter of fact, and regarding the play somewhat as an historical document, we find that he did not act for two months or so. If he procrastinates, it is because he is shown procrastinating. To put it another way, it is not sufficient that delay should be negatively implicit in the play; it is necessary, for its dramatic existence, that it should be positively demonstrated. The delay, in a word, exists just inasmuch as and just to the degree in which it is conveyed.

Evidently we ought to trouble ourselves less than we do with the old leading question, 'Why does Hamlet delay?'

At all events, we ought not to put too much effort into answering it in psychological terms. The more profitable answer is that which explains the delay as one of the playwright's devices for keeping us in suspense. L. L. Schücking in *Character Problems in Shakespeare's Plays* and E. E. Stoll in *Art and Artifice in Shakespeare: A Study in Dramatic Contrast and Illusion* take this line. Their books tell us much about the technique but little about the significance and the value of *Hamlet* and the other plays they discuss. In a similar fashion, Lily B. Campbell in *Shakespeare's Tragic Heroes: Slaves of Passion* makes Shakespeare so much 'of an age'—the Elizabethan—that he can hardly aspire to be 'for all time'. This is the trouble with the realists: the plays become more meagre and more provincial things as they talk about them.

Other critics object that Bradley, in his excessive reliance upon character analysis, unduly neglects Shakespeare's poetry. They feel that they can discuss *Hamlet* or any other tragedy to better effect if they regard it, as G. Wilson Knight puts it in the first chapter of *The Wheel of Fire,* 'as a visionary whole, close-knit in personification, atmospheric suggestion, and direct poetic-symbolism'. Wilson Knight evidently hopes that his studies of the plays as symbolist poems will extend rather than contradict the findings of the character analysts. Others, however, have been less respectful of tradition.

Whereas the stricter realists try to limit Shakespeare too narrowly to the thoughts current in his day and the modes of expression usual in the theatre, the symbolist critics feel freer to acknowledge whatever they believe they have found in his work. Certain of them claim to have discerned some very strange things there. But this is no place for reviewing the merely eccentric. The best of the symbolist critics dwell upon the play's poetry in the widest sense, and especially upon its poetic imagery. Consideration of these leads D. A. Traversi in *An Approach to Shakespeare* to a diagnosis of 'Hamlet's malady and its relation to "the state of Denmark" '. Like Tillyard, he classifies *Hamlet* as one of the problem plays. By her writings on Shakespeare's imagery, Caroline F. E. Spurgeon no doubt helped him, as she has certainly helped others, to perceive that the distinctive atmosphere of the work is partly due 'to the number of images of sickness, disease, or blemish of the body' in it and that 'the idea of an ulcer or tumour, as descriptive of the unwholesome condition of Denmark morally, is, on the whole, the dominating one.' In the light of the poetic imagery, she sees the problem in *Hamlet*

> *not as the problem of an individual at all,* but as something greater and even more mysterious, as a *condition* for which the individual himself is apparently not responsible, any more than the sick man is to blame for the cancer which strikes and devours him, but which, nevertheless, in its course and development impartially and relentlessly annihilates him and others, innocent and guilty alike. That is the tragedy of Hamlet, as it is, perhaps, the chief tragic mystery of life.

Wolfgang H. Clemen in *The Development of Shakespeare's Imagery* shows how language and imagery contribute to define Hamlet himself for us. But Caroline Spurgeon has not been alone in wondering whether the problem of *Hamlet* is perhaps not the problem of an individual at all. In a challenging lecture entitled *Hamlet: the Prince or the Poem?* C. S. Lewis says, 'I believe that we read Hamlet's speeches with interest chiefly because they describe so well a certain spiritual region through which most of us have passed and anyone in his circumstances might be expected to pass, rather than because of our concern to understand how and why this particular man entered it.' In Lewis's eyes, the true hero of the play

> is man—haunted man—man with his mind on the frontier of two worlds, man unable either quite to reject or quite to admit the supernatural, man struggling to get something done as man has struggled from the beginning, yet incapable of achievement because of his inability to understand either himself or his fellows or the real quality of the universe which has produced him.

If some twentieth-century critics have questioned the conviction, expressed by Shaftesbury as early as 1710, that the play 'has only ONE *Character* or *principal Part*', others have failed to detect in that character the sweetness and nobility traditionally ascribed to him. Wilson Knight sees him as a sick, cynical, and inhuman prince corrupting a world that is, 'except for the original murder of Hamlet's father . . . one of healthy and robust life, good-nature, humour, romantic strength, and welfare'. In the same essays, included in *The Wheel of Fire*, he discovers in the Claudius whom we are permitted to observe in the play simply 'a good and gentle king, enmeshed by the chain of causality linking him with his crime. And this chain he might, perhaps, have broken except for Hamlet, and all would have been well.' But does not Wilson Knight sweep aside the murder rather too easily? Claudius was no impulsive offender, suddenly acting out of character. He deliberately and treacherously poisoned his mistress's husband, a man who was his brother and his king. His crime discloses the nature of its perpetrator. Can 'all' ever be 'well' while such a man rules?

L. C. Knights rejects Wilson Knight's benevolent view of Claudius but develops his harsh view of Hamlet. He declares that Hamlet's 'attitudes of hatred, revulsion, self-complacence and self-reproach . . . are, in their one-sided insistence, forms of escape from the difficult process of complex adjustment which normal living demands and which Hamlet finds beyond his powers.' This seems excessively censorious. Within the five acts of Shakespeare's play, Hamlet is never lucky enough to face merely the demands of 'normal living'. He confronts an extraordinarily evil situation which is not of his making but which he must set right.

Knights's earlier statement of his opinions occurs in an essay of 1940 which he reprinted in *Explorations*. He does not modify his opinions greatly, though he elaborates them considerably, in *An Approach to 'Hamlet'*. No longer does he charge Hamlet with an inability to face 'normal living'; but he does blame him for 'a sterile concentration on death and evil'.

One other denigrator of Hamlet calls for mention in passing. This is Salvador de Madariaga, who in *On Hamlet* portrays the prince as a ruthless Renaissance egoist.

Those who insist that Hamlet is an unamiable character labour under the same disadvantage as those who maintain that the play is a failure: the testimony of the vast majority of the readers and theatre-goers of more than three centuries contradicts them. Recently critics seem to have become readier once more to acknowledge his sweetness and nobility. Helen Gardner, for example, justifying the historical approach in *The Business of Criticism*, points out that in Elizabethan revenge-plays generally the initiator of the action is the initiator of its resolution, that the villain, in other words, is to some extent the involuntary agent of his own destruction. This being so, the revenging hero does not so much create an opportunity as wait for the one that his victim will unintentionally provide. Hamlet is typical in that he has this waiting role. His guilelessness in it wins our affection, his constancy our approval. Talk of his delay is largely, though not entirely, beside the point.

The constancy which Helen Gardner praises is what Knights blames as 'a sterile concentration on death and evil'. Knights argues his case with sensitivity and subtlety. But it has met with considerable resistance. One of the more genial and persuasive retorts comes from Patrick Cruttwell, who follows Helen Gardner in stressing the prince's constancy and other soldierly virtues. These are not regarded as virtues by those twentieth-century liberal intellectuals whose thinking is dominated by 'very powerful quasi-pacifist emotions'. Hence Leavis's portrait of Othello, and Traversi's of Henry V. Hence, too, Knights's reference to Hamlet's 'murder' of Rosencrantz and Guildenstern. Cruttwell objects to the term, protesting that Hamlet was engaged in a just war such as might be held to sanction extreme measures. What Hamlet really is, he summarizes at the end of his essay, 'is a conscript in a war. He has done things, as we all do in wars, he would rather not have done; but he believes it to be a just war, and all in all, he has borne himself well.'

Many of the most recent critics, however, are trying to provide not an interpretation of Hamlet's behaviour but an interpretation of the tragedy as a whole. Even D. G. James, who in *The Dream of Learning* ascribes Hamlet's delay to his metaphysical and moral scepticism, feels obliged to recognize 'that we must not see the play as merely an affair of the character of its hero'. Maynard Mack, in 'The World of *Hamlet*', attempts to describe 'the imaginative environment that the play asks us to enter'. He discusses three attributes of this world: 'its mysteriousness, its baffling appearances, its deep conscious-ness of infection, frailty, and loss'. Following Bradley, he represents Hamlet as a sensitive and idealistic young man, deeply shocked by the events immediately preceding the action of the play. But in the Hamlet who returns from the sea voyage, he discerns a readiness to accept the world as it is. Like Helen Gardner, Mack reminds us that the situation which Hamlet has to face is one that he has done nothing to bring about.

H. D. F. Kitto in *Form and Meaning in Drama* and John Holloway in *The Story of the Night* would presumably be ready to echo this reminder. According to Kitto, Hamlet is inevitably engulfed by the evil that others have set in motion; but he himself becomes the cause of further disaster. The tragedy as a whole shows how evil, once started on its course, so works as to attack and destroy alike the good and the bad; it presents 'the complexive, menacing spread of ruin'. Holloway, too, sees *Hamlet* as a religious drama. In his eyes, the developing spectacle is that of a diseased society deferring to, and placing in distinguished isolation, the revenger who has reluctantly undertaken the role of its purifier, which Providence has forced upon him. Holloway interestingly compares Shake-speare's tragedies with the scapegoat ceremonies that have been performed in many communities.

To these attempts to formulate the total significance of the play may be added Harry Levin's *The Question of 'Hamlet'*, in which he emphasizes its questioning, its doubt, and its irony, and the essay in Jan Kott's *Shakespeare Our Contemporary*, a book which has influenced stage production of the works discussed in it to a quite extraordinary degree. Writing in Poland, a country which has known modern political totalitarianism in a variety of forms, Kott sees *Hamlet* as a political play in which not only the prince but also Laertes, Ophelia, and Fortinbras act parts 'imposed on them from outside'. His purpose is to portray Hamlet for our own times. This is no less the purpose of Helen Gardner and Patrick Cruttwell. But, whereas they try to see him historically, in relation to the Elizabethan age, before suggesting his significance for the twentieth century, Kott proceeds more directly to choose his twentieth-century Hamlet from those which he knows to be realizable on the stage. His best insights as a critic come from his intimacy with the theatre, his worst blunders from his determination at all costs to be modern. . . .

In 'The Decline of Hamlet', his contribution to Stratford-upon-Avon Studies 5, T. J. B. Spencer records with evident regret that some twentieth-century critics have 'tried to convince us that we should abandon the long theatrical tradition of Hamlet as "the Darling of the English Audience" '. In wishing to resist the denigration of Hamlet,

Spencer is by no means alone. A number of the most recent critics, without the slightest intention of pushing character analysis as far as does Bradley, or of dwelling excessively upon Hamlet's delay, find the prince a most sympathetic character. He is a likeable young man upon whom an almost intolerable burden has been laid, the action of the tragedy being largely the outcome of his reluctant but dutiful shouldering of it. The world in which he has to act is one in which there is little or no certainty, the society with which he is involved one that is sinking into decay. Such, in outline, is the account of the play that seems to emerge from much that has been said about it in the 1950s and 1960s.

Since the 1960s, when Jump's account concludes, the variety of interpretations of *Hamlet* has not decreased. The play today still gives rise to hugely contradictory readings, just as it has throughout its history.

The apparent plausibility of so many interpretations of *Hamlet* paradoxically supports both the notion that texts constrain interpretation and that they do not! If that is the case, how can you tell whether there are any boundaries in texts that constrain meaning? If boundary conditions do inhere in texts, it seems very clear that different readers infer different boundaries. Both the history of *Hamlet* criticism and our students' reactions certainly suggest this conclusion. One student argued, for example:

> Many of the texts we read in class seem to allow for two or three possible interpretations, but none—so far—allows for as many interpretations as *Hamlet*. The text, therefore, must have some role in determining how many interpretations of it one can make. Perhaps it's the evocative power of Shakespeare's language, or perhaps it's because the text deals with so many moral issues that readers can read it in such diverse ways.

Such a reaction shows one reader struggling to maintain the residual notion that there are still, somewhere, boundaries to interpretation marked *by* the text itself. Other students, however, argued that reading criticism on *Hamlet* demonstrated to them that readers *create* rather than *discover* meanings in texts. As one student wrote:

> Readers seem to think they're getting a certain meaning *out of* the text when actually they're getting it out of their own repertoire of knowledge.

Some students vehemently argued that Ernest Jones's Freudian interpretation seemed to them (at least at first) particularly bizarre. Jones reads *Hamlet* in terms of the Oedipal complex, focusing on Hamlet's seemingly excessive love for his mother. How could Hamlet (a dramatic character created in the early seventeenth century) have an Oedipal complex (a psychological condition named by Sigmund Freud late in the nineteenth)? Presumably, the reason is the condition existed long before there was a name for it. But for many students, the interpretation seemed absurd because they had read little or nothing of Freud or Jones. Nonetheless, they were able to entertain this interpretation of Hamlet simply because someone (and, moreover, an apparent expert) had offered a persuasive argument defending it. Thus notions of "correct" and "incorrect" interpretation came to be seen as constrained much more by a reader's repertoire and by the persuasiveness of the interpretation than by the text.

What you can discover from this exercise is that expert readers (like student readers) are influenced by cultural and literary assumptions, and consequently have no greater access to the "true" meaning of a text than you do. In fact, by studying the shifts in interpretation of *Hamlet,* you can see how meanings certainly cannot be said to be "in" a text. Because expert readers have more extensive literary repertoires from which to draw, they can write more complex and potentially persuasive analyses of texts than students. Your decisions on whether one critic's interpretation seems better or more correct than another's will always be influenced by your own prior knowledge; for many readers, this recognition provides an incentive to learn more about a given subject before reading and judging critical opinions about it.

As you seek to develop more complex and more interesting strong readings of texts, you will increasingly find that you need to do research along the lines we gave you with *Hamlet* so that you can discover how other readers—in different periods or in your own—respond to and culturally position a text.

Writing a Formal Research Paper

Before you begin to do any kind of research, it's often a good idea to have a sense of what particular issues are important to you. In this way, you are less likely to feel overwhelmed by the amount of material you will find on a given subject. We therefore suggest, whether you are assigned one in class or not, that you write a response statement (or even a series of them) on the literary text you are researching before you begin your research. Allow the issues raised in your response statement to help focus your paper. Read the critics attentively, but in the process don't forget that you too are a critic, and your repertoires must come under as close scrutiny as those of the critics you are reading. Allow yourself to reread the literary text at various points in your research to see if your responses have changed as a result of confronting those of other readers. In what follows, we present a research paper topic we frequently assign, a research paper written by one of our students, and some extensive commentary by the teacher.

Research Paper Topic

Writing a research paper often involves doing some detailed investigation of historical, cultural, or intellectual material. Here is a research paper assignment that can be adapted to a variety of texts:

1. Select a play, piece of fiction, essay, film, group of poems (by a single poet), or group of songs.

2. Find three or four critical discussions of the work in either books or articles. Try if possible to find articles from different critical perspectives.
3. Analyze aspects of the critics' general and literary repertoires. Focus on what you perceive as the social, cultural, literary, and institutional factors that work to influence the kinds of questions they ask about the text. Do not simply summarize their arguments or give your personal reaction to them; rather, you must discover and analyze their general repertoires (such matters as their ideals of success, their views of women's place in America, their opinions about what "good" music is, their sense of moral integrity); their literary repertoires (their notion of the text, the reader, character development, unity, multiple meanings, and their beliefs about literature's importance in society); and perhaps the institutional pressures on them (what type of journal their article is published in, what the critic's reputation is, and so forth).
4. Analyze some of the social, cultural, literary, and institutional factors that influence the kinds of questions *you* ask of the text and the kinds of answers you develop. Compare and contrast *your* general and literary repertoires with those of the critics.

What follows is a sample student paper; the student used research to enlarge her repertoires and to discover how readers with diverse backgrounds culturally positioned certain texts.[1]

---

[1] See Appendix for guidelines for formatting research papers.

Teacher's Comments

Nice idea to use an epigraph—establishes _____
an interesting tone for paper.

You might note (perhaps you do later!) _____
how text-centered is Hillis Miller's definition of literature. What kind of role does
he imply is left for the reader?

Perhaps you underestimate the *text's* role in all this? _____
What part does it play? Perhaps you need a slightly
more interactive view of reading?

Jennifer J. Even

Professor McCormick

76-242

April 28, 1986

"Unending Dream of Commentary": How Critics Engage with
Doris Lessing's Summer Before the Dark

As the reader drowns under the ever accumulating
flood of criticism, he is justified in asking, why is
there criticism instead of silent admiration? What
ineluctable necessity in literature makes it generate unending oceans of commentary, wave after wave
covering the primary textual rocks, hiding them,
washing them, uncovering them again, but leaving
them, after all, just as they were?

J. Hillis Miller

Criticism, according to J. Hillis Miller, is "an ever-
renewed, ever-successful attempt" to "get it right," to "name
things by their right names" (Miller 331). I would like to disagree with Miller's definition that criticism's aim is to establish "right" or correct labels for things. This implies that
once we have established these labels, criticism comes to an end.
My view is rather that criticism is a particular reading of the
text based on the critic's literary, historical, and cultural
repertoires, and that certain readings often seem unacceptable if
the critic's repertoire differs from the reader's. In this paper
I would like, first, to explain briefly the notion of repertoire,
and second, to examine several critical readings of Doris Lessing's Summer Before the Dark to illustrate how these critics of-

Why do you think "universality" and objectivity remain such tempting goals ————
for criticism? Remember the distinction between "interpretation" and "strong
reading."

Are you implying there aren't *better* in- ————
terpretations? You sound as if you're
claiming objectivity yourself!

Presumably you'll not exclude yourself! Don't forget ————
that cognitive self-awareness is an important aspect
of the way of reading you're advocating.

Good—you show an excellent ————
awareness of your own as-
sumptions about reading.

ten assume the universality of their particular repertoires and thus seem to come up with "wrong" interpretations in the eyes of readers with different repertoires. Then finally I attempt to deal with Hillis Miller's question: Why is there criticism?

A reader's repertoire is a subset of cultural, historical, and literary assumptions derived from the ideology that surrounds him or her. The reader's literary repertoire contains strategies for reading a piece of discourse. With fiction, for instance, the reader may have such traditional strategies as the expectation of full plot development, unity of detail, and resolution, based upon the author's intended meaning. But the reader may also have more untraditional strategies (what we may call Hillis Millerish strategies), such as deconstructionist assumptions, including expectations of multiple meanings, floating signifiers, and lots of abysses that produce "no true meaning." The general reper- toire consists of ideas about such matters as male and female roles, the importance (or lack of importance) of the family unit, religion, politics, and so forth. Whenever one reads a piece of discourse, his or her repertoire plays an important role in de- termining the significance of the piece.

The criticism of Doris Lessing's novel Summer Before the Dark takes many conflicting approaches to the work, none of which I be- lieve is "right" or "wrong" but each is, rather, a reflection of each critic's repertoire. This view, of course, reflects an aspect of my literary repertoire that believes that a text has no final meaning.

I am very moved by the novel since it reflects on matters in which I am very interested—maturation, private fulfillment, and public responsibility. Its form appeals to me as well: as I read it, I realized that its seeming randomness captures the spirit of

Do you think these observations are, in ——————
their turn, derived from *your* ideology?

Clear sense of your own read- ——————
ing strategies and preferences.

Were these reasons for choosing these par- ——————
ticular periodicals? They are, after all,
widely different in their assumptions
about their audiences. Is this reflected in
the *kinds* of criticism they would favor?

To what extent do these critics show any self-awareness of their own historical ——————
situatedness? Or of their writing that they claim to be an "interpretation"? Do
you see the difference between their writing and a "strong reading"? Which are
they doing?

life as modern society seems to lead it, or at least many members of modern society.

Randomness, unpredictability, even inconsistency are what strike me about the characters' lives—especially on a rereading. The novel's form, with its seeming loose ends and unresolved questions, provides a perfect vehicle for its concerns. But such a reading, I am aware, depends on a reader who is willing to forgo the traditional delights of rounded plots and coherently presented issues.

I am also aware that my enthusiastic reading of the novel is not shared by many reviewers and critics—and that when a critic has been favorable, it is often because he or she seems to be able to find coherent plots and themes. Have such critics, to use Miller's phrase, gotten it "right"? Have I gotten it wrong?

For instance, articles that appeared in the New York Times and Time magazine reflect very traditional literary assumptions and base their views of the merits of Lessing's novel on her ability to uphold these literary "musts." An article in Modern Fiction Studies, which provides a strong feminist reading of the novel, finds Lessing's work a satire, since Kate Brown is too "frail" a "vessel for a message of importance"; and a chapter from Betsy Draine's book, Substance Under Pressure, employing a less militant feminist viewpoint, finds Kate Brown emotionally engaging and instructive. There are of course many more aspects to each of these readings, and as I examine the criticism in depth, I will fill in these gaps and also explain how my repertoire meshes with or differs from those of the critics.

In examining the literary assumptions in the New York Times and Time magazine, I will admit right now that my literary assumptions and theirs have little in common. First, I find an inherent contradiction in a point made by Timothy Foote in Time, based on

Where do these assumptions come from? ———
Can you find general as well as literary
ideological origins for them?

Isn't the point rather that this writer assumes that plot and style are primary? ———
You do mention them as matters on which your own repertoire contains distinctive
preferences, but you need to make the contrast between his repertoire and yours
more explicit. His metaphors are, I agree, a little tacky, but you might acknowledge that's caused by the journalistic mode.

This comes close to being a "subjective" reading and implying that only an ———
exact matching of repertoires can get the meaning right. You surely don't mean
that! Don't forget a "strong reading" develops out of self-consciousness *and*
knowledge.

what seems to be an assumption that fiction writing must be constantly spontaneous, engaging, and witty. He writes:

> Kate Brown and the reader, accordingly, must face
> the shock of age, the loss of beauty, with dramatic
> speed. And if that means the plot must groan like a
> Paris elevator, or the prose sometimes has to scuff
> along in rundown slippers and an old dressing gown,
> Doris Lessing has never been one to take the cosmet-
> ics of fiction seriously. (99)

I believe that the aging process entails lots of groaning and
scuffing and that Doris Lessing, by making her text groan and
scuff, has indeed taken the "cosmetics" of her fiction
seriously.

Elizabeth Hardwick, in the New York Times Book Review, seems
to hold a set of assumptions similar to Foote's:

> The madness out of which Kate Brown is to retrieve
> herself is altogether unacceptable to me. Aestheti-
> cally it is undramatic, living in fevered dreams,
> long, depressed sleeps, general deterioration.
> Morally it is utterly wasteful and even shocking
> when presented as a value out of which a woman may
> find self-knowledge, fulfillment, the truth of
> herself. (1)

With my repertoire it seems to me that Lessing has produced a wonderful sense of madness—it reflects much of my sense of what such
disturbances might mean, and, as I read it, it made me squirm and
begin to have doubts.

Finally, John Leonard in an article in the New York Times seems
particularly traditionally bound in his literary assumptions. He
pans Lessing's The Golden Notebook and The Four-Gated City,
saying:

Here you show yourself as "traditional" as the writers you criticize: the feeling/ ————
style equation is one of the most traditional—and crudest, perhaps—assumptions
of expressive realism. Your argument nonetheless is a very interesting one—
that the *disorder* you find in the novel is somehow *more* realistic than less.

Well done! ————

A rather rough and ungraceful transition. ————

> . . . emotion and intellect were not brought into a
> satisfying proximity. Both novels stopped because
> they ran into a brick wall: not a resolution, but a
> giving up to despair. The artfulness that makes the
> difference between information and wisdom was miss-
> ing. (47)

He finds this artfulness in <u>Summer Before the Dark,</u> though:
"There is little that is unnecessary in this novel," he argues,
"little that is not indispensable. Its power is in its contain-
ment . . . a resolution, achieved with fine economy" (47).

My literary repertoire is much less traditional than these
journalists'. I assume that literary texts need not be dramatic
at all times; in fact I tend to believe that a text is most effective when the writing can mimic the feeling of the content. I also
believe that a novel need not come to a neat, unifying resolution.
The end of the novel should leave the reader with the same feeling
as the character with whom he or she was to identify (it is, of
course, an assumption in my repertoire that there is a character
with whom to identify). If the plot is unresolved at the end of the
novel, then why should the reader demand a sense of resolution? In
short, the increasing self-consciousness I am developing about
many of my literary assumptions is helping me to recognize that
the reviewers I have quoted are also bringing unstated assumptions from their own repertoires to bear on their readings—and,
more significantly, they don't acknowledge this fact.

Moving on to social and cultural repertoires, Lorelei Cederstrom's social and cultural repertoire, as demonstrated in her
article "Doris Lessing's Use of Satire in <u>Summer Before the
Dark</u>," seems quite different from mine. The assumptions at work
in Cederstrom's repertoire seem to be that conformity and acceptance of duty before personal integrity are "the easy way out"

You could do a lot more with this—by probing the moral and philosophical
assumptions, you could expose a whole view of what literature "should" do.
That would be a very interesting observation to make—but perhaps in another
paper!

> You are consistently making a number of good points,
> but your paper would be more persuasive if it were
> organized more obviously by major ideas into which
> certain critics fit rather than by successively sum-
> marizing and commenting on critics.

> If you respect this view, or at least argue
> that it differs from yours, how do you
> account for your desire, stated earlier, to
> identify with characters?

(132), that those people who choose to conform are limited and "lack the imagination to see any alternatives" (135), and, most important, that a person has a "real" self beyond role-playing that is supreme and should be attended to before all else. Because, as she puts it, "at face value" Lessing's novel fails on these issues, Cederstrom sees the novel as satire; otherwise it would be a failure. Therefore, Lessing must have <u>intended</u> it as such.

In light of her assumptions, Cederstrom's criticism can be interestingly contrasted with the different assumptions of Betsy Draine in Chapter 6 ("<u>The Summer Before the Dark</u>: An Achievement in Integration") of her book <u>Substance Under Pressure</u>. First, I noticed right away that Draine acknowledges a difference of opinion with Cederstrom. Draine seems to believe that the ordinary, when well portrayed, can intimately convey not only the feelings of daily life but the deep emotion that can be felt in such a routine. This is in opposition to both Cederstrom and Foote, who find that monotony, especially when portrayed as such, is rather meaningless and a good foundation for satire. But like Cederstrom, Draine assumes that there is an <u>essential self</u> and that <u>authorial intent</u> is a deciding factor in establishing a novel's meaning. Yet Cederstrom believes that Lessing intended the novel to be read as satire, while Draine believes that Lessing wrote an apologue! Finally, Draine, like Leonard, seems to hold the same traditional literary assumption that a work is best when it pulls "disparate plots into unity" (129) and moves toward a single resolution.

Another aspect of both Draine's and Cederstrom's criticism, which is interesting to explore for underlying assumptions, is the difference between their interpretations of Kate's dream sequence. Once again Draine seems to be countering Cederstrom by

One criticism of your approach, indeed, might be to say it's *too* open: you seem ——————
dangerously close to saying a strong reading depends *solely* on the reader's
repertoires. What part does the repertoire of the text *play?*

Are different repertoires merely a matter of "sub- ——————
jective differences?" Can we try to explain what
produces them? Are there "better"—richer, more
interesting, flexible, "humane"—repertoires?

Good analysis of your literary ——————
repertoire on fiction.

Interesting that you still want to see fiction as "reflecting" life. Again, that's a ——————
fascinating assumption.

saying that the dream is not a flat, mundane allegory, but rather a full, rich dream with an exciting idea of the seal as a floating signifier with multiple meanings. This seems to contradict her idea that the story is a didactic apologue with "ethical, spiritual, or philosophical imperatives" (112). But I am not one to complain when I see an open mind! Meanwhile, Cederstrom seems to have trapped herself by imposing satire upon the story, and thus I think that she is in a way forcing herself into such a strong reading that she is missing some of Lessing's marvelous subtleties. Draine's literary repertoire seems much broader since it not only encompasses the traditional reading strategies of looking for unity, resolution, and authorial intention, but also accepts the idea that sometimes meaning is best left open.

In my own case, a desire to leave things open is a very important aspect of both my literary and cultural repertoires. I disagree with the assumptions that resolution and unity are the strong points of "good" fiction, that the "true" meaning of a work can be found in the author's intentions, or that there is an 'essential self" that reigns supreme. Such notions lead critics down alleys that this reader, at least, won't follow! As I have already discussed, I think that the reviewers in the New York Times and Time magazine unfairly judge books on the question of their unity. Is life unified and always tied up neatly? No. Then why should the literature that is supposed to be a reflection of our lives possess such qualities? I also question the nature of, if not the very existence of, the essential self. The closest thing to an essential self is perhaps what is contained in one's repertoire. Yet this is constantly changing and growing as we experience new happenings. Thus, how can there be an essential self which remains unchanged?

Do you think your repertoire is closer to Lessing's than Cederstrom's? That ———— wouldn't of course make your reading more or less authentic. But you don't raise the question of the *text's* repertoire. While it would take you outside the bounds of the paper, it's another interesting question.

This ties in nicely with your introduction; ———— it shows a firm sense of organization.

A good answer to Hillis Miller. ————

The issue of your "feminism" needs to be developed. It is probably quite ———— important to your reading of Lessing, but here it comes rather out of the blue.

But does it still remain his or her "own"? In short, you need to probe the *cultural* ———— roots of your own changing repertoire. Needs more analysis here.

Cederstrom and I seem to clash most violently on this notion of the importance of the essential self She holds this "real," "true" self to be some sort of supreme deity that should be worshipped above all else. With this stance, as with her strong reading of the novel as satire, I think she has lost sight of some of the main components of other people's repertoires. She neglects the importance of relationships, and she certainly seems to have no concept of nurturing relationships since she says that this "limited woman" whom the author "did not intend us to identify with" took the "easy" way out.

All of this ties neatly (for those who still yearn for resolution and unity) back into the larger question: Why do we have criticism? This could be reworded as follows: Do people like flaunting their repertoires when they know that the stronger the reading they do of the text, the fewer repertoires they will mesh with? My answer is that although criticism may cover, hide, wash, uncover again, and essentially leave a piece of literature just as it was, criticism has a more productive effect on the reader. In revealing a particular repertoire in a strong critical reading of a text, the critic is exposing his or her readers to new ideas that could be incorporated into their own repertoires. After reading first Lessing's novel and then several pieces of criticism, I reaffirmed my belief that my literary repertoire is less traditional than most, and I discovered that the portion of my general repertoire that I thought was strongly "feminist" was really much more traditional in its ideas on commitment, responsibility, and conformity. Unlike a text, which is really untouched by criticism, the reader of criticism can have his or her repertoire, if not changed, then illuminated, reaffirmed, or maybe stretched just a bit.

Works Cited

Cederstrom, Lorelei. ''Doris Lessing's Use of Satire in Summer Before the Dark.'' Modern Fiction Studies 26 (1980): 131–145.

Draine, Betsy. Substance Under Pressure: Artistic Coherence and Evolving Form in the Novels of Doris Lessing. Madison: U of Wisconsin P, 1983.

Foote, Timothy. ''Portrait of a Lady.'' Time. May 21, 1973. p. 99.

Hardwick, Elizabeth. ''The Summer Before the Dark.'' New York Times Book Review. May 13, 1973. p. 1.

Leonard, John. ''More on Lessing.'' New York Times. May 13, 1973. p. 47.

Lessing, Doris. Summer Before the Dark. New York: Knopf, 1973.

Miller, J. Hillis. ''Steven's Rock and Criticism as Cure, II.'' Georgia Review 14 (1983): 330–48.

As you can see, our student set herself the task of writing a formal research paper that did not abandon the personally involved nature of the response statement, but which was more tightly organized and more formally documented. Unlike a traditional text-based interpretation in which the primary goal is to say objectively what the text means, the goal of this paper is to show that the reading experience is an interactive process and to examine how the reader's repertoire plays a crucial role in this process. Moreover, she attempted to incorporate in her paper her own strong reading of the text she was studying. But her main goal—and in this her paper differs from the previous one we analyzed for you—is to establish a dialogue with a number of critics. A formal research paper using critical sources is the most advanced, seemingly authoritative, kind of formal paper, and yet, as you can see from reading this student's paper, in writing it you should not abandon the strategies and goals of the response statement. In fact, writing a formal paper in which you investigate the criticism and scholarship dealing with a text provides an excellent opportunity to probe the cognitive and cultural assumptions of *other* readers—in this case, some distinguished critics. Reviewers and critics are readers like you. They have their own strategies and goals, their own general and literary repertoires, which are inevitably brought into play when they read.

No paper is ever perfect—even if it receives a high grade. This paper is, we think, very good, but it could certainly be improved; we commented on some possible ways its argument could be strengthened. But it has some virtues that we urge you to follow. Even if it occasionally uses too much summary, it is quite well organized. It starts with a quotation from J. Hillis Miller, argues with Miller's opinion, and returns to that argument at the end. When it uses unusual technical terms—the necessary terminology of literary criticism—it defines them succinctly. It is therefore easy to read. It is detailed, but never becomes a mere summary. Its argument is coherent. It is, we think, persuasive.

It also illustrates very well how the cultural and cognitive self-awareness that emerges from a response statement can be incorporated into a formal paper. Note how the student analyzes (if only briefly) the assumptions she perceives to be within the reviewers' and critics' remarks. Note, too, how she tries to probe her own literary and general repertoires insofar as they are relevant to her topic. We think she might have extended her analysis of her own repertoires—but as we have pointed out, it is often very difficult to analyze one's *own* involvement in a society's ideology; it is much easier to analyze someone else's.

Reading criticism of a work is never a substitute for reading the work itself, but it allows you to realize that criticism is *not* objective and authoritative. It arises, as does any reading, from the engagement between text and reader, in the various matchings of repertoires that occur whenever a reader picks up a text—whether poem, novel, play, or critical essay—and reads. A formal paper is one particular way—often a very powerful way—of articulating your analysis of what occurs in that fascinating and ever-changing dialogue between reader and text.

Part 3

Reading, Responding, Writing

船 Chapter 5
Reading Poetry

Creating Your Text

When you read, you create a text of your own—whether that takes the form of a mental response, a verbal response, a written response statement, a term paper, or even a book. It is *your* text, created out of your experience of reading another's text. But, of course, as we've demonstrated in earlier chapters, the notion of something being "yours" is not a simple one, in that you yourself are also "written" by your culture, your history, and the very language you read, speak, and write.

In the next three chapters, we will introduce you to ways of reading three traditional forms, or *genres,* of literary texts—poetry (Chapter 5), fiction (Chapter 6), and drama (Chapter 7). These are the standard divisions of literature today, although many works seem to be a mixture of these forms. There are "factual" or "documentary" novels like Truman Capote's *In Cold Blood* or Norman Mailer's *Miami and the Siege of Chicago.* There are prose poems, poetic dramas, and novels that include poetry and dialogue. In fact, the traditional kinds of literature are always shifting around, and what in one age would not be considered literature at all will often in another age be perfectly acceptable as such. In the same way, of course, the *canon,* or the recognized masterpieces of literature, is always changing. The poetry of John Donne, for example, was barely read before this century; now Donne is usually regarded as one of the major poets of our literary history.

Distinctions among genres break down for other reasons as well. As you know by now, when you distinguish between a poem, a story, and a play, you are distinguishing as much between *ways of reading* texts as between *kinds* of texts. In the following chapters, we will suggest that certain reading strategies are dominant with each of these genres, such as reading for multiple meanings and word play with poetry; reading to naturalize (or, conversely, to refuse to naturalize) with fiction; and reading imaginatively to visualize with drama. We will explore in detail why these strategies work particularly well and tend to be dominant for a certain genre, but we will also suggest that your reading of each genre can be enriched by *any* of these strategies. As you become increasingly self-conscious about how you can use certain strategies in one genre, we hope you will feel more comfortable using them with other genres. Readers can (and frequently do) blur the distinctions among reading strategies: often readers will read a novel like James Joyce's *Ulysses* as closely and with as much attunement to wordplay, metaphor, and symbolism as they would a poem. Similarly, the strategies readers adopt with a long narrative poem like Byron's *Don Juan* may be similar to those they use when reading a novel.

The concept of "literature," then, is closely bound up with a way of reading a text *as* literature. In the same way, the concepts of "poetry," "drama," and "fiction" are bound up with certain expectations about and strategies for reading in different ways.

In Chapter 8, we will turn to what we call (rather strangely, you may think) the "texts of media." We will suggest that the same interactive model of reading we have developed for literary texts can apply also to the "texts" of television, film, advertising, comics, rock music, and other media.

Poetry Is a Way of Reading

The very question "What *is* poetry?" has been given very different answers across the ages and between cultures. Does poetry have to rhyme? Must it conform to particular metrical or stanzaic patterns? What is "free" verse? The answers to such *technical* questions are not fixed and universal, and it seems fair to say that it isn't even very helpful to raise the question, "Is this or that *really* a poem?" A much more relevant question is, "Is this or that poem interesting, lively, stimulating?" Or another even more provocative question is, "How can I read this or that poem to *make* it interesting, powerful, fun?" These are certainly the kinds of questions we will encourage you to ask rather than "Is this *really* a poem?" As with the other kinds of literature you read, we suggest you emphasize:

1. Exploring the experience of reading the poem—asking what effect the poem had on you.
2. Understanding how that effect was produced (by the interaction of the repertoires of text and reader) and understanding the distinctive ideologies from which these repertoires are produced.
3. Developing goals and strategies for constructing a powerful and persuasive reading of the poem.

We are suggesting that poetry is just as much a way of reading as it is a way of writing. In this chapter we will present you with some strategies and goals for reading poetry, some of which may be new to you, which we hope can help make your experience of reading poetry more enjoyable.

When you read a poem, what kinds of strategies do you use? How are they different from your reading of other types of texts? Look, for example, at the following:

If you have
only
one
phone,
borrow one from a
friend
or
neighbor.

How might you go about reading this text? You might note that it is directly addressing you, the reader—it is possibly about your life. What could it mean to "have only one phone"? Perhaps this is a metaphor for having only one connection to the outside world, and the poem is therefore telling you, if you are shy, lonely, and isolated, that you should try to become more gregarious, more outgoing. But why then would it tell you to "borrow one" from a friend or neighbor rather than, say, "make a friend" or "meet a neighbor"? One student suggested a possible answer in this response statement:

This poem is highly ironic and cynical. It suggests that relationships are mechanical and disposable, that in fact they are
not even worth buying but can, rather, be "borrowed," implying
the impermanence and lack of commitment involved. This reminds me
of what it was like for some people preparing for our senior prom.
A number of us (myself not included) didn't have dates or had recently broken up with their boyfriend or girlfriend ("if you only
have one phone"), and so they "borrowed" a date "from a friend
or neighbor." This girl on our street "borrowed" my younger
brother. She hardly knew him and didn't even seem to want to get to
know him. I think she just liked him because he looks like Sting.
After the prom, she "disposed" of him quickly. I think this dis-
posing of people goes on a lot in our society in much more serious
ways than getting dates for a prom. With a 50 percent divorce rate
in our country, one can easily replace "phone" with "husband"
or "wife": it's a sad statement about our society, but it's true.

What strategies did this student use to read this text? First, knowing it was a poem, he read it accordingly: he read it *figuratively* rather than literally. Second, he focused on particular key words, such as "phone" and "borrow," exploring their **connotations**. Third, from these key words he determined a **mood** or **voice** of the poem. Fourth, he then explained how his personal **repertoire** helped to inform the development of this interpretation, and he finally *generalized his interpretation*, and presumably its significance to the larger American society. All in all, our student filled in a lot of gaps.

This last strategy is one that you would use with any literary text. But the first three—reading the text figuratively, focusing on the connotative power of individual words, establishing the mood or voice—are strategies that suit the reading of poetry particularly well.

If this text were presented to you in a different context—in a novel or a play, for instance—you would probably read it quite differently. Most likely, it would be a line of dialogue, advancing the plot in some way. Or if you read this line in a different context entirely, in the source from which it in fact was taken—the Bell of Pennsylvania telephone book, under instructions on how to check your telephone before calling the repair service—you would read it very differently. You would read it monovalently, not polyvalently—unless, like us, you were trying to make a point about reading poetically.

Writing Suggestions

1. The "poem" we quoted from the telephone book is what is called a "found poem." Find one for yourself, arranging it on a page like a poem. Try it out, as we did, on your class or a friend.
2. (a) Analyze your "found" poem by self-consciously recording your reactions to it, both in its original context and in its new context as a poem.
   (b) How do your reading strategies change as you move from one context to another?

Don't feel that we've attempted to trick or manipulate you (or our students) by this example. Quite the contrary. What it indicates is that (1) readers bring very specific assumptions about poetry to their reading of it, and that (2) all of us have power as readers to manipulate the texts we read by choosing to read them with certain kinds of reading strategies. Poetry is a form that employs certain types of *text strategies* that lend themselves particularly well to certain types of *reading strategies*.

Poetry as Playing with Language

As it is possible to read a sentence from the phone book as if it were a poem, so too is it possible to read a poem as if it were from the phone book—that is, to summarize, to read it *monovalently,* to read it as if it should denote one meaning or message. But we suggest that the first is more fun than the second. To try to read a poem as if it were the phone book, with the goal of "finding its meaning," is to mismatch your reading strategies with some of poetry's best text strategies and to take much of the enjoyment out of reading poetry.

Of all the traditional kinds of literature, we have frequently found that poetry *initially* generates the least enthusiasm among students. Unless you yourself write poetry, or have been lucky enough to come to enjoy it in high school, you might regard studying poetry as a real chore. This may be because the goals and reading strategies you find comfortable and natural are more suited to reading monovalently than to reading polyvalently. Perhaps you were taught that you had to learn *the* meaning of every word or line, pick out "images" as though the poem was an archaeological dig site, or work your way through impenetrable references to classical gods, mythical countries, or obscure personal experiences undergone by the poet. Or perhaps you were told that you should summarize a poem to get its "message" and that without this kind of knowledge you could not discover what the "real" meaning of the poem is.

Unquestionably reading poetry *does* require careful concentration—indeed careful and close *re*reading. There are also some "great" poems you won't warm to, either at first or perhaps even after studying them. Tastes vary: what matters is that you should understand how your tastes are formed, what assumptions about poetry you bring to the reading of it, and how you might find ways of enjoying more poetry more fully. If you can get over seeing poetry as boring and solemn, as difficult language deliberately disguising its message, this allows you to liberate a little of your sense of fun. Again, there's a real sense in which poetry is a kind of playing with language—and when you read a poem, or attend a lively poetry reading, you are being invited to play as well.

Involving the Reader

Our approach to reading and writing can help you to develop this sense of playfulness by encouraging you not to try to pin the text down to one "correct" meaning but to allow multiple, diverse, and often contradictory readings of a text to exist simultaneously. While we advocate cognitively and culturally self-aware reading of all genres, it particularly enhances your reading of poetry, which most consistently requires you to read for multiple meanings. We want you to become self-conscious about the ways you make meanings and to provide you with an increased number of options for doing so.

When you read a poem, then, you should not just ask, "What does it mean?" or "What does the author intend?" The most important questions, initially, are, "How do I respond to that?" and "Why do I respond as I do?" A poem is an arrangement of words that are asking to be read and responded to within different readers' pre-existing expectations, associations, or attitudes—attitudes that even within a single reader may be multiple and contradictory. Particularly because of its economical use of language, poetry asks its readers to shape the poem into their own reading by filling in gaps and by exploring the rich connotative power of language. Part of the problem about some of the less interesting ways of reading poetry—like summarizing or developing an "objective" interpretation—is that sometimes students are discouraged from seeing a poem as being as much about *their* own experiences as it is about the author's. Students are also discouraged from seeing a poem as evoking, perhaps simultaneously, several different reactions in them.

Let's get this point very clear: Poems may start their written lives as a poet tries to express his or her fascination with what words can or can't say—to express feelings, explore experiences, reveal personality, or comment on some public issues. But those origins of a poem don't provide its readers with the only meaning or meanings they can take from it. In the first place, poets inevitably bring more into their writing than they may be consciously aware of, even if they employ deliberately ambiguous or playful text strategies. The poet is (as we put it earlier) "written" by his or her culture—especially by its ideology. Language, history, and culture together in a sense "write" the poet. In the second place, a poem is a set of words waiting to be read, over and over, by *different* readers. It is you, the poem's reader, who bring those words to life—and you do so by bringing your reading strategies and goals, your culture's attitudes and experiences, or your interests in public issues to bear on your reading. If you choose to read denotatively or monovalently, a poem simply remains those dead black words on a page.

Reading Poetry and Reading Rock Lyrics

Even if you have trouble reading poems for English classes, most of you probably already know how to read "poetically" because you have a lot of experience reading our culture's most popular form of poetry, rock lyrics. In Chapter 8, we will have more to say on popular culture, but here it provides a useful way into thinking about reading poetry. Think of the way you "read" rock music. You listen to it over and over, sing along with the radio, dance to it at parties, watch videos on MTV, hum songs to yourself in the shower, memorize the words; you play this music at important and enjoyable times. When you hear this music even years later—whether it's Led Zeppelin's "Stairway to Heaven," Simon and Garfunkel's "Parsley, Sage, Rosemary, and Thyme," Crosby, Stills, Nash and Young's "Woodstock," or The Police's "Every Step You Take"—you may still resonate strongly to it. Why is this so?

The reason is that you have listened to the song many times, and developed strong associations to it because you "read" it in a rich public and personal context of friends, lovers, presidential elections, international political upheavals, college fads, and so forth. You probably didn't worry about what it meant to the person who wrote it. Nonetheless, it is the product of a particular cultural period. If you are a part of that same culture, your shared repertoire allows you to see certain significances in the song that someone from a different culture, or even a different age group, cannot. The repertoires of reader and text match readily. The lyrics of rock music, therefore, like the language of more traditional poetry, often require you to fill in its gaps, but the context in which you listen to music is often fuller and richer than the context in which you read poetry.

Here are the words of "Money for Nothing," written by Mark Knopfler of the British rock group, Dire Straits. As you read these words, think about your associations with and interpretations of the song; think about the knowledge in your repertoire that informs your reading of the song.

MARK KNOPFLER (b. 1955)

Money for Nothing

Now look at them yo-yos that's the way you do it
You play the guitar on the MTV
That ain't workin' that's the way you do it
Money for nothin' and chicks for free

Now that ain't workin' that's the way you do it　　　　　　　5
Lemme tell ya them guys ain't dumb
Maybe get a blister on your little finger
Maybe get a blister on your thumb

We gotta install microwave ovens
Custom kitchen deliveries　　　　　　　　　　　　　　　10
We gotta move these refrigerators
We gotta move these colour TV's

See the little faggot with the earring and the makeup
Yeah buddy that's his own hair
That little faggot got his own jet airplane　　　　　　　　15
That little faggot he's a millionaire
We gotta install microwave ovens
Custom kitchen deliveries
We gotta move these refrigerators
We gotta move these colour TV's　　　　　　　　　　　　20

I shoulda learned to play the guitar
I shoulda learned to play them drums
Look at that mama, she got it stickin' in the camera
Man we could have some fun
And he's up there, what's that? Hawaiian noises?　　　　25
Bangin' on the bongoes like a chimpanzee
That ain't workin' that's the way you do it
Get your money for nothin' get your chicks for free

We gotta install microwave ovens
Custom kitchen deliveries　　　　　　　　　　　　　　30
We gotta move these refrigerators
We gotta move these colour TV's, Lord

Now that ain't workin' that's the way you do it
You play the guitar on the MTV
That ain't workin' that's the way you do it　　　　　　　35
Money for nothin' and your chicks for free
Money for nothin' and chicks for free

Do you remember what you were doing when this song came out in 1985? What did you think of it then, and what do you think of it now? Sung with the crisp and sometimes amusing musicianship of the band, this is a delightful and provocative piece of entertainment. But it is also a "text" in the sense that we are using the term in this book—it is a product not just of a single individual, its author, but also of a whole culture. Like any human cultural product, it articulates the desires and contradictions of its time. Particularly noticeable here are the contradictory views of the success of the rock musician. The dramatic speakers—in the video of the song, two robotlike moving men—articulate a common, dismissive (but still envious) view of rock musicians as trivial, escapist, weird, and scandalously overpaid—and not only in money! You can (if you want) agree with that view, but you might also want to point to the years of dedication, practice, and often poverty that go into a musician's life. Should a musician refuse the material rewards? Does accepting them—does becoming successful in this or any other field—mean that someone has sold out? Interestingly the song is very contradictory on these questions, certainly reflecting the ideological ambivalence not just of its writer but the ideological contradictions of the culture at large.

In short, when you interpret this lyric (this *poem,* if you like), you are not required to limit yourself to one single meaning. The lyric opens up a debate. Although you are (probably!) neither a famous musician nor a robotlike moving man, you may find ways to relate this song to your life. You have particular views on the subject, and they in turn are derived from your presuppositions, your ideological positioning within your culture—and often the particular events that were occurring in your life when you first heard the song. It might remind you of a complicated situation in your own life or in our country's politics about which you had mixed feelings. Or it might remind you of somebody winning something, of succeeding or not succeeding, or of a particular night when you first heard the song, the person you were with, and so forth. Inevitably you make these associations part of the song, so that whenever you hear it, those associations come back to you. The formal properties of the lyric, its text strategies—words, music, setting—become the occasion for different "readings."

Writing Suggestions

1. Write a response statement on an aspect of "Money for Nothing" you consider important, which our remarks did not address.
2. Write a response statement on another contemporary lyric, paying special attention to the cognitive and cultural factors influencing your response.

The Context of Poetry Today

Compare this rich context of reading "Money for Nothing" with the generally impoverished social context in which you may often read poetry: alone, hurriedly, to yourself rather than aloud, without listening to the way it sounds, without rereading it frequently (if at all), without a sense that the poetry can have rich associations for you, that you can recite it in the shower, and share it with friends. One of the reasons most people pay so little attention to poetry, unless they write poetry themselves, is that it has a marginal status in our society; consequently, there are few social situations of which it is a part. Of course the writing, publishing, and reading of poetry is still widely felt to be a significant and prestigious activity in some communities. Every city and town, and every college campus, has poetry readings, poetry groups, and visits by individual poets. Many well-known poets teach in college departments of English; nonetheless, there is no P(oetry) TV. So your sense of the contexts in which poetry can be read and enjoyed may be limited because poetry is not popularized in our culture in the same ways as rock music.

In studying a poem, we want you to try to develop and deepen the contexts in which you can read it. Read it aloud, talk about it with your friends, and spend time exploring the personal and cultural associations it evokes in you. Return to the poem at various points in the semester, noting how your reactions to it might have changed as your general and literary repertoires change. Above all, if there are poetry readings at your school or town, try going to them with friends, and if possible, become familiar with the poetry being read. Remember that even at rock concerts you always like best those songs you know best.

Connotative Richness

The quality that distinguishes most poetry from the latest song lyric is that its power of rich association can be much deeper and more permanent. Rock songs, of necessity, have to make immediate impressions. Because they are set to music, the words usually have to be relatively simple so they can be remembered easily (although some of the songs by Bob Dylan, for example, reveal very complex and richly associative lyrics). Whereas songs are meant to give their listeners a kind of instant gratification, most poems don't try for just an immediate hit. Poems are usually trying to summon in their readers more complex and often contradictory reactions that may take much rereading to develop.

But the strategies by which you should "read" these texts are basically the same, whether the text is Madonna's "Material Girl" with its jaunty cynicism or the following poem. Read this poem aloud and reread it a number of times so that you can become familiar with the way it sounds and with the thoughts and emotions it evokes in you.

WILLIAM STAFFORD (b. 1914)

Traveling Through the Dark

Traveling through the dark I found a deer
dead on the edge of the Wilson River road.
It is usually best to roll them into the canyon:
that road is narrow; to swerve might make more dead.

By glow of the tail-light I stumbled back of the car   5
and stood by the heap, a doe, a recent killing;
she had stiffened already, almost cold.
I dragged her off; she was large in the belly.

My fingers touching her side brought me the reason—
her side was warm; her fawn lay there waiting,   10
alive, still, never to be born.
Beside that mountain road I hesitated.

The car aimed ahead its lowered parking lights;
under the hood purred the steady engine.
I stood in the glare of the warm exhaust turning red;   15
around our group I could hear the wilderness listen.

I thought hard for us all—my only swerving—
then pushed her over the edge into the river.

How do you respond to this poem, particularly to its use of language? In one respect, this poem reads like a narrative, like a little short story, and were it not written in stanza form, you might not pay attention to the creative power of the language. You might read it more monovalently than polyvalently. For example, you might say this poem is about a man who finds a dead doe whose unborn fawn is still alive; he feels bad for the doe but after some consideration pushes it into the river. Such a reading looks more at the poem's simple denotations than its complex connotations.

Let's play with a couple of the connotations—let's read this poem poetically. Look for example at "swerve" in line 4 and again in the next to the last line. In the first usage, the poet suggests that swerving the car to avoid a deer lying in the road might result in the killing of others. But what does "swerving" suggest in the next to the last line? He "thought hard for us all." But how? And why does he say this was "my only swerving"? You may think of the context for "swerve" in line 2, and wonder in what way could his thinking hard "make more dead"?

What are the denotations and connotations of "hesitate"? What is the effect on you of the poet's calling himself, the deer, and his car (which, oddly, he vividly describes) "our group"? And what about his hearing the "wilderness listen" and pushing the fawn "over the edge"? Read this poem again and allow its words to trigger in you multiple and varied associations. Feel the play of language and, in this poem, its tension.

In reading and responding to this poem, you may find that you have to concentrate on the complex emotions it may produce in you—pity for the dead deer and its never to be born but still living fawn, the complex feelings of the driver and how they affect you. You are asked to face some difficult moral choices. What would you have done if you were in the position of the poet? What reasons would you have given for your actions? Can you (or do you already) read the whole poem, not just individual words and phrases, connotatively, about something other than what it is literally describing? On a richly connotative level, the poem seems to be asking its readers to consider that life is much more ambiguous and complex than any of us often wants to realize— and it is one function of poems to awaken us to that realization, to help us become more sensitive to it, and perhaps share that sensitivity with others. Thus one reading strategy that we suggested in the previous section—allowing yourself to develop multiple, even contradictory, readings of a text—may help you respond more deeply to this poem. In the following sections, we will suggest various other kinds of reading strategies that can help you enjoy poetry by enriching the context in which you read it.

Writing Suggestions

1. (a) What aspects of "Traveling Through the Dark" that we did not discuss strike you as especially interesting?
   (b) What strategies did you use in your reading?

2. (*a*) Read the following poem or another you are studying and show ways in which its connotations work to evoke certain responses in you.

(*b*) What intersections of your and the text's general or literary repertoire account for your response?

WILLIAM SHAKESPEARE (1564–1616)

Sonnet 65

Since brass, nor stone, nor earth, nor boundless sea,
But sad mortality o'ersways their power,
How with this rage shall beauty hold a plea,
Whose action is no stronger than a flower?
O, how shall summer's honey breath hold out   5
Against the wrackful siege of battering days,
When rocks impregnable are not so stout,
Nor gates of steel so strong, but Time decays?
O fearful meditation! Where, alack,
Shall Time's best jewel from Time's chest lie hid?   10
Or what strong hand can hold his swift foot back?
Or who his spoil of beauty can forbid?
    O, none, unless this miracle have might,
    That in black ink my love may still shine bright.

A Common Pattern for Reading Poetry

In Chapter 3, we presented you with a menu of six different task definitions for reading and writing (pp. 88–91). Recall that while we favored using response statements, we did not dismiss summarizing, free-associating, and traditional interpreting but rather suggested that they were useful starting points. In actuality these six task definitions, and their attendant goals and strategies, overlap in the reading process, particularly in the process of rereading a poem. Because its language is so compressed, a poem requires you to pay closer attention to details and to the connotative power of individual words than you would with prose texts such as novels and short stories.

The following is a common pattern for reading poetry, which we will discuss in detail throughout the rest of this chapter.

1. Analyze individual word meanings (both denotations and connotations) and construct your sense of the poem's argument (summarize).
2. Formulate your initial response to the poem (by free-associating) and develop a tentative interpretation.
3. Establish a *context* for the poem's argument, that is, fill out some aspect of

its repertoire—literary or general—by analyzing its text strategies (as we did with Stafford's "Traveling Through the Dark"), or by situating the poem in its culture (as we did with Knopfler's "Money for Nothing"). This may require some research. When establishing a context, look not only at the cultural attitudes and ideas that are explicit in the poem but at those that are implicit as well. Look for interesting contradictions in the poem's repertoire.

4. Contrast the repertoire of the text with your own. Combine your initial response to the text with your analysis of its cultural situation. Highlight some of your cognitive and cultural assumptions. Use your reactions to the text to make discoveries about your own reading strategies and cultural situation.

5. Do a strong reading of the poem in which you actively acknowledge the cultural imperatives underlying your response to or interpretation of the poem and analyze the implications of your response.

You should be aware that while different poems will require that you spend more time on one aspect than another—say, analyzing their argument or filling out their repertoire—with all poems you seek finally to do a strong reading, to make the poem your own by integrating it into your larger cultural experience.

Writing Suggestions

1. Reread the section in Chapter 3 dealing with the costs and benefits of different reading strategies. Then take a poem of your own choosing and briefly work out the costs and benefits of each strategy in relation to that poem.
2. (a) Which of these strategies do you find most familiar?
   (b) Which do you find most interesting?

Reconstructing the Poem's Argument

Some poems, like John Donne's "A Valediction: Forbidding Mourning," written in the early seventeenth century, almost defy an easy first reading. They have highly concentrated arguments that require their readers to puzzle them out before they can start the *re*reading that will allow the experience of reading the poem to be enlightening and enjoyable. Let's look at this poem.

JOHN DONNE (1572–1631)

A Valediction: Forbidding Mourning

As virtuous men pass mildly away,
  And whisper to their souls to go,
Whilst some of their sad friends do say
  The breath goes now, and some say, no:

So let us melt, and make no noise,
    No tear-floods, nor sigh-tempests move;
'Twere profanation of our joys
    To tell the laity our love.

Moving of the earth brings harms and fears;
    Men reckon what it did and meant,
But trepidation of the spheres,
    Though greater far, is innocent.

Dull sublunary lovers' love
    (Whose soul is sense) cannot admit
Absence, because it doth remove
    Those things which elemented it.

But we, by a love so much refined
    That our selves know not what it is,
Inter-assurèd of the mind,
    Care less, eyes, lips, and hands to miss.

Our two souls, therefore, which are one,
    Though I must go, endure not yet
A breach, but an expansion,
    Like gold to airy thinness beat.

If they be two, they are two so
    As stiff twin compasses are two,
Thy soul the fixed foot, makes no show
    To move, but doth, if the other do.

And though it in the center sit,
    Yet when the other far doth roam,
It leans, and hearkens after it,
    And grows erect, as that comes home.

Such wilt thou be to me, who must,
    Like the other foot, obliquely run;
Thy firmness makes my circle just,
    And makes me end where I begun.

It's often a useful preliminary step in reading a poem (especially if you are eventually going to write about it) to record some initial reactions—maybe scribbling some notes on a note pad, in the margin, or just marking lines that seem to you most significant. It's also worthwhile, at this early stage, to pause over unusual or strange words, or key words that seem to be thrust at you with unusual insistence—or words that, when considered together, seem to reinforce another word's meanings. Here "melt," "laity," "sublunary," "compasses," and "just" might appear to be such key words. They are clearly chosen to have intellectual and perhaps emotional impact. Whatever way you choose to move into the poem (and there is no one right way), initially you should think about the poem's first impact on you, and then play with the denotations and connotations of some of the unfamiliar words, and then with those that seem to you to be especially important.

The poem seems to be dramatizing a domestic situation: the "I" of the poem is speaking to a lover or a wife, trying to persuade her not to complain about an absence, let us suppose a business trip, a vacation. Note that even in summarizing the poem's argument to this extent we are already inevitably bringing in our own presuppositions and experiences. You, perhaps, will summarize the poem to yourself in a somewhat different way. It is impossible to let the poem speak for "itself"; it can speak only within your interpretation of it.

This is an intricately thought-out poem, one that doesn't demand a single interpretation but *does* require some initial close attention to the argument. It's constructed carefully and logically. Almost too much so, some readers might think: it is, after all, supposed to be a love poem! Its slowly developing argument might even be read as rather patronizing—the rational, powerful male talking down to the irrational woman.

Look at such details as the "as . . . so" structure of the first two stanzas, in which the reader is inserted into a carefully argued comparison that compares the lovers' parting to the peaceful way virtuous men die. Do you find that a strange comparison? Perhaps you find it odd, but often people who are in a very close relationship feel that parting, even for a short time, is very painful. Think of, let's say, lovers who can't be together at Christmas or over the summer. Or—a common enough experience now—two people who must live in different cities because of their jobs.

So the woman (let's call the "other" a woman since, at the time the poem was written, the expected gender of the one who stayed home patiently and waited would be female) is asked not to overreact ("no tear-floods") to the man's departure. He pleads with her—not desperately but rather with a good sense of humor. He flatters her intelligence: she must be bright to appreciate those references to the planets' movements, to religion—or do you think the poet is just trying to display his learning to you, his audience? By line 24, the poem has tried to explain why their love would not be, in any final sense, affected by the speaker's absence. It is because their love isn't merely physical but rather is a bonding together of their minds. Their love, the poem suggests, is like gold leaf (a thin layer of gold placed over a surface): the thinner it is stretched (that is, the farther apart the two of them are), the clearer and more beautiful it becomes.

But the poem doesn't end there (why it doesn't we'll look into later). The poet has another comparison for his lover—one that requires very close attention. It is between the man and the woman and the two arms (or "feet," as he calls them) of an ordinary geometrical compass. In order to draw a perfect circle, the foot in the center must stay firmly in one place: "she" is like that "fixed foot," while "he" moves around. Then, once he has drawn his circle, he can return down the radius to her at exactly where he started.

It is a startling comparison, even a bizarre one for today's readers. (How would you like it if your boyfriend or girlfriend said, "Gee, I think you're great—you're just like a compass.") The comparison is not, however, intrinsically odd. It just seems unusual to readers today because, although their repertoires regarding love may intersect fairly closely with those of the poet and his original audience, their repertoires regarding compasses probably do not. Today we may rarely even see one, except in art class. But in order to judge the effect of the comparison, a reader needs to follow it carefully, "leaning and harkening after" the argument.

To summarize the argument in this way (and there are other, different ways of doing so that would still be fair to the poem), however, is not to provide a complete or strong reading of it. In generating a response statement for instance, or even a more formal paper, probably none of the above statements would be written down. To reconstruct a poem's argument is a useful thing to do, but only as an explanation of what the poem is "about." There are many other more significant things to be said: the poem's ideological assumptions—about the relations between men and women, activity and passivity, love and work—have not been questioned at all in the reading thus far. Nor have we explicitly analyzed the reader's possible side of the argument. The reader's response to the poem has so far been played down. All that has been provided is a summary.

Writing Suggestions

1. Compare your *own* summary of Donne's poem with the one provided. How does it differ and why?
2. Choose another poem that you think requires careful summarizing before other more interesting things can be done with it. Provide a summary and indicate what aspects of your reading might lend themselves to more advanced reading strategies.

Formulating Your Initial Response: Filling in Gaps

We've insisted, throughout this book, that writers and readers alike bring powerful ideological contradictions into the acts of reading, interpreting, and writing. The ideas a poem explicitly "contains" are not the only ones relevant to a discussion of it—and its unspoken assumptions can become the starting point for some more interesting kinds of analyses. We suggested that you could respond to Donne's "A Valediction: Forbidding Mourning" only after you had carefully followed the logic of its argument. But if you have as your only reading goal to summarize the poem's argument, your initial response will probably be quite dull.

For *you* to develop a strong reading of any poem—especially so demanding a poem as "A Valediction: Forbidding Mourning"—you need to insert yourselves into the poem. Because of its compressed language, poetry has many gaps and indeterminacies that allow you to begin to develop your own reading. Look at the gap at line 24 mentioned earlier; the poem might well end there. The argument is complete at that point; it provides a logical working out of the implications of some metaphors about their love. But this poem depicts not only a dramatic speaker but also another character, a dramatic listener—the woman, as we have called her. She has been asked to accept his decision without "giving him any grief," as one student put it. What do you think she might reply to the speaker's argument? The way you fill in such gaps will later help you develop a comparison between your cultural situation and the poem's. Do you imagine the woman is flattered that the speaker wants her to wait for him? Enraged that he would want to leave without taking her and that he would try to placate her sorrow with a few metaphors? Or do you imagine her passively, unquestioningly, but perhaps somewhat unhappily, accepting a role in which she cannot initiate action but in which she must always be strong enough to hold things together?

There may be a clue to what she might say between stanzas 6 and 7. But like the best clues in poetry, it is playful and has contradictory connotations. Look carefully at what happens to the poem at that point. By line 24, the poem has proved that their love will remain one because their souls are one. Now look at line 25: "If they be two, . . ." That "if" may suggest to some of you that the woman perhaps hasn't been at all convinced. However, it could also be read that she is probably convinced that they are "one" and that the notion of their being "two" is now only conjecture. The way you read the "if," therefore, because it is ambiguous, will depend on what you've already decided the woman's response would or should be.

Personal Associations

Let's construct some modern equivalents of what her response might have been. Perhaps she argued, "What do you mean we're spiritually together? It's all very well for you to fly off to that sales convention and have a good time. I know what you are up to there. What am I supposed to do about getting the children to school? I wanted to get back to full-time work this year. And I wanted to visit my sister in St. Louis this weekend. When do you start taking some responsibility in this relationship?" Or do you imagine her saying, "Yes, dear, off you go. Have a good time. I'll take care of the children, pay all the bills, take your messages. Maybe if you have time, you could call from the hotel. Don't forget to take an extra shirt. Let me fold it for you." By imagining how the woman might respond to the poet's argument, you are filling in gaps suggested, but not explained, by the poem.

It seems then that in stanza 7 the speaker starts his argument again. He argues with even more ingenuity, with the famous compass metaphor. And what do you imagine might be said when he has concluded (he no doubt imagines concluded triumphantly) his argument in the next three stanzas? Presumably what the poem wants all its readers to accept by the end is that the speaker has, at last, won the argument.

But what if you decide that the issues the poem has raised really can't be dismissed without opposition? Let's stand back and ask a few questions. Is "he" trying to overcome "her" with his sheer brilliance? Does *she* think that the compass comparison was so ingenious and funny that she'd forgive him almost anything ("Oh, you're impossible—off you go, you great idiot"). Does she have any choice? What does that tell you about her, her cultural situation, and their relationship? Or can you perhaps imagine her *rejecting* the argument? ("Twin compasses! What drivel! I'll make you end where you began—if you go off again, I won't be here when you get back!") In her cultural context, does she actually have a choice? If she doesn't accept his argument, does that spoil the poem for you?

The more interesting question, in any case, is how do *you* react to the argument? How would *you* deal with a similar situation? When you consider this question, does it matter whether you are a man or a woman? Can you see how *your* own assumptions about relationships, fairness, and commitment are relevant to the poem? How are they like or unlike those of the poem? When you start to answer those questions, you are beginning to assert yourself, asking *your* questions of the text, and becoming a strong reader.

Writing Suggestion

Using some of the issues we've just raised, and developing your own, do a strong reading of the Donne poem from either a male or female perspective.

Expanding Your Knowledge of a Poem's Repertoire: Discovering Contradictions

Another step in becoming a strong reader is to develop a background for the poem's argument by filling out its repertoire. Because they were written in an earlier culture or an unfamiliar society, many poems bring to the foreground ideas, attitudes, and assumptions that may be unfamiliar to you. If you don't investigate these, you may wrongly assume that words (and concepts) don't change their meanings through history, when it is clear that such key words in our culture as "democracy" and "love," even "person" and "self," have changed their meanings significantly.

Often, however, a poem will be difficult to understand even after you have done such research. This is because texts—some much more blatantly than others—almost always incorporate the conflicts within an age's ideology. In teasing out a text's unconscious assumptions—about politics, religion, lifestyles, social organizations, and so forth—you often bring to light ideas or attitudes that the poem takes for granted or of which the author might not have been aware. You can also find contradictions in a poem's ideas or assumptions— places where the ideology to which the poem gives voice is uncertain or confused. The reason for this is that the dominant ideology of any period is always under pressure from counter-dominant forces, and poems—and texts in general— often display these conflicts in the form of verbal contradictions and tensions. Frequently a poem will try to ignore these contradictions or try to smooth them over—to reassert that what the author and the dominant culture take for granted is, in fact, universally "true." But sometimes a poem's energy will arise from trying to grapple with and overcome these conflicts. The poet will try to bring together disturbing, contradictory, irreconcilable ideas, and the result will be the energy and power that make the poem memorable. The poem won't solve the problem and neither, probably, can you; but the struggle makes it fascinating to read, and often you can seize upon the problem as one of the most interesting things about it.

Ideological Conflict in the Text

A famous poem that can help illustrate this process is the following lyric written in the late eighteenth century:

WILLIAM BLAKE (1757–1827)

London

I wander thro' each charter'd street,
Near where the charter'd Thames does flow,
And mark in every face I meet
Marks of weakness, marks of woe.

In every cry of every Man,   5
In every Infant's cry of fear,
In every voice, in every ban,
The mind-forg'd manacles I hear.

How the Chimney-sweeper's cry
Every blackning Church appalls,   10
And the hapless Soldier's sigh
Runs in blood down Palace walls.

But most thro' midnight streets I hear
How the youthful Harlot's curse
Blasts the new-born Infant's tear,   15
And blights with plagues the Marriage hearse.

In this poem, it is the words and the associations they accumulate that carry the ideological conflicts. Words, as we have discussed previously, are not simple signifiers with a single signified. Words do have meanings that you can read in a dictionary, but the richer and more powerful the word, the more likely there will be a range of meanings, some of which are dominant in a given period or culture. The meanings of a word in a poem always depend on context and are inevitably multiple, and reading for multiple meaning is part of the particular pleasure you can derive from reading poetry. When you read the second stanza, for example, at first you probably think that "ban" means prohibition, which would quite obviously be a kind of manacle. But when you read in the last stanza about the harlot's curse blighting the marriage hearse, you may think that "ban" of line 7 could also mean marriage bans or marriage announcements. The coming together of these two quite disparate meanings of "ban" implicitly stresses the ideological conflicts associated with the institution of marriage that are more explicitly addressed in the final stanza.

You are most likely to feel that a word suggests a range of associations when you react to it emotionally. Words like "chartered," "palace," and "midnight" in this poem give you *suggestions* for taking a particular attitude towards the city of London and (since "London," like today's "New York" or "Los Angeles," has such rich connotations) towards the large modern city of the industrial world—and all that it stands for.

What does "London" mean to you? What do large cities in general represent for you today? Excitement? Terror? What "London" stands for, what it *connotes,* is where ideology is found. Such words are like little battlegrounds: they are sites where different meanings struggle for supremacy. You can learn to read the text of a poem just to explicate the surface meaning, but such a strategy results in a dry and detached reading. Poems are concentrations of energy and conflict packed into words. A richer, more enjoyable, and, we suggest, more "poetical" strategy for reading a poem reveals how words betray themselves, not just as caught up in *verbal* conflict (multiple or ambiguous), but as caught up in the conflicts of *history.* By reading the poem in relation to history, you can understand how the real and vital contradictions of society—between industrial progress and the individual, morality and the social structure, marriage and death (the marriage "hearse")—enter the poem and fight for mastery over its language. Different philosophies of life, different kinds of lifestyles, are fighting in the lines, and you can determine them by looking at the conflicting connotations of the poem's words.

On this level of analysis, can you find the *true* meaning of "London"? Can you ask what it "really" means? "London" means many contradictory things that struggle for supremacy in *your* reading of the poem. These contradictions (which are *historical,* not just linguistic, contradictions) can also be seen not just in what the text says but in its gaps and absences, in what is *not* there. What Blake's poem alludes to, therefore, is both "in" the poem and "absent" from it—the complex interactions of the whole social formation and the ideological struggles that produce the bitterness, helplessness, and condemnation of "London."

As we explained in discussing *history* in Chapter 2, texts speak out of the ideological conflicts of their time, and part of your goal in reading is to reveal those conflicts. Although you get a glimpse in "London," you can fill out the repertoire of this text with further historical research into Blake's society. The poem articulates the moral and emotional anguish of suffering and exploited individuals. What you don't get in the poem and what you must fill in are the complex historical causes for the anguish that the poem articulates. Perhaps when you do some historical research, you can find out such things—the terrifying poverty of late eighteenth-century London, the appalling health conditions, the spread of venereal disease throughout Europe, and so forth. The poet's indignation and horror at aspects of his society are not mentioned in detail because they are, in fact, all around him; they are implicit in the repertoire of the poem.

Writing Suggestions

1. (*a*) What other aspects of Blake's poem carry strong ideological conflicts?
   (*b*) Do you discover these from your own knowledge of Blake's time or from your contemporary views on the issues the poem raises?
2. Choose another poem with interesting ideological conflicts and subject it to the same kind of **symptomatic analysis** we offered on the Blake poem.

What is essential in this activity of producing such a reading for Blake's poem is *your* role as reader. It becomes *your* task not just to explain the text but to fill out its absences, gaps, and indeterminacies; one way to do this is by filling out its repertoire. From your present-day perspective, you can look back in history and perhaps understand in more detail the complex forces of which Blake saw only a glimpse. You try to show how the poem was produced by articulating what it has said only implicitly. And then *you* enter into the debate. In doing so, you begin to become a strong reader. You bring your late 1980s perspective to bear on the issues the poem raises—issues of individuality, exploitation, marriage, social responsibility, and so forth. After all, like the poem, you are the product of *your* place in history, your ideological tensions. You bring your feelings, ideas, and apprehensions to bear upon the text. If the poem's repertoire conflicts significantly with your own, you may find that this conflict can help you to realize that all your assumptions and expectations are learned, not natural—the products of your particular cultural situation.

Analyzing Your Repertoire

After you have become as informed as possible about the forces that produced the text and *its* history, you then must explore those forces that have produced your reading and *your* history. That means becoming aware of the factors that make your reading different from other people's. You discover these factors by listening to them and debating, not in order to change your (or their) readings (though that may happen), but to bring out the reasons for the differences. The reasons may include social backgrounds, gender, age, prior knowledge, political or religious beliefs, or assumptions. Those are, after all, what make you read the way you do, and the more you are aware of such factors, the more powerful your reading will become.

Once you realize that poems do not dictate meanings to their readers (nor do poets!), but that readers, because of their diverse repertoires, produce different readings, then your enjoyment of poetry can become much greater. Read this poem by Emily Dickinson:

> Apparently with no surprise
> To any happy Flower
> The Frost beheads it at its play—
> In accidental power—

The blond Assassin passes on—
The sun proceeds unmoved
To measure off another Day
For an Approving God.

What can you do with this poem? First, try to get a sense of its text strategies and general argument. What does the poem offer you as you read it? Eight short, cryptic lines—perhaps surprising in the direction of their logic. The poem appears to ask its readers to set two apparently contradictory scenes alongside each other. The first is the seemingly inexplicable unconcern of nature for a flower, which despite its beauty is killed by frost. The second, just briefly hinted at in the last line, is "an approving God." With the first, the destruction of flowers by frost, many readers are likely to be sympathetic but not, probably, deeply upset—although look how the poem tries to deepen your sympathy by the use of words that make the flower almost human—"happy," "beheads," "assassin." When those words are drawn to your attention, perhaps you become a little more sympathetic, recognizing the power that language can have to move you. But what about God? To what extent can God be accused of "approving" of this destruction?

It is here that different readers will react differently largely because of their different religious repertoires. But sometimes you don't know why you react as you do to a poem, and that's particularly when you need to probe your own repertoire. For example, one student's initial reaction to this poem was, "I just don't like it, and I don't know why." Later she said that it made her nervous; finally she said she thought it was "blasphemous." If you, like this student, believe in a traditional Christian God, you may be disturbed by the poem's accusation. Why would God approve of destruction? You might say that the poem points to a great and worrying mystery, traditionally known as the "problem of evil in the universe." You might point out the poet's seeming lack of faith. If a deep religious faith is part of your repertoire, and you believe that God's ways can't be understood by men and women, then you would want to argue that these ways cannot be criticized. Your repertoire would clash with the poem's, and you would probably suggest that "approving" in line 8 might be unfair, or even, as our student said, blasphemous.

If, however, you are an atheist or just skeptical about such traditional views of God, your reaction will be completely different. You might, for example, say that the anguish and fear expressed in the poem articulate very effectively one of the major problems of traditional religion. You might argue that such a view of God is exactly what Christianity implies—an uncaring power who approves of the destruction of beauty. In this case, your repertoire would intersect with the poem's.

We've given you two brief, somewhat extreme reactions thus far, in which it is easy to see what the reader's repertoire is and whether it conflicts or intersects with the poem's repertoire. Frequently, however, things are not so obvious because your repertoire is not so clearly defined. Imagine the reader—and you may be like this—who is confused about what to think about God, who simultaneously wants to believe in God's goodness and yet feels skeptical about it because of all the war, poverty, and destruction in the world.

Such a reader might read the flower as a symbol for all humans, thinking about the inexplicability of evil and destruction—and especially their unpredictability in this world. Such thoughts are a recurring human anxiety—and indeed, some anthropologists and philosophers have argued that the idea of God, or certain concepts of God, has grown up in human societies precisely to try to explain such mysteries. In this particular reading context, you may find yourself not so much agreeing or disagreeing with the poem as seeing it as a catalyst for you to try to clarify confusions in your own repertoire.

This little poem, then, might well direct you to think about matters far beyond the merely "literary." The problems of evil and pain, the existence of God, and the place of religion in human life are all matters that many readers care greatly about and that you may want to think about. When you read this poem, you bring your assumptions about these issues to bear, and the different readings you produce in turn have implications for the way your beliefs may be challenged or reinforced, and for the ways you act in the world.

Writing Suggestions

1. What other aspects of Dickinson's poem do you find ideologically contradictory? Reread the section in Chapter 2 on "absences" (pp. 47–48) and write an analysis of the poem in terms of the suggestions given there.
2. Choose another poem where quite contradictory strong readings can be easily made. Construct a case for each reading.

A Strong Reading:
Developing a Differing Perspective

The best and most interesting readers of poetry are those we have called "strong" or "powerful": informed, aggressive, lively, they bring to a poem important and interesting questions and issues of their own choosing. By all means, the poem will have its say, and indeed you should do everything to let it speak to you as powerfully as possible. But finally it is *you* who are going to let it speak, to let its words come alive.

Let's look at a poem by a seventeenth-century Cavalier poet.

RICHARD LOVELACE (1618–1658)

To Lucasta, Going to the Wars

Tell me not, sweet, I am unkind
That from the nunnery
Of thy chaste breast and quiet mind,
To war and arms I fly.

True, a new mistress now I chase,   5
The first foe in the field;
And with a stronger faith embrace
A sword, a horse, a shield.

Yet this inconsistency is such
As you too shall adore;   10
I could not love thee, dear, so much
Loved I not honor more.

If you were asked to write a response statement on your initial reading of this poem, what are the kinds of things you might note as a way of coming to grips with it? You might try to compare some aspect of its general or literary repertoire with the same aspect of your own, taking into account the ideological conditions that helped produce yours and the text's. You might note that it is a love poem, seemingly addressed by a man (the "I" of the poem) to a woman (the "sweet" of the opening line). Next, if you were trying to compare some aspects of your general repertoire on love relationships with those of the poem, you might consider two questions:

1. What kinds of attitudes to love, both explicit and implicit, does the poem embody?
2. Equally important, how and why do *you,* as a modern reader, react to those attitudes?

The first question is directed to the *text:* it suggests that the poem may assume attitudes about love that it doesn't explicitly articulate but that are taken for granted by its writer—and in a sense by the poem itself. They would have also been taken for granted by his initial audience. They are the product of the dominant, shared ideology of a particular society and, as such, may have seemed "natural" or "normal" to the poet and his initial audience. A first step in doing a strong reading of a text is to explore some of its unarticulated assumptions in an attempt both to contrast its implicit with its explicit repertoire and to contrast its underlying ideological presuppositions with those of your own cultural setting.

The relationships between the sexes—love, courtship, family structure, marriage, questions of dominance and subordination—are always, in any age, a central issue of the ideology of the time. It is therefore important not to assume that the views of love articulated by the poem are necessarily the same as your own. The further back in history a poem was written, the more likely it is that the meanings of its words and the assumptions they embody will have changed over time.

This poem, of course, does not say that its assumptions about love are conventional or ideological: they are simply so obviously true and "natural" to the writer and his presumed audience that they don't have to be defined or defended. They are therefore not explicitly stated, but they are nonetheless part of the poem's repertoire, which you can discover if you try to read the poem **symptomatically.** There is a dominant male, and a female who is seen as a "nunnery" (in other words, as something pure, as an escape from the world) and who occupies an essentially passive role. *She* stays in the nunnery with her "chaste breast" and "quiet mind"; *he* goes chasing off in the field of war, neither quiet nor (necessarily) chaste. Constancy, like chastity, seems to be valued very highly, though clearly it is more required of women than men.

Historical Research

Next you might probe a little further and find out just exactly what kind of society had such values. Here doing a little historical research can help you. You will discover that seventeenth-century England was in fact a stratified, hierarchical society where relationships between the sexes were highly organized and where a woman was legally the property of her husband. Given that information, consider the attitude of the last two lines: clearly the male "I" of the poem estimates that the values associated with a man's going to war to defend his country (values undefined because, once again, taken for granted) are regarded as more important than the values associated with loving a woman. Overall, you may see "To Lucasta," as many students suggest in their response statements, as a very sexist poem. Men are aggressive, active, powerful, and have all the authority; women wait patiently for them at home and embody virtues like tolerance, patience, and passivity.

Obviously such a reading would almost certainly not have been intended (let alone appreciated!) by the poem's author. The poem is, after all, meant as a love poem—and presumably, therefore, as a compliment. Would the woman to whom it might have been sent (Lucasta or whomever) have appreciated it? Presumably, if she didn't, she might have been abandoned by the man. So perhaps the woman to whom the poem was originally addressed would have accepted such attitudes as givens. The poem certainly takes it for granted that she wouldn't protest.

Note that the reading of this poem we have just offered is not just a summary of its ideas. It is also deeply influenced by its modern readers. Their particular ideological positioning enables them to distance themselves sufficiently from the poem to recognize its distinctive assumptions. The above reading takes the form it does because of what many, even most, people living in the late twentieth century bring to their reading of such a poem. Whether your values are conscious or unconscious, as modern readers you probably expect women to be treated equally to men, and consequently you may be disturbed by poems that embody values different from yours.

You are not, of course, required to read the poem in this way, but it is a typical late twentieth-century reaction to it. Here, to give you an instance, is a sample from a response statement written by one of our (female) students:

```
At first I thought this narrator was sincere as well as clever,
talking about his love for her in religious language. But toward
the end I asked myself just what kind of commitment did he have to
her? Isn't he saying how much he loves her and then saying, "Well
yes, but there are more important things in my life than love."
```

That would be fine if she could have other things as well—move
around freely, be adventurous, and so forth. But no, she has to
sit around and wait for him in the nunnery or quietly at home while
he's out having wider experiences—even other women. You know
what soldiers are like.

Like our reading, this student's response was clearly not intended by the author.
But it becomes a possible and even a common interpretation for readers today
because the poem is being read in a different age by a reader who brings a typical
late twentieth-century repertoire to bear on the poem.

A self-conscious reading from a perspective that differs from that of the text
results in an interesting, lively, and engaging response to the poem. The poem
does not mean only what its author intended; nor does it mean only what a
contemporary reader projects upon it. It is open for different readings—for
discussion, debate, dissension—and thereby for enjoyment.

Implications Beyond the Classroom

One characteristic of a strong reading of a poem is that it has implications beyond
the classroom, beyond merely "literary" study. Just as you bring your own
assumptions and interests into your readings, so the readings you construct may
affect the decisions and choices you make in other aspects of your lives; that is,
literary reading doesn't end with books. Just as there are *didactic* texts, which
advocate distinct moral or political positions, so your readings likewise have
moral or political implications.

What are the implications for your understanding of male-female differences
if you take up a reading like the one just proposed for Lovelace's "To Lucasta"
or for Donne's "Valediction"? What are the implications of your reading of
Blake's "London" for your views on politics, the individual, and poverty? All
the readings you adopt as your own do have implications for your behavior and
commitments in the world. Reading is not just an aesthetic or academic activity:
it is the process by which you describe and, in a real sense, create your world.

Writing Suggestions

1. Explain what is meant by a *strong reading*.
2. Develop a strong reading of a poem of your choice.
3. Explore some of the non-literary implications of your strong reading.

Enjoying Poetry Together

Part of the reason reading poetry doesn't always strike modern readers as an
exciting activity is the impoverished context in which they put it. Throughout
this chapter, therefore, we have discussed ways in which you can enrich your
reading context by exploring your own and the text's repertoire and by becoming
a strong reader of poems. But the best way to sense the excitement of reading
poetry is to participate in it. We'd like at this point to suggest you write your

own poetry, listen to other poets reading their work, and perhaps above all choose your own favorite poems and read and enjoy them with others. We'd like to close with an account of our experience with a poem that students have repeatedly found provoking and exciting. The poem we'll discuss is one of our favorites.

ROBERT HASS (b. 1941)

Meditation at Lagunitas

All the new thinking is about loss.
In this it resembles all the old thinking.
The idea, for example, that each particular erases
the luminous clarity of a general idea. That the clown-
faced woodpecker probing the dead sculpted trunk   5
of that black birch is, by his presence,
some tragic falling off from a first world
of undivided light. Or the other notion that,
because there is in this world no one thing
to which the bramble of *blackberry* corresponds,   10
a word is elegy to what it signifies.
We talked about it late last night and in the voice
of my friend, there was a thin wire of grief, a tone
almost querulous. After a while I understood that,
talking this way, everything dissolves: *justice,*   15
pine, hair, woman, you and *I.* There was a woman
I made love to and I remembered how, holding
her small shoulders in my hands sometimes,
I felt a violent wonder at her presence
like a thirst for salt, for my childhood river   20
with its island willows, silly music from the pleasure boat,
muddy places where we caught the little orange-silver fish
called *pumpkinseed.* It hardly had to do with her.
Longing, we say, because desire is full
of endless distances. I must have been the same to her.   25
But I remember so much, the way her hands dismantled bread,
the thing her father said that hurt her, what
she dreamed. There are moments when the body is as numinous
as words, days that are the good flesh continuing.
Such tenderness, those afternoons and evenings,   30
saying *blackberry, blackberry, blackberry.*

In a number of our classes, this poem has become the focus of animated discussion, sometimes with a few other poems by Robert Hass. A different person has read the poem aloud in class each day, and the discussion has often developed in quite different and unpredictable directions.

What Is the Poem "About"?

As a group, we have usually found it difficult to say exactly what this poem is about. Yet from the first time we read it, many of us found the repetition of the word "blackberry" to be very seductive, and so our discussion has often focused there. Most students liked the last lines better than the first eleven because they were less abstract. Yet they could see that those opening lines were setting up an argument that would be examined as the poem developed. Those opening lines, therefore, might deserve some detailed attention. So together we launched into the first stage of reading a poem, working through word meanings and text strategies toward a restatement of the argument, keeping in mind that this *summary* can only be a starting point, not a conclusion.

In the first two lines, the poet is, many suggested, complaining about "new thinking." What is that? The more you think about contemporary life and the more you read contemporary literature, the more you become aware of the fragmentation, alienation, and general lack of unity of individuals, texts, and cultures. Our students have proved sympathetic to the poet's complaint: much that the twentieth century has done to us has been for our material good, yet a widespread feeling is one of "loss." Loss of what? Religion, innocence, a feeling of being at home in the world? Many students argued that they still want, as you may, to believe in "general ideas," that is, in a kind of transcendent essence, even though they know that such ideas and assumptions are specific to a culture and not universal, and that the modern world seems to have destroyed many possibilities of believing in them.

So most readers responded to a sense of nostalgia—for "general ideas," for a time when people weren't overwhelmed by details, when "a first world/ of undivided light" was still somehow part of a universal experience. But they recalled that the poem argued that much of the "old thinking" was also about loss. A number recognized that "the first world of undivided light" refers to the Garden of Eden and suggested that the myth of Adam and Eve's expulsion from Eden shows how "loss" has been a major preoccupation of our cultural history. They saw some suggestion of the idea of loss as an ideological continuity that has been aggravated and increased in the twentieth century.

Students knew that birches are white, not black, and were confused by what lines 5–6 might possibly be suggesting. Some argued that they were just particular dead birches in the landscape that the poet was looking at. They interpreted them literally. Others wanted to see these lines in the context of the whole argument. The poet is arguing that "loss" is so disturbing that life, represented by the woodpecker, seeks to overcome the "black birches" (a possible symbol for anything from forest fires to a general presence of evil in the world). Most readers felt that the woodpecker's presence in these lines suddenly introduced a note of brilliance, even fun. After all, the woodpecker is "clown-faced."

What happens next—with the "or" in line 8? To most readers, the poet tries to restate his argument, as if worrying about getting it across to his audience, trying to share with us his exploration of a difficult but important and intriguing observation. He's arguing that just because the word "blackberry" is only a word and doesn't mean one particular blackberry—the juicy black fruit we eat in pies or jelly or straight off the bush—we shouldn't think a word is "elegy to what it signifies." What does *elegy* mean here? ("Maybe I don't like this poem so much after all," one student remarked at this point, as the poem continued to be abstract.) What *does* "elegy" mean here? An elegy is usually a poem of mourning. How can a word be an elegy? Perhaps because it's a kind of nostalgic memory. What about "what it signifies"? A signifier is what a word stands for. For example, the word *chair* stands for or signifies those things you sit on. But words never fully capture the reality they supposedly describe, as we discussed in Chapters 1 and 2. So the argument is perhaps saying that the word "blackberry" can stand for many things, but it never captures the real taste or look or smell—or, as some students who had picked blackberries said, the feel of the thorns!

Bringing Associations to the Poem

We can give other examples of different words or sentences that have many connotations in which the words never quite give us access to the experience being described. Love poems are a good example. However evocative and moving they are, words like "lips," "kiss," "eyes," "hair," and "passion" remain just words. They never magically bring the man or woman they "signify" into existence. That's part of the fascination and the frustration of language.

So far we had let ourselves slowly enter into the poem's argument, freely responding to it and thinking of examples that supported it or countered it; and we had discovered a lot about one another's literary and general repertoires in the process. Some people said they felt that life with its losses is quite "tragic," others that it is "great" despite the losses, others that language is so slippery that it's amazing that we can communicate at all. That's what reading poetically can do: you don't just stay with the formal text features, summarize the argument, or launch into personal associations. You start to develop a coherent response to a text that allows you to analyze the connotative power of language, not merely for its own sake but to explore larger literary and cultural issues.

Finally, we moved on to what most agreed was the easier part of the poem. The poet and his friend, like the class, had been talking about the way "everything dissolves" when it is put into words. Then we became aware of a paradox: the poem itself is words! With *words*, the poet recounts some of his finest memories—of a woman, the river where he fished as a child. He gives what many readers feel to be very *un*abstract, very emotional descriptions—especially of the woman and her hands, her dreams, and the restful, happy, Eden-like scene of fishing.

Here most students felt the poet was inviting them to bring their own favorite memories into play: the house one lived in as a child, a first kiss, moonlight in Vermont, the first sight of the Golden Gate Bridge, the Rockies on a sunny day. These memories, like those in the poem, are always a mixture of scenes in nature and human relationships. Despite what the poet has said about everything dissolving and about the inadequacy of words, he managed for most of us to make his memories seem very real and concrete by means of those words. Simultaneously but in different ways, members of the class were moved by the poet's descriptive powers, and the poem's strange and striking incantatory ending, as the poet recalled "those afternoons/and evenings," repeating three times the final word: "blackberry, blackberry, blackberry."

Blackberry or "Blackberry"?

Students were divided strongly over whether the poem was, in the final analysis, optimistic or pessimistic—and of course, we could not resolve this issue because students' responses were contingent on their different repertoires.

Interestingly, some of the debate hinged on the particular connotations students had for "blackberry." Some saw the word as signifying anything natural or associated with nature and found the poem to be positive because it somehow asserted the value of natural things; in this case blackberry became a kind of symbol for all that is living. Other students quickly argued against this position saying these students were falling prey to a particular ideology of nature which romanticizes all things natural. "Have you ever picked blackberries?" one student cried out. "They're buried in thorny bushes, and you could bleed to death getting enough out for a mouthful, and then when you eat them, their little seeds get stuck in your teeth." For this woman, "blackberry" related to the line in the poem, "desire is full of endless distances," because, she argued, "blackberries look desirable, but they're hard to get hold of, and when you do, just like everything in life, they're disappointing."

On the other hand, another student, whose repertoire also included picking blackberries as a child, remarked in rather shocked horror: "I love blackberries. We just wore gloves and spit out the seeds. To me they symbolize something that's hard to find, but when you get it, it's all worth the trouble."

Finally, one student argued that he felt what was really important about "blackberry" was the way it sounded: he argued that it didn't matter if it was natural or not, it was just that, when repeated, it produced a hypnotic effect. This position, however, was countered by a student who laughingly argued that the poem just wouldn't be the same if it said "Tupperware, tupperware, tupperware!" We never developed a consensus interpretation of the poem, but we did get a better sense of how our repertoires (particularly on nature and language) influenced our reactions as well as a sense of how vast and varied our repertoires were.

The way that we make language signify for us is a complex and endless process. Poetry is a particularly rich genre to read in this way because it allows so much interpretive freedom. To learn to articulate your responses to language, to see their cultural antecedents, and to share your reading experiences with others can be a kind of playing in which you watch your own ideas, those of others, and those of the poet solidify and dissolve in language—that medium we can never totally pin down. If you read or write poetry, particularly if you share it with your friends, you too may find "such tenderness, those afternoons and evenings, / saying *blackberry, blackberry, blackberry.*"

Checkpoints for Chapter 5

1. Poetry is as much a way of reading as of writing.
2. Learning to read poetically means concentrating with unusual attention to detail on individual word meanings, your responses, and your and the text's repertoires.
3. Poems are both written and read within the ideological constraints of their whole history, from the time in which they were written to the present.
4. As with other texts, you develop strong readings of poetry by asking questions of the text that are different from the ones it may explicitly refer to.
5. Part of the pleasure of reading poetry is becoming aware of, and sharing, the multiple possibilities of reading.

Chapter 6
Reading Fiction

Fiction in Our Lives

Reading prose fiction—short stories or novels—retains a peculiar hold over most people. We say "retains" both because a hundred years ago reading fiction was one of the most common forms of leisure, and because as adults people still retain much of the **literary repertoire** regarding fiction that they were taught as children. Although most people today spend more time watching movies and television or listening to their stereos, reading stories and novels is still a favorite pastime for many of us. Best-selling novelists make what for most people are fabulous sums of money; even many "serious" novelists whose writing never makes the best-seller list are well known and prosperous. Poetry does not command a mass audience, but fiction still retains something of the cultural centrality of fifty or a hundred years ago—before the development of the electronic mass media.

Reading fiction, therefore, is particularly interesting to consider in the context of our approach to reading and writing. The conventions by which you read fiction are no doubt so engrained in you that you probably think of reading a novel or a story as a "natural" activity: you settle down in an armchair or in bed or on a plane, and you read, seemingly automatically, without too much effort. Depending on your taste, you may pick up the latest best-seller, a thriller, or a historical romance. You may read all of the books available by Raymond Chandler, Iris Murdoch, or Norman Mailer. You may be one of the millions who read every new book by Louis L'Amour or Judith Krantz—or all those pulp romances by writers with names like Violet Winspear.

Why Do You Read Fiction?

Why do people like fiction so much? What particular pleasures do *you* get from reading it? Why is it so prominent a part of most people's general and literary repertoires? When asked to discuss their own reading habits, our students respond with a variety of reasons to account for the residual power of fiction. One is simply entertainment: novels and stories that are a "good read" provide an escape from either a routine or a hectic life. They are relaxing; they "pass the time."

A second and related reason is the pleasure provided by narrative closure, that sense of resolution that comes at the end of both "realistic" stories like traditional novels and most "imaginative" or self-consciously unrealistic stories like space fantasies, which follow a traditional narrative structure. In both those cases, the pleasure seems to be closely related to the childhood (some people would say universal) pleasure in "hearing a story," a narrative that sets up certain tensions and problems that are resolved over the course of the telling. For many adults, those moments of closure frequently recall the "and they lived happily ever after" ending of fairy stories. They reinforce the safe feelings people felt as children being read to by a protective parent whose voice lulled them off to sleep. The closure of the story symbolized the close of the day and perhaps for many symbolized the security of their lives. Thus, at a very early age, your literary and general repertoires may well have been formed by this rich context in which the reading of a story became associated with all sorts of comforting things.

A third assumption most contemporary readers bring to fiction, which in some ways contradicts the second, is that it should be "believable" and "true to life." Fiction, so this common assumption goes, is "about" life: it is written to communicate a personal view of the world that readers can "relate to." This assumption seems commonsensical enough. One student, analyzing his assumptions about what "literature" is, wrote:

> Literature reflects on life in general and in particular. It tells truths we might otherwise miss about human nature. The greatest fiction, therefore, has a "message" or vision to communicate.

This view is what the critic Catherine Belsey calls **expressive realism,** a set of reading strategies that still seem commonsensical, even though the nineteenth-century world outlook they are built upon—of an orderly and rational universe—has been largely abandoned. Expressive realism assumes that the plots of fiction reflect this view of the world. It assumes that real people and, like them, fictional characters are consistent and unified. It assumes that however chaotic or relativistic the world may look, it is built upon rational and verifiable truths that can be expressed from a coherent point of view. The narrators of traditional fiction generally attempt to express this coherent point of view. In short, the traditional notions of plot, character, point of view, and theme—still so natural to most readers—grow out of a wider view of the world, which, even though its basis has been largely called into question, still retains its power in the late twentieth century. Such beliefs still dominate the literary and general repertoires of most modern readers. They imply that you don't need to analyze why you take pleasure in reading fiction: you just read it "naturally," to consume it, to get the message it "expresses." Further, the belief that such fiction—with its tidy plots, unified characters, coherent points of view, and themes or messages—is like life comes to support its inverse: that life is like traditional fiction, a reassuring (though clearly untrue) assumption. If you feel comfortable with such strategies, and so regard reading fiction as natural rather than conventional, you may be unwilling to attempt **strong readings** of fiction.

Writing Suggestions

1. Do you agree or disagree with the reasons given for reading fiction? Why do *you* read fiction?
2. Choose one novel or story you have read and liked, and give an account of why you liked it.

Reading Fiction as "Natural"

People assume reading fiction is a "natural" activity only because they are members of a society that has used fiction as a major form of leisure for so long. But what happens when you encounter a piece of fiction that does not conform to your expectations? Either you will have to treat that fiction as confusing and perhaps unreadable, or you will have to enlarge your literary repertoire by developing new reading strategies to interact with it. Later you will discover that you can also apply these new reading strategies to traditional texts to help you to read them "against the grain" and to become a stronger reader. For it is only after you first recognize and then challenge the strategies by which a text is written that you can actively choose the way in which you will read it.

In this chapter, we will first introduce you to some conventional text strategies for fiction. We will then contrast these with more unconventional strategies. We will show you how to do strong readings of texts by using various combinations of conventional and unconventional reading strategies. Finally, we will explore how your cultural context influences the ways you read and interpret fiction.

Do you think that if you become too self-conscious about reading fiction it will lose its special pleasure for you? We don't think so. If you become more aware of what reading fiction (and other kinds of literature) involves, you will become more capable of deciding how you will read. You will no longer be a consumer but a producer of your *own* texts, as Roland Barthes puts it.

We will not argue that conventional reading and text strategies are in any way inferior to unconventional strategies. But we will argue that a near-perfect intersection of reading and text strategies, as often occurs when you read conventional stories conventionally, can lead to comfortable but complacent reading patterns in which you have little desire to explore the ideological forces that produced the story and that are implicitly supported and reinforced in you by reading it. Unconventional stories are much more likely to disrupt you initially and cause you to develop some new reading strategies. It is our hope that, after reading some unconventional stories, you can then return to conventional stories with a wider range of reading strategies.

Conventional Reading and
Text Strategies for Fiction

It is fascinating to discover the extent to which our repertoires of reading strategies for fiction match the text strategies of most works of fiction we read. Such a close matching of repertoires becomes especially apparent in the commonly held traditional assumptions about **plot, character, point of view, and theme.**

Plot

When you read fiction, you usually assume that the events you read about and piece together will all fit together. Thus one of the major reading strategies you probably employ is **consistency building;** that is, you work to create an inner logic, a sense of a consistent whole in the structure of events in a story. Generally, most texts will encourage such reading strategies. Plots can be very complex, and often readers must reread earlier details to get them "straight," but a major assumption most readers have about fiction is that it all should *cohere.* Much fiction, if read in this way, certainly appears to. Even if a story uses flashback or flashforward techniques, like, for example, Hemingway's story "The Short Happy Life of Francis Macomber," readers assume that such strategies are used to accomplish particular effects, perhaps to achieve suspense or to provide information from the past that will account for an event in the present.

In "The Short Happy Life of Francis Macomber," the flashback strategy works in both these ways. The first sentence of the story reads, "It was now lunch time and they were all sitting under the double green fly of the dining tent pretending nothing had happened." Obviously something has happened: the reader's curiosity is aroused, and his or her questions will be answered in a flashback a few pages later. One common strategy readers adopt in reaction to such text strategies is to allow the story to increase their sense of suspense but to remain relatively passive. Readers often don't try to piece its confusing bits together because they feel confident that eventually the story itself will do that for them. Consequently, such ambiguous lines as: "Francis Macomber . . . had just shown himself, very publicly, to be a coward"; "let's not talk about the lion"; and "I wish it hadn't happened" both build suspense and allow the reader to feel confident that the story will soon explain and resolve itself. As one of our students commented after reading the pages of the story before the flashback occurs:

> I'm very familiar with this kind of text strategy: the story drops hints about what has happened in the past in order to get the reader interested. This technique occurs often in detective stories when the reader comes in after the murder has already taken place. I didn't try to figure out what Macomber had done. I just read quickly, waiting for the story to give me all the answers.

Thus the twists, turns, and dramatic ironies of the plot are elements that generally can be read so that they cohere in the final analysis. There is no "natural" reason why plots should cohere, but because they do in many texts such as "Francis Macomber" and because readers' literary repertoires are in part formed by reading these kinds of stories, readers generally think that a unified plot is both "natural" and "realistic."

Paradoxically, a coherent plot is not, in fact, "realistic" at all. Most people don't experience their lives that way: often their lives feel like a collection of random, unpredictable details in which events occur by chance and suddenly end without a sense of closure. People do not continually experience sudden revelations (what James Joyce called *epiphanies*) in their lives. Of course you may well wish your life was indeed a well-planned, coherent plot, with startling (and regular) epiphanies! That wish may account for such a long-standing preference for nicely rounded plots—as the adult equivalent of the child's desire for a "happily ever after" ending before going off to sleep.

But some fiction doesn't cohere; it twists and turns but comes to no resolution—and even has contradictory endings. You will have to change some of your reading strategies and expectations about some contemporary (and some earlier experimental) fiction and become a more self-conscious reader if you are to enjoy these stories.

Writing Suggestions

1. Choose two stories with very different kinds of plot.
   (*a*) Briefly summarize each plot.
   (*b*) Which kind of plot did you prefer and why?

Character

Most readers tend to assume that **characters** in fiction should be coherent, consistent, and unified. And again, many stories appear to bear this out: their characters will seem consistent if readers try to read them in a consistent fashion. One strategy for doing this is to classify characters according to patterns with which you have become familiar from other fiction. Or you may set them in opposition to each other: this character is good, this one evil; or this character is the victim, this one the persecutor. For example, in Flannery O'Connor's story "The Artificial Nigger," you might classify Nelson as the typical young know-it-all; and his grandfather as the typical old know-it-all. This story can then be read as a study of character: after a series of humiliating events, they both learn a lot about themselves and about their lack of importance in their society. Their development follows a familiar structure of movement from innocence to experience.

Another common strategy for establishing the unity of characters is to "identify" with them—despite the fact that they are fictional, not real. According to this strategy, the character is not completely like you but may resemble one part of you or have learned lessons that perhaps you have learned. So you may say you can "relate to" the characters. Yet everyone has felt **decentered** by the often bewildering variety of events or roles that each of us is called upon to play in our lives: you are one person with your parents, another with your friends, another in class, another in a job interview. Who can possibly say which is "the real you"? All these selves are you, and all these selves are real, but they are neither consistent nor unified. People are all made up of contradictory fragments that cannot be summed up in a word or phrase. Thus only by simplifying your own complexity can you see characters as likewise unified and realistic. People's lives continually call into question the notion of a stable, coherent "self." In the often unpredictable world we all live in, the continuing expectation of such stability in fiction may—like the rounded plot—be a kind of cultural nostalgia. But, as we will see later in the chapter, all stories do not present unified characters.

Writing Suggestions

1. (a) When you read fiction, do you habitually "identify" with characters?
   (b) Why do you do this? What reading strategies are involved?
2. Choose a novel or short story you have read and analyze:
   (a) to what extent you find the characters "realistic."
   (b) what "realistic" means in this context.

Point of View

Another conventional assumption most readers have about fiction is that it should be told from a consistent **point of view**—whether first- or third-person, omniscient or limited—and that the consistency of the point of view makes the story seem realistic and believable. Again, readers have these assumptions about point of view in their literary repertoire because they have read many stories that use a single viewpoint. They also know that different viewpoints give distinctive effects and pleasures and require different reading strategies. For example, the **first-person** point of view in Edgar Allan Poe's story "The Tell-Tale Heart" probably gives you a sense of immediacy and heightened involvement in the story. One of your strategies may be to believe the "I" because it seems so "real." As the narrator in Poe's story implores you not to think that he is mad, only "dreadfully nervous," you allow the first-person strategy to draw you in, perhaps becoming more "dreadfully nervous" yourself.

The distance provided by the **third-person omniscient** perspective in, for example, Willa Cather's story "Paul's Case" lets you get inside each of the characters' minds, and what you lose in intimacy, you gain in knowledge: "Paul stated, politely enough, that he wanted to come back to school. This was a lie, but Paul was quite accustomed to lying; found it, indeed, indispensable for overcoming friction." Your reading strategies are perhaps most passive in this narrative situation. Faced with an all-knowing narrator, what else can you do but sit back and believe? We will suggest later in this chapter some alternative strategies by which you can actively choose to read such texts against the grain.

In other situations, however, readers are confronted with an *untrustworthy* or otherwise **limited** narrator. In reading Emily Brontë's novel *Wuthering Heights,* you may well feel that one of the main narrators, Nelly Dean, has a biased, hostile view of the love affair between Heathcliff and Cathy. If so, their love affair may take on a mysterious aura for you. Such a narrative situation can force you to become a more active reader, puzzling over and trying to detach your view of the love affair from Mrs. Dean's.

Surprisingly, this limited point of view is often one that readers like least, even though it is more "realistic" than the other two, particularly more than third-person omniscient. If you ever study the different perspectives taken by various reporters on a news story, or witness two friends arguing, or hear the account of a divorce case, you know that there is no "true" story—no objective point of view that takes everyone's perspective into account. But why, if readers know this, do they still readily accept the highly artificial and conventional notion of a single viewpoint, and (even stranger!) often regard such stories as more realistic than stories with multiple viewpoints?

As with expectations about plot and character, expectations about point of view have been built up by literary traditions spanning the last two hundred years—traditions, in this case, of a unified narrative voice. Thus most readers today assume that one of the distinctive pleasures people *always* get from fiction comes from being addressed by the *voice* of the text—just as when they were children, they were addressed by the voice of one of their parents "telling them a story." Readers have **naturalized** the conventional expectations about fiction that they have accumulated in their literary repertoires and so have ceased to see them as conventional—unless they are challenged by stories that do not conform to these conventions.

Writing Suggestions

1. Outline what are for you, with your particular assumptions and reading strategies, the advantages and disadvantages of two different points of view in fiction.
2. Choose a story or novel you have read and show how the point of view helped you to construct your reading of it.

Theme

Another common expectation readers have about fiction is that it will always have a point or **theme,** and many stories readily offer readers actions, symbols, or events that can be linked thematically. Your recognition of a theme in one part of a story usually leads you to assume that it will recur in the rest of the story. When readers find in a story a continuing concern with the theme, their initial reading strategy is reinforced. Most readers of Hawthorne's *The Scarlet Letter,* for example, notice the description of the roses growing around the jailhouse door in the opening chapter, or the light and dark imagery in the forest, or Arthur Dimmesdale's repeated gesture of putting his hand on his heart. A reader attuned to reading for the "point" or the underlying meaning will probably read Dimmesdale's gesture not only as a revelation of illness but also as a **symbol** of his lack of moral courage. The main symbol of the book, the embroidered scarlet letter A, likewise "stands for" many things—adulteress and angel, among others.

Readers who have become used to reading *The Scarlet Letter* for its underlying meanings have no difficulty reading such passages figuratively rather than literally and trying to get all the symbols to conform to one major point. They have in their repertoire a set of expectations about *symbolic* or underlying meanings—and one of their major strategies is to look for them individually and then build consistency among them. But even readers who don't read figuratively can read this book fairly comfortably because it does make sense on a literal level. The "theme" of good versus evil simply isn't as rich if one says, "The forest is dark because there are lots of trees in it." Some stories, however, do not seem to have a unified theme—whether they are read literally or figuratively— and they pose new problems for readers who try to find a consistent theme.

Unconventional Reading and Text Strategies for Fiction

The assumptions we've discussed have traditionally been powerful ones in the reading and writing of fiction. But it's important to see that while they allow you to manipulate stories in certain ways—to read, we might say, *fictionally*— they also can constrain your reading. They may lead you to read conventional texts only in conventional ways and to reject all unconventional texts, many of which can offer you great fun. Probably the major distinction between reading fiction conventionally and unconventionally is that conventional reading looks for *coherence* and *closure* (in accordance with the meaning that the text strategies encourage), whereas unconventional reading enables the reader to develop alternative meanings. Unconventional strategies can make you a strong, self-aware reader and can empower you to decide actively rather than by default how you will read a piece of fiction. Deciding to disturb a complacent text can be an exciting and enriching procedure that can reintroduce you to the playful, polyvalent power of language we discussed in Chapter 5. In this section, therefore, we turn to a discussion of some texts that defy traditional notions of unity of plot, character, point of view, or theme. We suggest ways in which you can develop new reading strategies so that you can interact with unconventional stories more effectively, as well as do strong readings of conventional texts. Only after you have learned to go *against* the strategies or arguments that a text is encouraging can you begin to do a strong reading of it.

Plot

What happens if you encounter a story for which the conventional strategy of reading for plot is unrewarding? Donald Barthelme's "Views of My Father Weeping" creates such a problem. It concerns a man who is searching for the "artistocrat whose carriage" has run his father down and killed him. But it is told in short, disconnected paragraphs that—if a reader adopts a traditional assumption that a story should have a recognizably realistic (or linear) plot—seem quite confusing. The story not only is jumbled in time (the father reappears alive) but also introduces anachronistic details, like the mention of a Ford Mustang in what seems to be a nineteenth-century setting and the appearance of seemingly extraneous characters.

> I don't know whether it is time to flee or will not be time to flee until later. He may suddenly stop, assume a sternness. I have kept the door open and nothing between me and the door, and moreover the screen unlatched, and on top of that the motor running, in the Mustang. But perhaps it is not my father weeping there, but another father: Tom's father, Phil's father, Pat's father, Pete's father, Paul's father. Apply some sort of test, voiceprint reading or . . .

One student wrote of this story:

> If I list all the details of plot and setting, I find far too many inconsistencies. There are many absurd details, and events occur out of place. It seems that nothing "really" takes place here at all. It's almost as if the author just selected words and phrases at random. The story certainly goes against every technique of fiction I know.

What specific reading strategies is this reader using? To make these assertions, he obviously was expecting a unified plot, and clearly such a reading strategy cannot deal adequately with the text strategies of this story. One conclusion might be to abandon the story as nonsensical, but a more rewarding one is to search for alternative reading strategies.

Naturalizing Strategies

The strategy of creating meaning from a story that initially seems odd or difficult is called **naturalizing.** The stranger a story appears to you, the more difficult and yet the more crucial it becomes to naturalize it. One of the text strategies of the **post-modern** short story is often to thwart rather than support the reader in this sense-making or naturalizing process.

One possible reading strategy you might use to naturalize "Views of My Father Weeping" would be to try to create a conventional plot by reassembling the details of the story; another, however, would be to accept and enjoy its disparateness. Barthelme himself has written of how the *collage* is a major principle of modern art. Collages, the seemingly random assembling of miscellaneous objects, are something most people have in their repertoires from a very early age when they were encouraged to make them in grade school—from paint, paper, pictures, shoelaces, or whatever. Barthelme's story, like much other post-modern fiction, can be fun if read as a collage—with its implication that the active reader will naturalize the story by accepting its randomness rather than by looking for a pre-existent, conventional plot.

The strategies you use to naturalize the seemingly surrealistic nature of dreams are also similar to the strategies you could use for reading such fiction. When you dream, you find yourself caught up in a world that often brings together a miscellany of details that are often causally disconnected but which you might connect by relating them to deeper psychological significances. Dreams, like "Views of My Father Weeping," do not appear to be rational, logical, or coherent, and thus they provide a similar challenge—to build linkages where none apparently exist "in" the text.

Readers may also draw analogies with music, pointing out the recurrent "motifs" or "themes" that make the story seem like a sonata or the movement of a symphony; they may draw a parallel with painting—with surrealism or cubism—where different elements of the ordinary, the fantastic, the clichéd, and the extraordinary are welded together. Such techniques are, of course, relatively common in some film and television comedy—*Monty Python's Flying Circus,* for example.

Reading stories with unconventional plots, therefore, can help you recognize the constructed nature of all plots. While a conventional story presents you with a fairly unified plot that moves toward resolution, an unconventional story may produce tension in you because it does not seem resolvable. Consequently, you realize that if a conventional resolution is to occur, *you* must create it with very active naturalization strategies.

Alternatively, you may begin to delight in the experience of reading a story like an irrational dream or a collage in which all the pieces never quite fit together or in which the relationships among them are so multiple that you cannot pin them down or interpret them with any assurance. This strategy of exploring and enjoying the fragmentation of a story can also be usefully applied to traditional stories. You might, for example, choose to find a way in which a story with a seemingly straightforward plot has in fact elements of the irrational that have to be ignored if you are to make conventional sense of it. In her book *Critical Practice,* Catherine Belsey demonstrates that while Arthur Conan Doyle's Sherlock Holmes stories are traditionally read as asserting the supremacy of rational thinking, this way of reading ignores the recurring irrational women whose very presence repeatedly initiates the plot. If you focus on these women, you contradict the dominant rational reading of the text and instead produce a reading that makes the stories more mysterious, even magical. When you perform such a reading, you often find yourself moving your analysis of text and reading strategies to a broader cultural level. You start to read *symptomatically.* You begin to explore some of the ideological reasons for the existence of certain dominant readings. The dominant readings of the Sherlock Holmes stories reflect the traditional nineteenth-century faith in the objectivity of science and the belief that the plots of fiction should, in turn, reflect that objectivity. In the twentieth century, we are more skeptical about nineteenth-century rationalism and therefore more able to construct alternative readings of such stories.

Writing Suggestions

1. What are the main differences in the strategies you would use to read what you consider "conventional" and "unconventional" fiction?
2. Choose an "unconventional" story you have read and show what strategies you used to read it.

Character

Much contemporary fiction emphasizes that characters have multiple or constructed selves rather than essential, unified ones. You may initially find it difficult to visualize these "multiple" characters. If, however, you enlarge your conception of characters from one in which they must be unified to one in which they can behave contradictorily in different situations, you can open up new possibilities for your reading of both traditional and untraditional stories.

Many contemporary stories, either implicitly or explicitly, call attention to the fictional nature of their characters. They destroy the illusion for the reader that the story is "real" and may also call into question whether one can make fact versus fiction distinctions about people in general, since so much of life seems to involve role-playing of one kind or another. John Barth's humorous short story "Life Story" explicitly addresses the fictional nature of characters. Its main character is a writer who is plagued by the fear that he is a character in a fictional work. He finally resolves his conflict by suggesting that, because no character he has ever read about in fiction knew he was fictional, he himself must be real. Of course, such logic can't convince the reader who has just read this story: characters who fear they are fictional really do exist—in fiction, that is—and so the character has come to the wrong conclusion. This story raises hilarious yet poignant questions about what it is to be "real."

Character in "The Hitchhiking Game"

Other stories address such issues more subtly, and we turn to one of these for some extended analysis of the nature of character. Milan Kundera's "The Hitchhiking Game" is a story about a man and woman who lose a sense of their own identity when they begin an elaborate role-playing game in which their "fictional" selves become indistinguishable from their "real" selves.

The two characters in "The Hitchhiking Game" begin by assuming that they both have a unified self—an essential self—within the context of their own relationship. The woman, however, fears that the man might be different in other contexts, that, for example, he may be flirtatious with more sophisticated and worldly women. The man encourages her insecurity although it seems basically groundless, because he finds her jealousy "touching." He, in contrast, assumes that he "knew everything that a man could know about women," and he certainly assumes that he understands her. You discover as the story develops that he imagines that she possesses a clear, unified, non-contradictory essence: "it had always seemed to him that her inward nature was *real* only within the bounds of fidelity and purity, and that beyond those bounds it simply didn't exist." Consequently, he is angry and crushed when he finds her character not clearly defined and certainly not unified, but rather "hopelessly ambiguous." For her part, the woman, who had "confidently entrusted every moment of her life" to her lover, becomes frightened and demeaned by the changes that occur in him over the course of the evening. Neither is able to distinguish the adopted *persona* from the essential self: "The game merged with life."

Viewed from the man's perspective, this story can be seen as a modern-day version of Hawthorne's story "Young Goodman Brown." It suggests that people's personalities are always ambiguous and that this recognition can be profoundly disturbing. Clearly the woman in the story is not secretly a whore, as the man almost begins to suspect: if she was able to play the role so well, he thought, "it meant she really *was* like that." Nor is the man really a "heartless tough guy," although we are told that "if he did not resemble such a man, nonetheless he had *longed* to be one at one time." To think that the woman is a whore or the man a ruthless exploiter of women is again to fall into the trap of assuming that people have essential traits rather than that they possess complex, often contradictory selves. The woman wants to be both pure *and* sexually experienced. The man wants to be both compassionate *and* abrasive.

This story also calls attention to the characters' fictional status by suggesting their—and by implication the readers'—inability to distinguish among their various roles: on one level, a reader can't tell what the man and woman are "really" like, but on another broader level, the man and woman—despite how real they seem to their readers in all their contradictions—are only characters in a piece of fiction.

What are your expectations about character? In the light of such a story, you can perhaps see how your general assumptions about love, reality, and the self influence your readings of the characters in "The Hitchhiking Game." How you perceive the man and the woman might depend, for instance, on your tolerance for ambiguity, on your willingness to entertain the possibility that characters—and people—are multiple. Your assumptions about the nature of the self, therefore, will to a large extent guide the way you respond to the contradictory details provided about these two characters.

If, however, you are unfamiliar with or resist the concept of multiple selves, you may try to give this story and its characters very different readings from the one presented above. You may attempt to "pin down" one or both of the characters. We have discovered that a number of our students who want to preserve their residual beliefs in a "real" unified self have done just this. Such a process of trying to determine the characters' essential natures can lead to a variety of interpretations, depending on the aspects of the text to which you become attuned. If you tried to pin the two characters down, how did you do it? What details about each did you pay attention to? What details did you ignore?

You might find that your gender also significantly influences the way you respond to "The Hitchhiking Game." Some students, usually women, have argued that the entire game is the man's fault. They suggest that right from the start he is presented as sexist and exploitive. They argue that he makes the woman walk to the gas station when he runs out of gas and maintains a double standard regarding male and female behavior, wanting the woman to be pure but liking her to be jealous of his sexual prowess. At one point in the story, the man recognizes "the law of universal transience, which made even his girl's shyness a precious thing to him." Defenders of the woman interpret this line as a statement that it was really the relationship that was transient for the man, not the woman's shyness, that his commitment to the relationship is minimal whereas hers is complete. They further argue that the woman's insecurity is caused by the mystery the man tries to develop about his other relationships with women. They point out the ridiculousness of his changing directions and driving to Nove Zamky, the cruelty of his toast, his inability to stop the game, his enjoyment at objectifying the woman as a whore, and the difficulty with which he summons compassion at the end when the woman is sobbing in his arms.

Other students have suggested, however, that to argue that the man is completely at fault ignores the fact that he did not start the game and that he tried to stop it early. These defenders of the man also point out that the narrator describes the woman as "the epitome of jealousy" and that she is said to be "grateful . . . for every bit of flattery." They argue that such lines imply that the woman's insecurity is innate and has nothing to do with this particular relationship. Students taking this position also argue that the woman enjoys and feels liberated by her role as a loose woman; they suggest, much like the man in the story, that the woman, though ostensibly shy, must really desire to lead a wild life.

Since arguments can be made equally forcefully in favor of either the man or the woman, why is it that so many readers of this story side with one particular character? As you can see clearly here, readers' gender and assumptions about male-female relationships may cause them to identify with either the man or the woman, and readers will usually be more sympathetic to the character with whom they identify.

Further, you may believe that clear distinctions can be made between right and wrong. You may, therefore, try to make these distinctions when reading this story even if doing so involves ignoring information about a particular character. It is important to see these interpretations not as wrong but as following from different (and, in the long run, ideological) presuppositions. We are not advocating that you adopt one interpretation over another, only that you recognize that your interpretations can be richer and your interpretive options can increase if you recognize that characters can be multiple—decentered rather than unified.

Our students' readings of the characters in "The Hitchhiking Game" suggest that strong forces in their general repertoire are influencing aspects of their literary repertoire. Changing your ideas about the nature of the self can help you not only to appreciate (and enjoy) what initially may seem to be odd text strategies in some contemporary fiction but also to do strong readings of characters in traditional fiction. If characters seem on the surface to be unified, instead of reading to reinforce that unity, you can read to disrupt it. You may decide to look for internal contradictions in those characters, to see the characters as sites of struggle, suppressing the conflicts within a given society. In doing so, you should explore the culture about which the text was written—in this case, contemporary Eastern Europe—as well as your own society for reasons why a particular type of unified character may have appealed to readers in one period and not in another. Then you will be reading the text against the grain and giving a strong reading of its characters.

Writing Suggestions

1. (a) Read "The Hitchhiking Game" and consider whether your analysis of character agrees with the one we have put forward.
   (b) How do you account for the differences?
2. Choose another story in which the traditional concept of character can be challenged, and write an essay analyzing how it can be done.

Point of View

Other contemporary fiction, such as John Barth's famous story "Lost in the Funhouse," will challenge your assumptions that a story should be told from a unified point of view. It is probable that the first four sentences will seem like a fairly conventional opening to a story, except perhaps for the rather strange italicizing of some phrases, apparently without explanation:

> For whom is the funhouse fun? Perhaps for lovers. For Ambrose it is *a place of fear and confusion.* He has come to the seashore with his family for the holiday, *the occasion of their visit is Independence Day, the most important secular holiday in the United States of America.*

Readers might be puzzled by the differences in typeface, since there seems so far to be no reason for it. But then, without pausing, this opening paragraph of the story goes on:

> A single straight underline is the manuscript mark for italic type, *which in turn* is the printed equivalent to oral emphasis of words and phrases as well as the customary type for titles of complete works, not to mention. Italics are also employed, in fiction stories especially, for "outside," intrusive, or artificial voices, such as radio announcements, the texts of telegrams and newspaper articles, et cetera.

For many reasons this will seem an illegitimate and odd shift. Where does this voice come from? Whose voice is it? For some readers, it will seem silly and inappropriate—as will many similar dislocations throughout the story in which you are given instructions on how to write stories.

The reason "Lost in the Funhouse" seems strange, even incomprehensible, to some readers is that they do not have an appropriate repertoire of strategies by which to naturalize it. If you expect a story to maintain a consistent point of view, to have believable and coherent characters, then it is at first difficult to read "Lost in the Funhouse" without irritation. A story, it would seem, should not be a textbook on how to write stories.

Yet John Barth is a famous author. How is it that so many readers find his fiction enjoyable? The answer is that they have developed a repertoire of strategies for dealing with such shifts in point of view. Let us look at this in a little detail. Early in the story the narrator explains what the story would be like if it followed a conventionally consistent point of view:

> Actually, if one imagines a story called "The Funhouse," or "Lost in the Funhouse" . . . The *beginning* should recount the events between Ambrose's first sight of the funhouse early in the afternoon . . . the *middle* would narrate all relevant events from the time he goes in to the time he loses his way . . . Then the *ending* would tell what Ambrose does while he's lost, how he finally finds his way out, and what everybody makes of the experience.

But the story disrupts these conventional expectations. It starts with an apparently *omniscient third-person narrator*—"Ambrose was 'at that awkward age.' His voice came out high-pitched as a child's"; later the reader realizes this narrator becomes an *unreliable third-person narrator*, as he turns out to be Ambrose, looking back with nostalgia and embarrassment on his youth:

> He wishes he had never entered the funhouse. But he has. Then he wishes he were dead. But he's not. Therefore he will construct funhouses for others and be their secret operator—though he would rather be among the lovers for whom funhouses are designed.

Here the "he" is close to an "I." How do readers deal with this situation? Most conventionally assume that stories will be told from a single viewpoint, and they have various strategies for reading each narrative perspective. What is unexpected for many readers in this story is the mixture of such points of view and the consequent need for a scheme to incorporate what is, to use Donald Barthelme's phrase again, a "collage" of perspectives. Yet there is a distinct pleasure in experiencing the shifts in viewpoint in a story like "Lost in the Funhouse": it invites the reader to play, to move back and forth, to find that it is fun to fill in the story's many gaps. From such reading strategy, you learn that the dominant narrative voice of any story, conventional or avant-garde, is the voice of the active *reader*.

If a story presents multiple points of view, try the strategy of reading it playfully as a collage. To naturalize it, look for links among the perspectives, but also keep in mind the chance element of a collage: sometimes a relationship of contiguity, closeness, or juxtaposition does not imply a relationship of significance. Thus you must be prepared to recognize that all perspectives of texts do not necessarily cohere. As Thomas Pynchon shows in his hilarious novel *The Crying of Lot 49*, the world is full of clues—but "clues to what?" is the question!

Once you have expanded your repertoire of reading strategies for handling several points of view, you may be more able to enjoy disruptive or post-modern texts—like Ronald Sukenick's novel *98.6*, John Fowles's *The French Lieutenant's Woman*, or the stories of Robert Coover, Jorge Luis Borges, or Vladimir Nabokov, many of which use shifting or unreliable narrative voices. Robert Coover's "The Babysitter" presents a series of unreliable narrators, many of whom mix fantasy with fact indiscriminately, while his story "The Elevator" presents alternative accounts of an event, neither of which may be accurate. Some older stories, however, also use such strategies. In his story "Ligeia," Edgar Allan Poe gives us a narrator with a confused mind, and Nikolai Gogol's "Diary of a Madman" makes it clear his narrator is a madman.

Your new strategies can also be applied to stories with more conventionally coherent viewpoints. Edgar Allan Poe's "The Cask of Amontillado," for example, is a story of a carefully planned murder of a man named Fortunato, told from the point of view of the murderer, Montresor. Its consistent first-person point of view tries to involve you in the intrigue of the crime and to prevent you from focusing on the plight of the victim. But what would happen if you reread the story from the point of view of Fortunato, who (we are told) remains largely silent at the end of the story, even though he is being walled up in a cellar by Montresor? Such an analysis might lead to a broader cultural point: characters who don't get to speak are in some sense all victims—perhaps not in such an extreme sense as Fortunato, but victims, nonetheless, of a particular narrative convention that allows only one point of view to be heard. To question the coherence of a story's point of view is to explore the ideological circumstances that give rise to particular narrative perspectives—whether authoritative, moralistic, gender-specific, unreliable, fragmented, or unified. What values are exposed and hidden, what cultural conflicts expressed or suppressed in the narrative voice? In asking such questions, you are acknowledging the limitations of expressive realism, with its belief in a single, unified point of view.

Writing Suggestion

Choose a contemporary story or novel you are studying and analyze how the point of view is "constructed," not "natural."

Theme

When we read, we naturally look for confirmation of or challenges to our general repertoire. One common way of explaining the issues a story raises for us is to talk about its *themes*. Themes generally are serious human issues, such as maturity, or appearance and reality, or initiation. We speak of them as being somehow "in" the text. What that inevitably means is that we project aspects of our general repertoire upon the text and naturalize the text by "finding" in it evidence for the themes. Themes arise not from the text itself but from the matching of the repertoires of text and reader. And sometimes these repertoires don't match that easily because some stories seem absurd or ridiculous. When reading such stories, many readers try to fall back on "theme" as a way of making sense of them but soon find that strategy not to be particularly rewarding.

Many readers of Donald Barthelme's stories, for example, have difficulty in constructing themes for them. His stories are short, whimsical, and often seem illogical. In "The Balloon," the first-person narrator describes how an enormous balloon, covering acres of ground, settles over Manhattan and soon becomes a familiar part of the landscape. At the end of the story, the balloon disappears, and the cause is attributed to the narrator's changing emotional life. In the same author's "Porcupines at the University," a dean of a university sees a flock of porcupines being driven by two cowboys along a highway and speculates on whether or not they will try to register for courses. To say such stories have serious themes—implying they raise moral or philosophical issues and questions—may seem far too solemn. One of our students who couldn't "make sense" of "Porcupines" wrote:

> This story reminds me of a fantasy story written by a child. Porcupines don't just appear on a freeway. Even if the story's jokes are funny, there isn't enough in it to make it believable.

What does such a reader's repertoire contain (or not contain) to produce this very disjunctive matching with the text's? Behind such a response is the assumption that all fiction ought to depict the ordered and coherent view of life typical of conventional fiction.

For other readers, however, ghost stories, science fiction, gothic novels, and fiction about the marvelous or fantastic immediately provoke expectations that the story does not have to be conventionally ordered and coherent. One of our students saw "Porcupines" as "fantastic" and "The Balloon" as "a magic story." She wrote of "The Balloon":

> The events are some sort of joke about New York. Since it is such a fantastic place anyhow, why not imagine it as even more fantastic? What the balloon means is up to the imagination. For the narrator it reflects his emotional life.

Two very interesting strategies are at work in this reader's response. The first is that she judges "The Balloon" not by realistic criteria but as an escape into the imagination. The pleasure of the story comes from the duality—the "real" place, New York, and the "fantastic" or magical balloon. Normal ideas about place, setting, cities, and people can be suspended—or put side by side with the abnormal.

Such writers as Kafka, Calvino, and Borges specialize in such effects: their readers find themselves caught between two worlds, one they recognize as realistic or normal, the other as magical, supernatural, or fantastic. But older stories, too, maintain this tension between the real and the magical or supernatural. In Henry James's story "The Jolly Corner," readers argue about how to interpret Spencer Brydon's experience of his phantom "self." If readers interpret the vision as a hallucination or neurosis, they are assuming that the story's events can be explained "realistically" by an appeal to psychology or psychopathology. But other readers point to the strange coincidence of Alice's dream, which suggests that the phantom self "really" exists. Such readers see the story as inexplicably magical.

The second strategy we can observe in our student's response to "The Balloon" is the desire to give an underlying meaning to the events that seem magical or strange. Rather than simply enjoying the pure fantasy of dream or magic, she wanted to find a way of saying what the story *really* means—of seeing the fantastic balloon as a metaphor or symbol for something in the real world. This is a dominant part of many readers' literary repertoires, whether the story they are reading is "realistic" or "unrealistic." One of our students wrote on Scott Fitzgerald's novel *The Great Gatsby:*

> What Gatsby stands for is the romance of the American dream. In the story he is just a crook, but in a reader's experience he represents something all Americans yearn for—romance, ambition, success, wealth, beauty. Even if we never find it, we go on looking.

Such a strategy is common in most reading. It is perhaps related, once again, to the childhood habit of looking for a "moral" or "message." Most people are habituated to expect fiction to have direct or indirect application to their lives, either as individuals or as a society. Otherwise, it is often said that fiction has no "point."

Theme, therefore, is one of the most common ways in which readers want to find or create coherence. But with unconventional stories, as we have suggested, readers must work very hard to create themes. Readers may get much reinforcement in a traditional story for trying to read for its point. Various images, symbols, and dialogue may all work together as different signifiers that point to the same signified meaning. Unconventional stories, in contrast, may seem aimless: their images, symbols, and dialogue might seem to be diverse signifiers to which no single signified can be attached with any degree of certainty. We saw a recognition (perhaps needing further elaboration) of this uncertainty in our student's comment: "What the balloon means is up to the imagination." This recognition is one of the most significant you can make in your reading of literature. It can help liberate you when you read both traditional and untraditional stories.

You can begin to realize that you have options when reading fiction. This can make you read more playfully, looking for multiple meanings not only in unconventional texts that encourage such reading strategies but in conventional texts as well. You may discover that some of the multiple meanings you develop are contradictory. If you choose to explore these contradictions, you will probably find that they derive from the society that produced the text. In discussing the multiple meanings of a text, as opposed to searching for a single meaning, you will still be naturalizing the text. But you will be doing so with a degree of self-consciousness about your reading strategies and assumptions, as well as about the assumptions of the text and of the larger culture.

Mixing Traditional and Untraditional Reading and Text Strategies with a Traditional Story

If you become more self-conscious about the reading strategies you use on some contemporary, particularly post-modern, stories, you may also be able to use them profitably with more traditional fiction. The point of doing so is not to be perverse or arbitrary. Rather, you will be able to produce powerful, insightful readings that are interesting to create and that reveal unresolved ideological struggles underlying much traditional fiction. To read in this way is to read **symptomatically**—what in Chapter 2, in discussing *history,* we termed reading for the "absences" of a text.

As an example, we will discuss a traditional story, Anton Chekhov's "The Lady with the Dog." It tells the story (from a limited third-person point of view) of a married man's obsession for a married woman—and of their affair. It is set in late nineteenth-century Russia. If you approach the story with the strategies of *expressive realism,* what kind of reading would you produce? The plot is a straightforward, linear narrative. It focuses on the internal debate of Dmitry Gurov, who is presented as a sentimental but manipulative womanizer, while his mistress, Anna Sergeyevna, is described primarily from the outside, and characterized as bored, vacillating, and guilty, but still willing to respond to Gurov's advances. The story seems to prefer a reader who will appreciate the difficulties of the two lovers, agree with the moral judgments hinted at in the narrative about Gurov's unreliability and womanizing, and be sympathetic to Gurov when he falls in love with Anna near the end of the story. In short, you are asked to accept the viewpoint of the narrator, who focuses almost exclusively on Gurov. Such a reading is not a simplistic one: the text strategies of Chekhov's story ask for a reading that is subtle and sensitive. As Virginia Woolf noted about Chekhov, "As we read these little stories about nothing at all, the horizon widens; the soul gains an astonishing sense of freedom."

A Symptomatic Reading of "The Lady with the Dog"

But if you have learned some different strategies for reading, you may be able to produce a **symptomatic reading** of great interest and power. You can, for instance, realize that the viewpoint you are asked to adopt is exclusively Gurov's; the plot lays out a set of incidents that are presented as inevitable and natural; the characters, especially Anna, seem inevitably tied to the situations and stereotypes of the author's society; the themes of the story, at least by the criteria of expressive realism, may seem obvious—innocence against experience, freedom against restriction, individuality against conformity. We want to emphasize that by using conventional strategies you can produce lively and coherent readings but that by becoming more cognitively and culturally aware you can produce even more interesting ones.

There is, in fact, such a reading: the contemporary fiction writer Joyce Carol Oates has written a version of Chekhov's story called "The Lady with the Pet Dog." Set in the 1970s in America, it is told from the woman's perspective. Whereas Chekhov's story is told in chronological order, Oates's story begins in the middle, with the woman's most intense experiences, and then moves forward and backward in time. Here are the openings of the two stories, first the Chekhov, then the Oates. As you read them, notice the differences in their setting, tone, and point of view—as well as the different event at which they begin.

Chekhov

A new person, it was said, had appeared on the esplanade: a lady with a pet dog. Dmitry Dmitrich Gurov, who had spent a fortnight at Yalta and had got used to the place, had also begun to take an interest in new arrivals. As he sat in Vernet's confectionery shop, he saw, walking on the esplanade, a fair-haired young woman of medium height, wearing a beret; a white Pomeranian was trotting behind her.

And afterwards he met her in the public garden and in the square several times a day. She walked alone, always wearing the same beret and always with the white dog; no one knew who she was and everyone called her simply "the lady with the pet dog."

"If she is here alone without husband or friends," Gurov reflected, "it wouldn't be a bad thing to make her acquaintance."

Oates

Strangers parted as if to make way for him.

There he stood. He was there in the aisle, a few yards away, watching her.

She leaned forward at once in her seat, her hand jerked up to her face as if to ward off a blow—but then the crowd in the aisle hid him, he was gone. She pressed both hands against her cheeks. He was not there, she had imagined him.

"My God," she whispered.

She was alone. Her husband had gone out to the foyer to make a telephone call; it was intermission at the concert, a Thursday evening.

Now she saw him again, clearly. He was standing there. He was staring at her. Her blood rocked in her body, draining out of her head . . . she was going to faint. . . . They stared at each other. They gave no sign of recognition. Only when he took a step forward did she shake her head *no—no—keep away.* It was not possible.

Oates's story, like Chekhov's, is written from a *limited third-person* point of view, but writing it from the woman's viewpoint provides an entirely different perspective on the events. Oates's story can be seen as a contemporary, mildly feminist, strong reading of Chekhov's story. We suggest to our students that they take a hint from Oates—and treating her as a fellow reader, construct their own strong reading of the Chekhov story. They are encouraged to refuse to be the kind of reader the story asks for, and to reject, like Oates, the apparent inevitabilities of character, plot, and viewpoint.

To adopt such a strategy makes you aware that the point of view the Chekhov story takes excludes any detailed consideration of the woman's perspective. That is, of course, the starting point for Oates's rewriting. In the Chekhov story, Anna's character is barely revealed, except as a series of reactions to her lover. The events of the story, which seem to flow naturally from the characterization and the point of view, seem equally naturally to produce a meaning (or "theme") that doesn't call into question the terms that Chekhov sets up. A reading of this story in terms of expressive realism is one apparently dictated by the text strategies.

Once you become aware of the way your reading strategies are being limited by such a reading, however, you can then proceed to a much more culturally aware reading. You begin to articulate what the text does *not* say—what, in a sense, it does *not allow* to be said. To do this, you could locate the story in its historical context and write about the limitations placed on women by the society. You would thus give the woman the voice she is denied by the story's point of view and by Gurov's characterization of women in general as "the inferior race." You could then focus on details such as the generalizations about women, regarded as "them," other-than-men, rather than as subjects in their own right:

> He was under forty, but he already had a daughter twelve years old, and two sons at school. They had found a wife for him when he was very young, a student in his second year, and by now she seemed half as old again as he. She was a tall, erect woman with dark eyebrows, stately and dignified and, as she said of herself, intellectual. She read a great deal, used simplified spelling in her letters, called her husband, not Dmitry, but Dimitry, while he privately considered her of limited intelligence, narrow-minded, dowdy, was afraid of her, and did not like to be at home. He had begun being unfaithful to her long ago—had been unfaithful to her often and, probably for that reason, almost always spoke ill of women, and when they were talked of in his presence used to call them "the inferior race."

If you wanted to do a particularly strong feminist reading, you could analyze some implications of the story's being written both by a man *and* from a male viewpoint. The readings and responses you develop would therefore be very different from those that seem to follow naturally from the text.

Focusing on the ways you read plot, character, point of view, and theme, you become aware that they are fictional and therefore able to be constructed differently by different readers. You can then start to produce distinctive, strong, culturally aware readings. Your *preferences* for certain kinds of reading strategies can be shown to have cultural origins different from those seemingly "required" by the story.

In looking at student reactions to these two stories, we have been surprised at how strongly their gender affects their response to the stories' literary and general repertoires. Many of our female students feel that Oates's storytelling technique is psychologically more realistic than Chekhov's because, they suggest, the mind never recalls an experience strictly chronologically but rather always gives priority to a person's most important moments, regardless of the order in which they were experienced. The men in the class, in contrast, quite frequently prefer Checkhov's more direct storytelling strategy, arguing that events in life *do* happen in a given time sequence and that stories should remain true to that sequence. Why these women and men respond differently to the narrative strategies of these stories is difficult to say. Perhaps their responses have less to do with the storytelling techniques and more to do with the point of view from which the story is told: the women may identify with Anna from whose point of view the Oates's story is told; the men with Gurov from whose point of view Chekhov's story is told.

One could also argue, however, that responses between men and women differ because they have learned certain values on the basis of the culturally produced assumptions of their gender. It may be that men have been trained in our culture to have a greater appreciation for logic and rationality than women, whose upbringing frequently emphasizes the importance of emotions and feelings. Whether such a difference *ought* to exist is, of course, very debatable. But until recently in our culture, such differences have often seemed to be "natural." Consequently men may find Chekhov's linear, orderly writing style compatible with their own culturally acquired appreciation of logic, and women may find Oates's dreamlike, circular style more compatible with their own emphasis on feelings. Perhaps these readers are also influenced by the gender of the author: the women might prefer Oates's story because Oates is a woman. We neither expect nor want to resolve questions such as these. We do, however, want to point out their existence and try to explore them as much as possible. For it is only by recognizing that readers among us differ in complex ways that we can begin to analyze *why* they differ and what the implications of those differences may be.

We have found that reading the Oates story definitely helps students produce stronger readings of the Chekhov. Whereas most of them initially accepted the plot, characterizations, male perspective, and themes in Chekhov's story, after reading Oates they were able to imagine some alternatives to what are presented in the Chekhov as inevitabilities. Contrasting the two stories also made all the students—male and female—much more conscious of the cultural ideology from which the text's general repertoire derives. The Anna of Oates's story simply has more options because of her historical situation than the Anna of Chekhov's story. Further, our students realized that it is because they are distanced in time from Chekhov's story that they were able to read it "against the grain."

The new reading strategies that we encourage you to learn should not supersede your older ones or be applied just to contemporary fiction. Our goal is to increase your repertoire of reading strategies so that you can have more interpretive options for all kinds of fiction—traditional and nontraditional—and so that you can use these to create strong readings of texts.

Writing Suggestions

1. Read the Chekhov and Oates stories, and compare your responses to them with those discussed in this section.

    (*a*) Which responses (if any) do you agree with and why?

    (*b*) What parts of your own literary and general repertoires influenced your reading?

    (*c*) What reading strategies did you find best suited to reading these two stories?

2. Choose another "traditional" story (for example, by Henry James, Sherwood Anderson, Scott Fitzgerald, Ernest Hemingway) and show how your new reading strategies can help you produce a strong reading of it.

Mixing Traditional and Untraditional
Strategies with a Contemporary Story

Let's now look at an odd kind of contemporary fairy tale. It is Gabriel García Márquez's story "The Incredible and Sad Tale of Innocent Eréndira and Her Heartless Grandmother," which has been widely anthologized and was recently made into a successful movie. We want to apply traditional and untraditional reading strategies to reading such a story. Fairy tales, or stories that work like fairy tales (as we showed in Chapter 4) often allow readers to draw on techniques of naturalization that go back to their childhoods—although sometimes readers feel they should have outgrown them. Garciá Márquez uses a mixture of straightforward plot and unbelievable "tall-tale" details: it relates how Eréndira accidentally burns down her grandmother's house and is made to pay for her misfortune by being made a prostitute, until after twenty years her grandmother is killed and she runs away.

Told like that, the story would appear to most readers to be rather bizarre, not only because of the events that occur in it but also because of the text's mixing of fantastical and realistic details.

> She picked up a feather fan and began to cool the implacable matron, who recited the list of nighttime orders as she sank into sleep.
>
> "Iron all the clothes before you to to bed so you can sleep with a clear conscience."
>
> "Yes, grandmother."
>
> "Check the clothes closets carefully because moths get hungrier on windy nights."
>
> "Yes, grandmother."
>
> "With the time you have left, take the flowers into the courtyard so they get a breath of air."
>
> "Yes, grandmother."
>
> "And feed the ostrich."
>
> The grandmother had fallen asleep but she was still giving orders, for it was from her that the granddaughter had inherited the ability to be alive while sleeping. Eréndira left the room without making any noise and did the final chores in the night, still replying to the sleeping grandmother's orders.
>
> "Give the graves some water."
>
> "Yes, grandmother."
>
> "And if the Amadíses arrive, tell them not to come in," the grandmother said, "because Porfirio Galán's gang is waiting to kill them."

Whether readers like or dislike this story and the ways in which they make sense of it will depend on their ability to mix traditional and untraditional reading strategies. In writing about the story, our students were asked to examine their reading strategies by focusing on the expectations they brought to it from their literary repertoires.

Questions to ask yourself in confronting such a story are these:

1. What *kind* of story is it?
2. Are its text strategies and conventions familiar?
3. After reading a page or two, what kinds of expectations do you have about how the story will develop and end?
4. Are these expectations confirmed or not?
5. What kinds of reading strategies do you find most useful in reading this story?

Surprisingly, a few of our students have read the García Márquez story as a terrifying tale about moral corruption. One of this group of students wrote:

> I felt increasingly indignant as I read about poor Eréndira's plight. This story may look like a fairy tale to some readers, but if it is, where's the happy ending? I think the story is serious. Such things used to happen and perhaps still do in those parts of the world like Central America where the law is not upheld. I felt like whipping the grandmother for her cruelty and was relieved when at last someone was able to rescue the poor girl from her terrible misery.

This student even suggested that the story was far too sordid to read, and that it was disgusting that she had been forced to study it in class! Her assumptions about *genre* (that is, about what kind of story it is—whether it is a fantasy or a realistic story) and *tone* (that is, whether it is serious, comic, or ironic) formed the basis of her reading. Some of the details of tone and setting pulled the story towards realism, and she chose to focus on them and so tried to read the story as realistic rather than fantastical. But despite her attempt at realistic reading, it is her contradictory recognition that the story looks like a fairy tale, coupled with her assumption that fairy tales should be sweet, asexual, and end happily, that made her enraged at what she found sordid. This student was angry largely because she could not classify the story into a well-established genre to which she could apply a given set of reading strategies, and she was unable to accept that she could *mix* strategies. She therefore chose to condemn the story as immoral.

A second group of students responded to the story not as morally reprehensible, but rather as allegorical or heavily symbolic. They worked to naturalize it by assuming that if any text doesn't seem to make sense literally, it might do so symbolically or metaphorically. For instance, one student wrote:

> Eréndira struggles for twenty years against the control of her grandmother. She is young, beautiful and trapped: she represents youth asserting itself. The grandmother represents age and experience. In order for youth to become truly free at the end, the grandmother must die.

This student, unlike the previous one, did not categorize "Eréndira" as a fairy tale at all, and hence did not have the genre expectations that caused her classmate to be outraged by it. By treating the story as an *allegory*, the second student found a way to read it comfortably and traditionally.

A third group of students, however, were willing to mix various kinds of reading strategies, and they probably enjoyed the story best. They read it as a "black humor" fairy story and found it hilarious, responding to the unbelievable accounts of Eréndira's life, as in this excerpt, with increasing jocularity.

> "Go right in, handsome," she told him good-naturedly, "but don't take too long. Your country needs you."
>
> The soldier went in but came right out again because Eréndira wanted to talk to her grandmother, who hung the basket of money on her arm and went into the tent. In the back, on an army cot, Eréndira was unable to repress the trembling in her body. She was in sorry shape, all dirty with soldier sweat.
>
> "Grandmother," she sobbed, "I'm dying."
>
> The grandmother felt her forehead and when she saw Eréndira had no fever, she tried to console her.
>
> "There are only ten soldiers left," she said.
>
> Eréndira began to weep with the shrieks of a frightened animal. Stroking her head, the grandmother murmured: "The trouble is you're weak. Come on, don't cry anymore. Take a bath in sage water to get your blood back in shape."
>
> She left the tent when Eréndira was calmer and she gave the soldier waiting his money back. "That's all for today," she told him. "Come back tomorrow and I'll give you the first place in line." Then she shouted to those lined up: "That's all, boys. Tomorrow morning at nine."
>
> Soldiers and civilians broke ranks with shouts of protest. The grandmother confronted them, brandishing the devastating crosier in earnest. "You're an inconsiderate bunch of slobs!" she shouted. "What do you think the girl is made of, iron? I'd like to see you in her place."

Although many of these students had never read a story like this before, they were willing to combine some strategies for reading fairy tales, particularly regarding character and plot (looking for the evil stepmother, waiting for the "happily ever after" ending), with some strategies for reading realistic stories, particularly searching for a theme (trying to make all the symbols in this story "mean" something). These readers found that the interaction of these two traditional, but not generally combined, strategies produced a comic effect because the story resisted conforming completely to their expectations for either type. The grandmother, the surrogate stepmother, is too evil; the "happy" ending, though a relief for Eréndera, lacks the sense of closure and well-being of traditional fairy tales, particularly because it is brought on by an unpleasant rather than pleasant event.

But if the story's events, as these readers contend, were too "realistic and grim" to fit their fairy tale expectations, so were they too fantastical to fit realistic reading strategies. They found that they could not relate symbolically Eréndera's becoming a prostitute to other events in the story, as did some other students, who were able to work toward a naturalistic point or theme. Once they recognized that traditional assumptions and strategies, even when mixed together, did not help them read the story coherently, this third group of students then adopted additional untraditional strategies and expectations. They felt that they could not satisfactorily read this story as having a focused plot, clearly defined "lifelike" characters, or a recognizably "realistic" theme. Once they had decided that "Eréndera" was an unconventional kind of fairy story, they didn't expect depth or consistency of character, motivation, or plausibility. They reveled in the disjunctive combination of absurdity and realistic detail, recognizing how the story's repertoire had challenged and expanded their own. One student wrote:

> This text is defying me to be shocked or get annoyed. But I won't. I'm one step ahead of it now—anticipating all sorts of strange events. I discovered that by the end, I had anticipated even more absurd things than actually happened. The story really sparked my imagination. I was a very active reader—and I think this is the best way to read the story.

All three groups of students were trying to call upon appropriate parts of their repertoires in order to make sense of the story. Because of their more flexible reading strategies, the third group was able to access more of their repertoires than the other two. They seemed to have the most fun with the story because they were able to mix and match reading strategies and enjoyed watching these strategies clash.

This assignment illustrates the means by which different readers naturalize their reading experiences. As you read more and become increasingly aware of the assumptions you bring to the texts you read, you will find your repertoires will expand significantly. As you read, you will focus on clues provided by the text, match them with different sets of expectations, and be able to construct more enjoyable and thought-provoking readings.

Writing Suggestions

1. Read "Eréndera" (*Innocent Eréndera and Other Stories,* Harper & Row, 1978) and discuss which of the comments by our students you agree with and why.
2. Choose another story or novel and outline different possible **strong readings** you might make of it, focusing on your mixing of traditional and untraditional reading strategies.

The Interconnection of Your Literary and General Repertoires

Although we have focused most of this chapter thus far on developing your literary repertoire, that is, on matching your reading strategies with text strategies, we have implied that your literary repertoire is interconnected with your general repertoire. Recognizing, for example, that characters are decentered has implications well beyond your reading of fiction. This recognition can drastically change the way you view yourself and your world. Assuming that fiction always has a point and that fiction is like life suggests that life is always directed and purposeful. We are arguing not only that all fiction is not unified, but also that all life is not unified. Thus while we are asking you to expand your repertoire of reading strategies for fiction, we may also be challenging some basic assumptions you have about the world in general. If you find yourself resistant to change—refusing, say, to read texts for multiple meanings, to consider that a particular character can be read in diverse ways, to see texts that mix genre expectations as humorous rather than annoying—it is probably because your reading strategies are rooted in some serious assumptions in your *general* as well as your literary repertoire, which we want you to begin to examine. We do not so much want to change them as to help you become self-conscious about what those assumptions are, so you can defend them forcefully and use them actively in your readings of texts.

The Interaction of the Reader's and the Text's General Repertoire: A Layering of Historical Periods

Nathaniel Hawthorne's story "The Maypole of Merry Mount" has provided interesting responses for analyzing the ideological dimensions of reading. The story is termed a "philosophical romance" by its author, and it traces in an allegorical tale the transformation of seventeenth-century England's "jollity" into the "gloom" of Puritan New England.

> Bright were the days at Merry Mount, when the Maypole was the banner staff of that gay colony! They who reared it, should their banner be triumphant, were to pour sunshine over New England's rugged hills, and scatter flower seeds throughout the soil. Jollity and gloom were contending for an empire. Midsummer eve had come, bringing deep verdure to the forest, and roses in her lap, of a more vivid hue than the tender buds of Spring. But May, or her mirthful spirit, dwelt all the year round at Merry Mount, sporting with the Summer months, and revelling with Autumn, and basking in the glow of Winter's fireside. Through a world of toil and care she flitted with a dreamlike smile, and came hither to find a home along the lightsome hearts of Merry Mount.
>
> Never had the Maypole been so gayly decked as at sunset on midsummer eve. This venerated emblem was a pine-tree, which had preserved the slender grace of youth, while it equalled the loftiest height of the old wood monarchs. From its top streamed a silken banner, colored like the rainbow. Down nearly to the ground the pole was dressed with birchen boughs, and others of the liveliest green, and some with silvery leaves, fastened by ribbons that fluttered in fantastic knots of twenty different colors, but no sad ones. Garden flowers, and blossoms of the wilderness, laughed gladly forth amid the verdure, so fresh and dewy that they must have grown by magic on that happy pine-tree. Where this green and flowery splendor terminated, the shaft of the Maypole was stained with the seven brilliant hues of the banner at its top. On the lowest green bough hung an abundant wreath of roses, some that had been gathered in the sunniest spots of the forest, and others, of still richer blush, which the colonists had reared from English seed. O, people of the Golden Age, the chief of your husbandry was to raise flowers!

When you read this story late in the twentieth century—as with Hawthorne's romance *The Scarlet Letter*—you are therefore looking back at Hawthorne's nineteenth-century fictional version of the founding of America over two hundred years before. Thus in your reading, there occurs a layering of three historical periods, all of which are subject to interpretation: seventeenth-century America, about which Hawthorne is writing and you are reading; nineteenth-century America, from which he is writing; and twentieth-century America, from which you are reading. We can also add a fourth historical period that is under interpretation—since in Hawthorne's view the Puritans were also "reading" or interpreting their inheritance from an earlier England. Here is an extract.

All the hereditary pastimes of Old England were transplanted hither. The King of Christmas was duly crowned, and the Lord of Misrule bore potent sway. On the Eve of St. John, they felled whole acres of the forest to make bonfires, and danced by the blaze all night, crowned with garlands, and throwing flowers into the flame. At harvest time, though their crop was of the smallest, they made an image with the sheaves of Indian corn, and wreathed it with autumnal garlands, and bore it home triumphantly. But what chiefly characterized the colonists of Merry Mount was their veneration for the Maypole. It has made their true history a poet's tale. Spring decked the hallowed emblem with young blossoms and fresh green boughs; Summer brought roses of the deepest blush, and the perfected foliage of the forest; Autumn enriched it with that red and yellow gorgeousness which converts each wildwood leaf into a painted flower; and Winter silvered it with sleet, and hung it round with icicles, till it flashed in the cold sunshine, itself a frozen sunbeam. Thus each alternate season did homage to the Maypole, and paid it a tribute of its own richest splendor. Its votaries danced round it, once, at least, in every month; sometimes they called it their religion, or their altar; but always, it was the banner staff of Merry Mount.

Unfortunately, there were men in the new world of a sterner faith than those Maypole worshippers. Not far from Merry Mount was a settlement of Puritans, most dismal wretches, who said their prayers before daylight, and then wrought in the forest or the cornfield till evening made it prayer time again. Their weapons were always at hand to shoot down the straggling savage. When they met in conclave, it was never to keep up the old English mirth, but to hear sermons three hours long, or to proclaim bounties on the heads of wolves and the scalps of Indians. Their festivals were fast days, and their chief pastime the singing of psalms. Woe to the youth or maiden who did but dream of a dance! The selectman nodded to the constable; and there sat the light-heeled reprobate in the stocks; or if he danced, it was round the whipping-post, which might be termed the Puritan Maypole.

Our students were given response statement assignments that directed them not only to the ideological tensions raised by the juxtaposition of various periods in the story but also to their own twentieth-century assumptions about the issues raised in those earlier periods. First, they were asked to analyze Hawthorne's assumptions about the Puritan founders of America. Second, they were directed to investigate the contradictions between the way Hawthorne *presents* the Puritans, the way they saw themselves, and the way contemporary historians see them. This assignment led students into some historical research, and as one student wrote:

I am puzzled by the rosy view Hawthorne has of the old English. "O, people of the Golden Age," he writes, "the chief of your husbandry was to raise flowers!" But it is clear that the early Americans left Britain out of fear of religious persecution, not just because "the Old World and its inhabitants became mutually weary of each other." Why is the author spinning out this myth of the Golden Age? Was there something in the *nineteenth* century that he was reacting against?

Such a response senses that speaking *through* the surface of the story is a set of beliefs and attitudes that aren't explicitly present *in* it. When Hawthorne contrasts the Puritan "whipping-post" with the Old World's "Maypole," he is not being historically accurate (or, for that matter, inaccurate): he is creating a "myth," a story by which he reveals his own values, even though the story is not on the surface "about" these values.

Next, our students were directed to investigate their *own* responses to the issues raised both explicitly and implicitly by the story. This part of the reading process is designed to show how all readers bring not only their literary but their general repertoires into the reading situation. Students are encouraged to take up distinctive contemporary viewpoints and pose their own questions to the text. Most of our students had firm ideas on many of the ideologically charged issues they perceived Hawthorne's story to be raising—what qualities make up a good society, the question of a proper balance between hedonism and duty, the value of the work ethic. Some readers even saw Hawthorne's contrast between America and Europe as relevant today.

Students writing on their ideological dialogue with "The Maypole of Merry Mount" were sharply divided. Some students saw Hawthorne's story as a prophetic insight into something they were also worried about in contemporary America. Such readers were responding to the story in ways Hawthorne would have wanted—except they were making associations with their own historical situation. Thus a student wrote:

Hawthorne's story makes us realize how destructive a narrow, moralistic legalism can be. In the seventeenth century, it was the narrowness of the Puritans. In Hawthorne's time it was the ruthless robber barons of the new industry. Perhaps today's equivalent is the military-industrial establishment, the Pentagon, and those who wish to turn our society more and more toward the political right.

Another student commented on what he perceived as the mixture of "fun" and "work" in contemporary America:

What Hawthorne perceived is still with us today. Think of the "myths" by which we live in contemporary America. There is the laid-back, cool California style, and the ambition of the business executive. Each is reflected in lifestyle, dress, morality. Hawthorne's sympathy seems to be with the anti-Puritan forces but I wonder if he would have approved of what they have become today.

Then there were students who found both Puritanism and Hawthorne's nineteenth-century moralizing rather tedious—"out of touch with the forward-looking nature of America," as one reader put it. Such a remark is equally revealing: no less than the previous reader, this reader is bringing ideological assumptions to bear on his reading.

Such opinions are not "right" or "wrong" in any absolute sense: you may agree or disagree. They result from the writers' considerations of their own political ideas alongside those they find suggested by the text.

The way you, as a late twentieth-century reader, respond to any work of fiction will be influenced by such concerns as your moral views, religious ideas, gender, and (as in this case) your sense of the "American dream." As you work on your response in relation to a text, try to ask not only what your ideas, feelings, and social practices are—but also where they came from. You will inevitably find that, though such ideas may have come to you from your other reading experiences, most have been formed by larger cultural forces. They are not just "subjective" or "personal": they are culturally produced, part of the general ideology of your society. Studying the ways you respond to texts challenges you to become critical of the ideology from which your assumptions and social practices are derived. This critical attitude, in turn, influences that ideology.

Writing Suggestions

1. Read "Young Goodman Brown" (or any Hawthorne story dealing with early New England) and discuss which of our students' comments you agree or disagree with, and why.
2. Write an analysis of any story or novel that has a historical setting and show how:

   (a) You can read it for its ideological absences (see Chapter 2, pages 47–48).

   (b) Your own general repertoire helps create your reading.

Gender-based Differences in Reading Fiction

The influence of your beliefs and assumptions on your reading becomes particularly acute when you read fiction that addresses controversial issues in your society or issues that affect you at crucial points in your life. Lynne Barrett's story "Inventory"[1] deals with the question of sexuality, specifically the interactions between a teenage girl working in a department store and her manager.

---

[1] Text may be found in Gary Waller, Kathleen McCormick, Lois Fowler, *Lexington Introduction to Literature* (Lexington, Mass.: Heath, 1987).

The girl is subject to what she feels to be sexual harassment by the manager who is promoting her. She takes a fairly cynical view of his clumsy attempts to touch her, knowing that she is not planning to stay long in the job but instead go off to college. But then she starts to wonder about her own feelings for a boy slightly younger than she is who works with her. The story ends with her running her hands over his body. It is a perceptive study of the contradictory demands made on young people by a complex society—of the pressures everyone has to deal with in peer groups and in the workplace.

When asked to give an account of the girl's behavior, many of the male readers in our class described her as a "slut," a "tramp." These readers were perhaps affronted by her frankness about sexual matters and in particular by the casual ways she thinks and talks about men. One student wrote:

> I feel repulsed by a girl who thinks so crudely about such explicitly physical things.
> She would not be the type I would go out with and seems to deserve all she gets.

Such views were common among the male students; the women in the class, however, were more divided. Some felt sympathetic to the girl, seeing her as a victim rather than as an exploiter. Others thought the girl tough, assertive, and realistic; others agreed with the male readers—she was not a particularly "nice" girl, as one of them put it.

Clearly, gender expectation, beliefs about appropriate sexual behavior, and upbringing all play a crucial part in determining these different readings. To be shocked at the frankness of the girl's thoughts may strike some of you as rather old-fashioned—although it is interesting that one woman student asserted that it was only men (or, as she said, "boys") who would be shocked:

> The story was very convincing on the matter of the girl's thoughts about herself
> and her sexual feelings. Boys often think girls should be pure and not think about
> such things. But we do, and like everyone else we are trying to find the best
> language to express ourselves. Only someone with unrealistic notions about girls
> would think of her as a "slut."

Obviously, in this disagreement, quite different repertoires were being brought to bear on the text. From one perspective, some argued that girls should be "good," that is, shy, gentle, demure, particularly about sex. From another perspective, others argued that girls should not be required to be "good," and that in fact they aren't. Such myths about women, these students held, are perpetuated by men who seek to dominate them professionally, socially, and sexually. One group of readers, therefore, was offended by the story; the second group found it honest and uplifting. The text was the "same"; the readers' gender and cultural assumptions were not.

Although gender has always been an important influence on the way people read, it has only become an accepted mode of study since the women's movement and feminist thinking have become such powerful forces in our society. In exploring gender-based differences in reading, you are thus doing two important things. First, you are recognizing the different ways in which our society creates its men and women as **subjects.** But, second, you are demonstrating that you are part of a period of history in which it is now *acceptable* for you to base arguments on gender-specific grounds. During a very heated argument on Milan Kundera's novel *The Unbearable Lightness of Being,* regarding whether women are trained to be more "passive-aggressive" than men, one of the women in the class stopped the debate to exclaim: "Look at us. Twenty years ago, we couldn't have had this debate. I'm sure the issues would have been just as relevant, but they would have been a taboo topic. I think it's great the way we can argue openly about such important issues."

As we have suggested throughout this book, you can construct powerful and effective readings of fiction by deliberately posing questions related to gender. What is it like to read Virginia Woolf's *A Room of One's Own* or Erica Jong's *Fear of Flying* as a woman as opposed to reading them as a man? Or many of the novels of Norman Mailer or John Updike? Or, further back, the novels of Samuel Richardson (whose long novel *Clarissa* is about the plight of a woman pursued and then seduced by a man), Jane Austen, or Herman Melville? Becoming conscious of your own gender-specific interests, questions, and assumptions is particularly important in today's cultural climate as we all become more aware of the importance of feminism and gender-related issues.

Increasingly, people have begun to recognize that women readers may well ask significantly different questions from those men ask about the texts they read. Because our cultural and literary history has been so dominated by men's values and language, people today are having to rethink very deeply which issues and interests are specific to each gender, and which are shared. These values may, of course, change from time to time through history and from text to text.

As you read in this context, you should try to concentrate on three matters:

1. Examine which aspects of your own and others' readings of texts are affected by gender.
2. Examine what kinds of questions or assumptions seem typical of men and of women. Are these the same at different periods of history? In different cultures?
3. Consider what differences these discoveries make to your own beliefs and actions. In short, what implications do they have for your lives as individuals and as members of your society?

Enjoying Fiction More— and Differently

Reading fiction is one of the distinctive activities of a literate culture. Many people read poetry, go to plays, or watch television, but there is still a widespread belief that a "good book" is one of the pleasures of life. How many of you have a novel partly read beside your bed? How many take a novel on the bus, to a doctor's waiting room, on a long plane flight? Reading fiction still seems like a natural activity.

To study the *reading* of fiction—the matching of repertoires (literary and general), the strategies readers use, the ideological strands of the text—is not thereby to reduce that pleasure. By becoming more conscious of what goes on in reading, you can expand your repertoires, develop your reading strategies, and so become increasingly open to more and more varied experiences of reading fiction.

Checkpoints for Chapter 6

1. Reading fiction seems a "natural" activity for most modern readers.
2. Conventional reading strategies involve your accepting plot, point of view, character, and theme as natural, transparent, and unproblematic.
3. Much contemporary fiction produces more interesting reading experiences if it is read with more unconventional strategies.
4. You can enjoy mixing conventional and unconventional reading strategies with both traditional and nontraditional fiction.
5. As with other texts, strong readings of fiction can be built on a self-conscious awareness of how your general and literary repertoires intersect with or differ from the text's.

ᛟᚹ Chapter 7
Reading Drama

The Distinctiveness of Drama:
The Text as Performance

In what ways is reading a play different from reading a poem or a story? We're sure you can imagine many ways in which it is similar, for there are many aspects of reading that are common among all forms of writing. Every text has a repertoire, general and literary, as does every reader. And when you read any kind of text, you look for the ways in which your repertoire and the text's intersect. But, as we've been emphasizing, certain reading strategies seem to be better suited for particular forms because the use of them significantly enhances your reading experience. With drama, it seems crucial that you *visualize* the play's action—what the characters look like, how they will act in relation to one another, what kind of space they will move around in, how the audience might react. Whether or not you have a chance to see a stage performance of the plays you are studying, almost all plays are written to be performed and you should try to stage them yourself in your own imagination.

We have suggested all along that in a real sense you produce your own particular version of *any* text you read. What distinguishes drama is that this strategy is made explicit: a play presents you with a script, generally with much dialogue but little description, which a director, actors, and the audience (you) must fill out. Part of the enjoyment of reading drama is that it calls upon you to read as "dramatically" as possible, to bring to life—in visual as well as conceptual form—the characters and events about which you are reading.

Visualizing a Scene

Look at the following passage from Act I of Oscar Wilde's much-acclaimed, witty play, *The Importance of Being Earnest,* and try to imagine how this scene could be performed. Two friends, Algernon and Jack, are discussing Gwendolen, Algernon's cousin:

ALGERNON   My dear fellow, the way you flirt with Gwendolen is perfectly disgraceful. It is almost as bad as the way Gwendolen flirts with you.

JACK   I am in love with Gwendolen. I have come up to town expressly to propose to her.

ALGERNON   I thought you had come up for pleasure? . . . I call that business.

JACK   How utterly unromantic you are!

ALGERNON   I really don't see anything romantic in proposing. It is very romantic to be in love. But there is nothing romantic about a definite proposal. Why, one may be accepted. One usually is, I believe. Then the excitement is all over. The very essence of romance is uncertainty. If ever I get married, I'll certainly try to forget the fact.

JACK   I have no doubt about that, dear Algy. The Divorce Court was specially invented for people whose memories are so curiously constituted.

ALGERNON   Oh! there is no use speculating on that subject. Divorces are made in Heaven—(JACK *puts out his hand to take a sandwich.* ALGERNON *at once interferes.*) Please don't touch the cucumber sandwiches. They are ordered specially for Aunt Augusta. (*Takes one and eats it.*)

JACK   Well, you have been eating them all the time.

ALGERNON   That is quite a different matter. She is my aunt. (*Takes plate from below.*) Have some bread and butter. The bread and butter is for Gwendolen. Gwendolen is devoted to bread and butter.

JACK (*advancing to table and helping himself*)   And very good bread and butter it is too.

ALGERNON   Well, my dear fellow, you need not eat as if you were going to eat it all. You behave as if you were married to her already. You are not married to her already, and I don't think you ever will be.

JACK   Why on earth do you say that?

ALGERNON   Well, in the first place, girls never marry the men they flirt with. Girls don't think it right.

JACK   Oh, that is nonsense!

ALGERNON   It isn't. It is a great truth. It accounts for the extraordinary number of bachelors that one sees all over the place.

What do you think Algernon and Jack look like? How do you distinguish one from the other? Are they handsome? Pale? Tanned? Tall or short? Plump or thin? Do they cross their legs when they sit down? Do either or both of them gesticulate a lot with their hands? Is either of them smoking? If so, how do they light their cigarettes? With matches? A flick of a Bic? With a solid gold lighter?

What do you think their voices sound like? Are they deep? Soft? High-pitched? How would you have them dressed? In tight designer jeans, Frye boots, a long-sleeved shirt with the cuffs rolled up, and a few gold chains? In polyester leisure suits? In tuxedos? In velvet vests with breeches? In bright oversized jackets, tee shirts, and baggy pants? Miami Vice style?

In what tone would you have them speak? Is either one or both of them serious? Which of their lines would you play for laughs?

What does the room in which they are talking look like? Are the chairs leather? Brocade? Are there crystal chandeliers? Are there tapestries, oil paintings, silver-framed prints or modern art, posters of Bogart, Rambo, or the Grateful Dead on the walls?

And what about the plate that those cucumber sandwiches are on? Is it Wedgwood? Silver? Corelle? And what do you imagine Gwendolen looks like—Gwendolen who is "devoted to bread and butter"?

What kind of stage are these actors performing on? How big is the theater? And on and on—and all this before we even begin to address what Jack and Algernon's dialogue might mean, with its strange inversion of moral and social values, its particular literary and general repertoires, and the ways they might intersect with yours. With drama, more fully than with any other genre, you participate actively in the reading since you have a greater range of variables to interpret. You must decide not only what characters' moral views are like, but also what they *look* like and how they will interact on stage.

Writing Suggestions

1. Describe how *you* visualize the scene from *The Importance of Being Earnest*.
2. Choose a short scene from a play of your choice. Explain how you visualize it and how you would stage it.

A Play Is Not a Novel

If you choose to read a play like a novel, focusing only on such matters as plot, character, or particular themes, you are missing out on an opportunity—that only drama offers you—to visualize the text as a spectacle, being performed on stage with a live audience. Paradoxically, *reading* a play, as opposed to seeing it, presents you with a unique opportunity: you get to be both actors and audience.

When you first read a play, you will most likely get caught up in its plot. On your first reading of Ibsen's *Hedda Gabler,* for example, you may not want to think about what Hedda is wearing when she first appears on stage. You are told in the stage directions only that she is wearing "an elegant, somewhat loose fitting morning gown." But as you reread the play and develop your reading in more detail, the question of her dress may become crucial. She is pregnant, but her husband, Tesman, doesn't notice, thinking only that she has "filled out." You can suggest by the way you dress her whether your audience thinks that Tesman is oblivious to Hedda or that Hedda is being secretive. Is her "morning gown" obviously a maternity dress? You get to decide.

Thinking about how you would stage a play gives you an interpretive freedom that can be great fun, particularly if your teacher asks you to act out various scenes from plays in your class. But this interpretive freedom can also be intimidating if you feel that you know very little about the conventions of drama.

Perhaps you have only occasionally been to the theater, or what theater you've seen hasn't impressed you. While theater-going is a common leisure activity, it is probably only in large cities that professionally acted plays can be found.

Drama Is Found in Everyday Life

You may, however, intuitively know more about drama than you think. The concept of "drama" is something everyone encounters in everyday life. Not all people write poems or novels or stories—even though they may sometimes interpret their lives according to narrative models or even describe someone they admire very much as "a poem"—poetry in motion, perhaps! But everyone acts. Most of us play parts in our lives, take on roles, and project different selves to the world—and then something like what happens in a theater is occurring. We are implicitly (and sometimes explicitly!) looking for an audience to respond to the "impression" that we are creating. And as the audience to another person's role-playing in this sense, you judge the performance according to its effects on you. When the "actor" seems to have no real commitment to the "sincerity" of his or her own role, you term such a person cynical or insincere. People tend to praise the "authentic" actor, whether in the theater or outside.

Perhaps the classic comparison of life to the stage is the cynical view (of both life and stage) voiced by Jaques in Shakespeare's *As You Like It:*

All the world's a stage,
And all the men and women merely players;
They have their exits and their entrances,
And one man in his time plays many parts,
His acts being seven ages. At first the infant,
Mewling and puking in the nurse's arms.
And then the whining schoolboy, with his satchel
And shining morning face, creeping like snail
Unwillingly to school. And then the lover,
Sighing like furnace, with a woeful ballad
Made to his mistress' eyebrow. Then a soldier,
Full of strange oaths, and bearded like the pard,
Jealous in honor, sudden and quick in quarrel,
Seeking the bubble reputation
Even in the cannon's mouth. And then the justice,
In fair round belly with good capon lin'd,
With eyes severe and beard of formal cut,
Full of wise saws and modern instances;
And so he plays his part. The sixth age shifts
Into the lean and slipper'd pantaloon,
With spectacles on nose, and pouch on side,
His youthful hose well saved, a world too wide
For his shrunk shank, and his big manly voice,
Turning again toward childish treble, pipes
And whistles in his sound. Last scene of all,

That ends this strange eventful history,
Is second childishness, and mere oblivion,
Sans teeth, sans eyes, sans taste, sans everything.

Here the different stages of human life are (rather cynically, as if the whole of life is at best a farce) likened to a stage presentation. But the comparison is a common and crucial one. In any human activity—in class, at a football game, at a dinner party—you find yourself inserted into roles, parts, dialogue, improvisation, scripts, all of which are likewise aspects of the stage. "All the world's a stage."

In what follows, we will present you with information about different acting spaces, various productions of different plays, how audience involvement has changed with different theatrical conventions over the last few centuries, as well as some examples of student responses to particular plays. All of this is designed to help you enlarge your repertoire of dramatic conventions and of possibilities for reading plays. In this way, you will be able to create, in greater detail and with more confidence, your own imaginative productions of the plays you read and to critique and enjoy more fully the productions of plays you see.

Acting Spaces and Audiences

Places in which poets and fiction writers read aloud from their work are generally spaces that are used primarily for other purposes—lecture halls, classrooms, coffee houses, or bars and restaurants in which tables and chairs are moved to give the speaker some (often not very much) room. Plays, however, are usually performed in a special "acting space," usually a theater.

Today when you go to plays, you can find yourselves visiting a huge variety of theaters. Some will be large auditoriums with variously shaped stages; others will be small and intimate theaters that are acoustically perfect and in which there are no "bad seats"; some perhaps are converted buildings, originally intended for other purposes, like churches; some will be outdoors in which the audience sits in bleachers under a large tent. There may be bright or subtle lighting; actors may wear period costumes or street clothes.

You may feel going to the theater is a special occasion and dress up for it, thus contributing to the spectacle of the event. You may go out to dinner before or after the performance, or picnic, or perhaps take a short vacation in order to go to a famous theater festival, such as those in Ashland, Oregon, or Stratford, Ontario. Some areas of our large cities are especially known for theater—Broadway in New York, the West End in London. New and impressive theaters, like new concert halls or football stadiums, are often seen as signs that a city is a highly livable place.

We dwell on these perhaps obvious details for an important reason. Theater spaces, like everything else, whether they are small and informal, large and elaborate, Broadway or basement, grow not just from an architect's or theater-owner's whim: they arise from wider social tastes and beliefs—they articulate the ideologies of our society. They all have in common what the British director Peter Brook calls an "open space," a place marked out for interaction between actors and audience. But the kinds of actors, audiences, and plays performed differ significantly. "Experimental theater," for example, is most frequently performed in small, informal theaters. This is in part because avant-garde theater, by its very nature, is on the margins of society. People who prefer a Broadway musical like *Funny Girl* or *Cats* would not always pay to see a more avant-garde play like Edward Bond's *Restoration*. But further, the very experimental nature of a play like *Restoration* would be undermined if it were staged in a huge Broadway theater. Thus, as you investigate different kinds of theater spaces, bear in mind that they embody various cultural values.

Acquainting yourself with different types of theaters in use today can help you greatly in trying to visualize a setting for a play you are reading. Studying the kinds of acting spaces that existed in earlier historical periods can also enlarge your repertoire. It enables you to imagine diverse ways to stage a play and thereby to reinforce or disrupt the traditional ways in which the play has been produced.

Writing Suggestions

1. (*a*) Describe the kinds of stages and other acting spaces that you have in your own area.
   (*b*) What different staging possibilities do they offer?
   (*c*) Describe how you might visualize a scene from any play you have read on one of these stages.
2. If you could design an ideal acting space, what features would it have?

Acting Spaces and Styles Through History

If you look back at the great periods of drama through history, you can discover ways in which each has developed distinctive styles of stages or theaters as well as distinctive styles of acting. The first great period of drama in the West was in ancient Greece. Sophocles' *Antigone,* for instance, was originally performed as part of a religious festival before an audience of nearly twenty thousand people. They sat on raised wooden seats around a circular *orchestra*, the dancing-place, which would have been about sixty feet across with an altar in the center. Behind was a wooden building, the *skene,* in front of which was a broad step, the *logeion,* where the actors stood. Such an acting space encouraged a view of drama as a community, even a religious, ritual. Unlike today, therefore, live theater was a much greater part of people's communal existence.

If you move forward almost two thousand years, you see how plays in the European Middle Ages, such as *Everyman* or *The Second Shepherd's Play,* both written in the late fifteenth century, were also originally performed as part of a festival by guilds of workmen, who each put on their own play or pageant. But the acting space and style were quite different from ancient Greece: the plays were performed on a movable stage mounted on carts, or sometimes in an open playing space with a rough scaffold erected behind. Sometimes they were performed on the steps of churches or even at the time of a special religious festival like the Feast of Corpus Christi. The informality of the acting spaces reflects the distinctive nature of theater in such a society. From the perspective of the commercialized modern theater, medieval plays seem marginal and informal. But the plays and actors of that period were closely tied to the dominant religious beliefs of the age: the popular theater was one of the institutions by which ordinary people were taught the mysteries of religion as well as entertained.

In contrast, a century or more later, the plays of Shakespeare's time were becoming distinctively more secular. Plays were increasingly performed in buildings—at first roofless and with dirt floors, but usually built specifically to present plays. By this time, plays had become part of the common commercial entertainment of most European cities. But the presentation of drama retained much of the medieval closeness between actors and audience. The theaters used "thrust" stages, projecting into the audience and surrounding the action on three sides—with some members of the audience actually on the stage itself. The stage normally had more than one level and thus could handle such devices as balcony scenes (as in Shakespeare's *Romeo and Juliet*), trap doors, flying machinery, and artificial lighting. Then gradually, beginning early in the seventeenth century, an increasing number of indoor theaters were built, thus allowing playwrights and actors to use more elaborate lighting, costumes, and stage effects.

From the late nineteenth century onwards, theaters started to develop something of the realism that viewers today associate especially with the television screen—conveying the sense that they are peering into a house or into a room and watching people act and talk. In most nineteenth-century plays in this tradition, an audience would see scenery painted to represent perhaps a recognizably ordinary setting of a room, with furniture, wallpaper, pictures, and lamps. All of these details would help create an atmosphere of realism, which would be underlined by the everyday, recognizable dress and speech of the characters. The lighting likewise was designed to stress that the audience was in the presence of people from their own time and place, creating the illusion that they were not in a theater at all—that by virtue of an invisible fourth wall between them and the stage, they were watching real people live their lives.

In the twentieth century, theatrical spaces and staging techniques have become much more diverse. There has been a widespread return to the bare stage, without many props or scenery. But much more elaborate kinds of staging are found, especially for musicals or in Broadway-style productions. Some performances will be very spectacular; others will have no lighting or other special effects whatsoever. Some will have "authentic" or anachronistic costumes and sets; others will have surrealistic settings—anything seems possible. Famous productions like Peter Brook's Royal Shakespeare Company (RSC) production of *A Midsummer Night's Dream*, with the fairies on trapezes, or the same company's eight-hour-long production of Dickens's *Nicholas Nickleby*, with its scheduled dinner breaks, show how varied and flexible theatrical experience has become. Theater, it seems today, can do anything and take place anywhere—whenever an audience gathers.

But keep in mind that particular acting spaces constrain performance. You, again, probably know this intuitively from your own life experiences. Special spaces in your lives seem to create their own kinds of theater. Restaurants, for instance. If you watch the interaction of a waiter and some diners, there is always the germ of a theatrical performance going on. The waiter's movement, his entrance, may be dignified or casual, with well-rehearsed and suave control of voice, movement, gesture. Or he may approach his patrons a little too obsequiously, a little too eager for their orders. As a patron, you may join in the play: you may play the wine expert, or the fussy eater, or the blasé sophisticate; you may be eager to impress the waiter, or your companion, or other diners. In a restaurant, too, you may be specially costumed, often more casually than the waiter, as if to stress that you can play at being more free, more in control of the whole act. The behavior on both sides is a kind of game—and all the ingredients of the theater are there—largely because the space of a restaurant makes it seem a place conducive to acting.

Writing Suggestions

1. Investigate the acting space available in a famous theater, for example, Shakespeare's Globe, one of Broadway's theaters, or Radio City Music Hall.
2. How do the venues where rock groups perform concerts affect the relationship between performers and audiences?

Cultural Influences on Theatrical Productions

The unpredictable and changing interaction of actors and audiences is a crucial consideration for your reading of a play. If you study a play's stage history, you will discover both how fluid an entity a play is and also how each age produces plays in terms of its own interests and assumptions—ultimately in terms of its ideological presuppositions.

Shakespeare's Plays in Performance

Shakespeare's plays are perhaps the best example for you to consider, since they are supposedly classics, and one thing we often assume about a classic is that it does not change. Shakespeare's plays are a cultural institution, almost a guarantee of the coherence of Western civilization. Not only in his birthplace, Stratford-on-Avon, but all over the world, there are Shakespeare memorials and festivals. There are magazines dedicated to his life and works; in most cities and towns all across the English-speaking world and beyond, there will be a production of at least one of his plays every year. Shakespeare is still the most widely studied author in our universities—frequently (we are afraid) to his plays' and his readers' detriment, but sometimes with wonderful results, as students learn different ways to explain the fascination of his plays. His works have been mystified into a timeless symbol of all that is best (and worst) about "great literature."

In this chapter, therefore, we will use a large number of examples from Shakespeare's plays. But, most emphatically, we do not want to suggest that they are timeless monuments, somehow immune to criticism. In fact there is, in one sense, no such thing as a Shakespeare play—at least there is no original meaning or single authentic way of presenting them. Like any other texts, they are sites where different readings and productions struggle for dominance. They are one of the most important places in literature where successive generations' understanding of themselves has been worked out. If Shakespeare's plays are "classics," therefore, that does not at all mean they are unchanging. They are classics because they *do* change.

We emphasize this point because of the ways traditional Shakespeare criticism and teaching have often tried to read his plays as embodying eternal truths, coherent and self-consistent meanings, to make readers respectful of his great genius, and above all to search for some "original" or "authentic" reading. We believe that a great disservice is done to Shakespeare if someone asserts there is an "authentic" or "original" meaning for his plays. Even in Shakespeare's own time, his plays were adaptable scripts. They were changed for different performances, cut or added to according to the demands of different theater spaces, audiences, or actors.

The great modern director and playwright Bertold Brecht (whose play *Galileo* we will discuss later on) is perhaps the clearest exponent this century of a **decentered** Shakespeare. He conceived of and directed some of Shakespeare's plays in much the same way as we have suggested you should construct a **strong reading** of any text. Brecht saw *Hamlet,* for instance, as displaying a man caught between two ideologies: an older, feudal ethic of revenge and a newer, as yet (for Hamlet) undefined ethic of negotiation, pragmatism, and compromise. In his production of the play, he read the final act (in which Hamlet returns and kills the king) as a relapse into the barbarity of revenge. To stress the point of his reading, Brecht wrote an additional scene for his actors in which Hamlet arrives in England and discovers that the Danish-Norwegian dispute has been settled by negotiation, and so the unthinking heroism, represented by Fortinbras and all the killing at the end, is shown up as outdated and unnecessary.

Something of the same decenteredness can, in fact, be seen in the history of Shakespearean productions. *Romeo and Juliet,* for instance, has been acted countless times since it was written by Shakespeare in about 1595—and in every style and setting imaginable, from Renaissance Italy to the New York streets. A happy ending was even introduced in the late seventeenth century, sometimes performed in tandem with the "authentic" ending. In the mid-nineteenth century, female Romeos were very fashionable (recall that in Shakespeare's time Juliet would have been played by a boy). An American production in 1877 used seven different Juliets in successive scenes.

Distinctive twentieth-century productions include the 1967 Royal Shakespeare Company production directed by Peter Brook, which used a miniature set of twelve-inch-high walls and buildings around which the characters acted and danced. The production was romantic, a little like a ballet, and the effect was that the "private" world of the lovers dwarfed the "public" world. A much darker version of the play reflecting the twentieth century's more pessimistic, cynical view of love was performed by the same company in 1976. It stressed the doomed quality of their love, with Romeo and Juliet overwhelmed by the power of family and state. The play can be seen as romantic or dark; Romeo can be played as mature or unlucky; Juliet as naive and romantic or as more adult than Romeo; the Friar can be seen as well intentioned but meddling, or as the moral center of the play.

The playscript itself is sufficiently fluid to incorporate all these—and more—interpretations. The test of a production is whether it works in the theater—whether it can provoke, disturb, or intrigue an audience. *Romeo and Juliet* owes its popularity in part to its dealing with a subject about which most people have strong, often confused, frequently nostalgic feelings—young love and its seemingly inevitable end in loss and failure (though, it is to be hoped, not generally death!). Those frequent ingredients of film and television drama, sex and violence, give *Romeo and Juliet* another part of its power—as can be seen in Leonard Bernstein's adaption of the play in the musical *West Side Story*.

Writing Suggestions

1. Choose a Shakespeare play you have read and write a detailed account of one scene in which you visualize how the scene would be presented.
2. Choose a Shakespeare play:
   (*a*) What aspects of its general repertoire strike you as being particularly archaic? How would you deal with that problem in a production?
   (*b*) What aspects of your general repertoire would you emphasize as especially relevant to developing a strong reading of the play?

How Plays Change Through History

But changes in productions are emphatically not merely a matter of taste any more than different kinds of theaters are merely a matter of architectural style. Like every other cultural practice, theater is influenced by the ideological forces that make up that society. This occurs in three main ways:

1. The text of a play—whether a tragedy or comedy, musical or monologue—articulates the ideological preoccupations of the period in which the script was originally written.
2. A production of a play articulates the ideological preoccupations of the period and culture in which it is being performed, even when it tries to be "authentic" or "faithful" to the time in which the play was originally written.
3. Ideological differences and contradictions within a given period give rise to the writing and acting of quite different types of drama.

We will deal with each of these points in turn.

Ideological Contradiction
in **Doctor Faustus**

First, the text articulates the ideology of its time: Marlowe's *Doctor Faustus*, for example, written in the late sixteenth century, takes for granted a world in which, regardless of how much an individual may struggle, there is no chance of escape or even of temporary freedom from a stern and all-powerful God. In the final soliloquy of the play, Faustus is carried off to hell by the devil to whom he has sold his soul, and you can see how—despite his determination and tragic anguish—the age's dominant beliefs make such a condemnation inevitable. He despairs that he has "but one bare hour to live/And then . . . must be damn'd perpetually." He wants time to stop; he even tries to "leap up" to God, but is unable to do so. He is carried off to hell.

When you read his magnificent speech, not only try to visualize how you might stage the scene but also try to imagine how the play would have been received in Marlowe's time—by a society in which Faustus' despair and help-lessness are the consequences of his being pitted against the inevitability of the universe itself. On the one hand, the play does not explicitly encourage you to question the justice of a universe that condemns the qualities that Faustus values—ambition, struggle, risk-taking. Yet, on the other hand, these are qualities that you may admire very much—and you might even believe (as many modern readers do) that the play, contradictorily, also sympathizes with Faustus. This sympathy is conveyed to many readers and spectators in the power and richness of the very poetry of Faustus' final speech. Thus, built into the text strategies of Marlowe's play are the ideological contradictions of his age. In recognizing the tensions between, on the one hand, the "dominant" ideology that condemns Faustus and sees his damnation as just and, on the other, the counter-dominant position that sees his ambition, drive, and self-affirmation as exciting and positive, you are isolating the ideological tensions of the period in which the play was written.

Writing Suggestions

1. Give a reading of *Doctor Faustus* in which you take issue with one or more of the points raised above. Account for the differences by reference to your own general and literary repertoires.
2. Choose another play you have read and in a **symptomatic reading** analyze its ideological contradictions.

Cultural Influences
on the History of Production

Second, the ideology of a culture influences the ways in which plays are *produced* and *read*. A production of *Dr. Faustus* today may stress, much more than an earlier period would have, the unfairness of Faustus' punishment, the accepta-bility of his desire for wealth and power, the religious neurosis of a world that would believe that Faustus could burn eternally in hell for his very human actions.

In earlier chapters, we talked about readers as the products of their cultural presuppositions. A director and an actor are likewise "produced" by their own time, and their interpretations of plays also reflect that time. Styles of productions address themselves to particular groups of people in a given society—usually, of course, the dominant theater-going classes. The production of a play is subject to prevailing market conditions, ideological assumptions, and expectations. A production is successful to a particular audience because its style of presentation seems familiar or acceptable to that audience's general mode of perceiving the world, its culture's general ideology. For example, American musicals like *Oklahoma* or *South Pacific* appeal to a sense of buoyancy, nationalism, and a desire for simple solutions to what in the real world are complex problems, such as the settling of the West or the invasion of the Pacific. To hear cheerful songs about these problems encourages audiences to believe that they could be easily solved—a desire for simple solutions, it is widely observed, has long been a dominant feature of the general ideology of Americans.

But the general ideology changes drastically from one period to another, so while a playwright like Marlowe might have written a play to suit what he perceived to be the demands of his particular audience, a director, many years or centuries later, may produce that play for an audience with a completely different set of demands and expectations.

That productions grow from the ideological conditions of their time can also be demonstrated by tracing the history of the productions of Shakespeare plays by the world's leading Shakespearean company, the Royal Shakespeare Company. The RSC performs primarily at Stratford-on-Avon and London, but it has made many successful tours of the United States with plays and musicals like *Cats* and *Nicholas Nickleby*. During the 1960s, the RSC's plays were deliberately chosen by their leading directors, including Peter Hall and Peter Brook, for what they saw as their political relevance to our time: their productions focused on showing how power operates through the mechanisms of society. But increasingly, RSC productions started to emphasize a very common anxiety of postwar Western society—the seeming helplessness of the individual before inexorable political and cultural events.

Peter Brook's 1962 production of *King Lear* (later turned into a film starring Paul Schofield), for instance, used a set of geometric sheets of rusty metal, worn leather, and glaring bright light to stress the hostility and brutality of the world. Brook omitted a scene in which two servants try to help the Earl of Gloucester against Goneril and Regan because he wanted to convey the lack of any reassurance in the play's political world. Brook's production is what we would call a **strong reading.** In a similar vein, *Henry V* has often been produced as a stirring patriotic epic (as in the film starring Laurence Olivier, made during World War II) rather than as a satire on the interaction of power and violence.

The women's movement has led to many productions of *The Taming of the Shrew* with feminist endings. It has also discouraged the happy-ever-after marriage ending of many of the other comedies. In Jonathan Miller's production of *Measure for Measure*, for example, Isabella refused the Duke's offer of marriage and walked off in the opposite direction, while a recent production in Canada had Isabella try to slap the Duke's face (as she had earlier slapped Angelo's) only to be prevented by the Provost, played as a kind of FBI bodyguard. In short, changes in the meanings of plays are not merely due to fashion or whim. They are ideologically based and grow out of the society in which they are acted.

Writing Suggestions

1. Research the history of performances or interpretations of a Shakespeare play. What ideological influences can you find on the history of production or criticism?
2. Investigate a production of a Shakespeare play in your local community. What ideological as well as theatrical factors do you see operating in the production?

Ideology Is Always Contradictory

Our third point is simple but important. In discussing both the writing of plays and the history of their production, we have stressed how both grew out of their age's dominant ideology. But the ideology of any given culture can influence people in diverse, contradictory ways. Any playwright, director, actor, or theatergoer possesses only a small subset of the society's ideological possibilities. Thus a label like "drama in the Age of Shakespeare" covers various types of plays (tragedies, comedies, histories and others), different audiences (courtly, popular, mixed), and different political, religious, or moral perspectives. Plays reflect the diversity in their age's ideology in different ways. Likewise, audiences that prefer different kinds of plays and productions can exist side by side within the same period.

These contradictions within a society can often produce surprise and confusion. Today those who go to a Shakespeare play expecting an "authentic" period costume production and find a performance featuring strobe lighting, rock music, violence, and contemporary costumes are likely to be disconcerted—and may even walk out. They do so because they have in their repertoire particular expectations of how Shakespeare should be produced that derive from one aspect of their culture's literary ideology: the belief that contemporary productions of well-known traditional plays should try, as much as possible, to be "authentic." This belief comes from an assumption that Shakespeare represents "high culture" and that his plays should not be tampered with. This assumption clashes with another aspect of our culture's literary ideology that seeks to emphasize that every production in some sense tampers with a play. There *is* no "original" Shakespeare at all. And there is therefore no unified, single, agreed-upon way of producing Shakespeare within a particular period. The effects of a culture's ideology are always diverse and contradictory, never monolithic.

Scripts, Actors, Audiences: The Interactive Nature of Performance

Drama differs only in degree from other kinds of literature in its insistence that its audience or its readers play an active role in producing it. In this section we want to focus on some of the various relationships that can develop between performances and audiences. We will look at ways in which the text strategies and reading (or spectator) strategies interact to produce the blurring of distinctions between intellectual and emotional responses, serious and comic effects, that is characteristic of much of the best theater.

Text Strategies and Reader Expectations: Comedy and Tragedy

One of the traditional distinctions among plays is between comedy and tragedy. Although there are certainly differences between the literary repertoires of these two forms of drama, the primary distinction between them is in their effects. With a *comedy*, the audience generally anticipates an experience in which all apparent illogicalities, incongruities, and disturbances will be reconciled. The audience's status as members of a social order is never ultimately threatened: they are made to feel at one with their society and with that of the play. Characters in comedies tend to be stereotypical; situations intrigue or amuse, but usually do not disturb the audience's sense of relaxed enjoyment. Plots tend to be improbable or fortuitous, as if offering their readers and viewers a pleasant fantasy about how they would like the world outside the theater to be. A comic ending is an emotionally reassuring text strategy, often represented by marriage or some other coherent reconstruction of all the pieces that had seemed broken. At the end of Shakespeare's *Twelfth Night,* for instance, the audience is caught up in a general mood of reconciliation:

> When that is known, and golden time convents,
> A solemn combination shall be made
> Of our dear souls. Mean time, sweet sister,
> We will not part from hence. Cesario, come—
> For so you shall be while you are a man;
> But when in other habits you are seen,
> Orsino's mistress, and his fancy's queen.

And off they go to be married.

In contrast, *tragedy* usually works by isolating its audience as individuals and then presenting them with emotionally threatening and intellectually disturbing experiences. Tragedies, as traditionally read, tend to focus on an individual character, isolating him (or occasionally her) from the world, inviting what Aristotle long ago termed our pity and fear as we watch his destruction. Often a tragedy will be built on the awful contradiction that it is precisely those characteristics the audience is led to admire in the tragic personage that are the basis of his downfall. The audience pities him—and simultaneously fears for itself. In the tragic experience, it is *their* own destruction people most fear, as when they witness the anguish of John Webster's heroine Vittoria in *The White Devil* as she faces her death, or the anguish of King Lear as he dies.

Tragedy and comedy represent the two main traditional forms of drama. But many of the most intriguing plays are a mixture of both—and your reactions as members of the audience, as readers, and as critics, may be correspondingly mixed. Many important contemporary plays, in fact, try to create a mixture of moods and effects—as if they recognized that people's lives today are likewise mixed. And many traditional tragedies like Shakespeare's *Macbeth* often use scenes that can be played for intensely comic effects—often to heighten the contrasting experiences of an audience.

The Blurring of Distinctions Between Entertaining and Serious Theater

We suggested in the previous section that while the traditional distinction between tragedy and comedy is a useful one, it can be misleading. Tragedies are conventionally regarded as "serious" plays while most comedies are widely considered to be light, merely escapist entertainment. Such a distinction is a false one, since many of the greatest, most "serious," plays are comedies, including most of Shakespeare's comedies (like *As You Like It*) and romances (like *The Winter's Tale*) and most of Shaw's comedies (*Major Barbara,* for instance). The subtitle of *The Importance of Being Earnest* is "a trivial comedy for serious people." As Wilde himself noted, the impression desired is all surface, all froth and lightness. But, in fact, Wilde's play is asking you to take comedy, even escapism, as a serious human activity. Such escapism—what we might call serious *wish fulfillment*—can be a profound experience. Light or comic drama (or film) provides important kinds of psychological relief in the same way that fantasies and dreams do. Many Shakespearian critics argue that *The Winter's Tale* and *The Tempest,* which include such "escapist" elements as oracles, fairy princesses, drunken songs, people miraculously restored to life, and magicians, are among the most profound, most "serious" plays Shakespeare wrote.

Nonetheless, a popular belief maintains that while tragedy is grim and serious, comedy should be diverting and light. Of course, a director (and you as a reader) can take the script of a comedy and give it a very anti-comic reading. What occurs in such examples is that the firm distinctions between these traditional kinds of plays break down. The text of a play may indeed suggest that it is light, frothy, entertaining—a "happy comedy," to use a phrase often applied to some of Shakespeare's comedies. But just as you can do a strong reading of any text, so a director (or a reader of the play) can direct (or read) it against the grain.

Writing Suggestions

1. Choose a comedy you have studied and show how aspects of tragedy can be detected in it—or might be brought out in a production.
2. Choose a tragedy you have studied and show how aspects of comedy can be detected in it—or might be brought out in a production.

"Entertaining" Plays and Provocative Productions

What happens when a director gives an audience a production of a comedy that deliberately undermines the lightness and entertainment it anticipates? The result is often disturbing to traditional playgoers. When the fairies in Shakespeare's *A Midsummer Night's Dream* are played as sinister and threatening, for instance, audiences may feel similarly threatened because they are being asked to react less passively, to be willing to have their expectations disturbed.

Yet there are undoubtedly plays that do encourage their audiences simply to relax and be entertained. Musicals or situation comedies are all examples of "light" entertainment, the primary purpose of which is to be diverting and undemanding. The established audiences for such plays support a theater that downplays social issues, complex or unresolved problems, or disturbing emotional experiences. Interestingly enough, such a view of the theater often goes along with a preference for "faithful" or "authentic" productions of the "serious" plays—*Romeo and Juliet* in Elizabethan costume, not in drag, or Molière's comedies performed in gorgeous period dress.

A preference for period dress is especially revealing. None of Shakespeare's plays were performed in "authentic" Roman or medieval dress—the actors wore variants on contemporary costumes. A liking for "period" dress helps to distance the audience historically from the characters and hence to distance it from the action of the play and any sense that it might be implicated by what is occurring on stage. Such a view of theater is that it should not be disturbing. In this view theater is rather like what the ancient Romans somewhat cynically called "bread and circuses"—entertainment devised to keep people happy and content with the current political regime. Another equivalent audience in the less distant past would have watched masques in Renaissance courts. The *masque* was a form of entertainment, mixing drama, song, dance, and spectacle, that very explicitly legitimized and praised the values and preferences of the ruling political regime. When you begin to visualize a play, therefore, pay attention to the way you imagine the characters to be dressed; this may give you a clue as to how involved in the play you want to become.

Most audiences for "light" dramatic productions enjoy being relatively passive. Like passive readers of fiction, they much prefer the play if it doesn't disturb them. They expect that they will not be threatened and that they will encounter familiar situations, which meet or reinforce their assumptions, legitimize their individual and social values, and don't offend their priorities or sense of appropriateness. Such a theatrical experience is a relief for some people from the complexities of their lives outside the theater. It often gives them a temporary emotional lift and provides a sense that all their problems can be overcome, even if only in fantasy.

"Problem" Plays

Some productions, then, show how directors and audiences can read plays much as the text strategies direct them; others show how much flexibility the dramatic script gives them. But some playwrights deliberately encourage such a confusion of experience by building into their scripts disruptive or disturbing passages— and often these are omitted or downplayed in timid or conventional productions. Shakespeare, for instance, wrote a group of plays, sometimes called "problem plays"—the most important of which are *Measure for Measure, All's Well That Ends Well,* and *Troilus and Cressida*. They have elements of romantic comedy, yet they contain as well scenes and issues that are very disturbing—of prostitution, consumption, violence, cynicism, betrayal. Before the twentieth century, they were rarely performed, or else heavily cut, as if directors and audiences were unsure of whether they were serious or light plays. Nowadays, because audiences are more used to disruptive theater experiences that blur the distinction between entertaining and disturbing the spectator, these plays have all claimed a legitimate place in the Shakespearian canon.

The "problem" plays have been given that name in part because they present directors and audiences with problems about how to read them, but also because they raise, very deliberately, "problems" for the audience. These plays evoke moral, religious, political, or philosophical issues for the audience to consider (as if it were part of a debate) and thus deliberately suggest that going to the theater is not just purely for entertainment.

Writing Suggestions

1. Choose a "light entertainment" play you have read or seen and discuss it in terms of serious issues that might be brought out in a production.
2. Choose a "serious" play and show how a director might make it as "entertaining" and enjoyable as possible.

Intellectual Theater as Entertainment

It is sometimes asserted that drama reflects the world around it—holding a "mirror up to nature," as Hamlet puts it:

> Suit the action to the word, the word to the action, with this special observance, that you o'erstep not the modesty of nature: for any thing so o'erdone is from the purpose of playing, whose end, both at the first and now, was and is, to hold as 'twere the mirror up to nature: to show virtue her feature, scorn her own image, and the very age and body of the time his form and pressure.

Instead of creating a romantic, fantasy world, with audiences content to have their fantasies satisfied, Hamlet argues that plays should provide audiences with insights into the great moral or political issues of their time, or of the past. David Mamet's *Glengarry Glenross* (1984), for instance, is a much heralded play about real estate salesmen and the pressure to sell; John Osborne's *Look Back in Anger* (1956) presented the restless post-World War II generation's rebellion and moral confusion; Shakespeare's *Coriolanus* (1607) reflects on the social unrest of Shakespeare's own time, the nature of democratic versus autocratic rule, and the personal nature of political leaders. It is not that the productions of these plays cannot be "entertaining" in the sense that audiences are riveted in their seats, engrossed, and fascinated. It is that these plays are deliberately trying to get their audiences to focus on moral and social problems—and not just be entertained.

But the degree to which a play can get you to focus on social problems depends significantly on the overlap of its repertoire with your own. "Social realist" plays, as they are called, were especially fashionable at the end of the nineteenth century when there was a movement—associated with such writers as Chekhov, Ibsen, and Shaw—to bring social issues firmly into the forefront of the theater's concerns. It was widely felt that the theater was exactly the place where important social issues should be aired. Many of the plays were, at the time, highly controversial, and many were commercially unsuccessful.

"Social realism" tries to give its audience the illusion that it is viewing a "slice of life," watching the enactment of issues and concerns that are part of the everyday social world. The language of these plays tends to be that of recognizably ordinary, educated, polite conversation. Ibsen, for instance, said that he tried to depict human beings, human emotions, and human destinies in relation to the social conditions and principles of his day.

In *Hedda Gabler,* for example, spectators observe a woman who senses that, while men can choose their own careers and lifestyles, her biology is her destiny, and she must remain dependent on men, despite her moral and intellectual superiority to them. Realizing that a world made by and for men will never be available to her, she kills herself in despair. Chekhov's *The Seagull* focuses on a playwright's emotional and professional life and unreturned love, and the interacting emotional lives of other characters. In each play, the setting and the atmosphere that the playwright attempts to create are very like those of realist novels—with a tension between what can be described or shown and the inner, psychological realities that are the work's real subject. The audience is invited, on the one hand, to recognize the setting as familiar and comforting; on the other, to acknowledge the problems and difficulties as disruptive of that familiar setting. Both the setting and the "real" or underlying subject of the play are seen as recognizable in the world the audience lives in when it leaves the theater.

A number of these plays are now considered part of the standard repertoire of modern theater, and it is often difficult for modern audiences to see them as disturbing or disruptive, especially if the social issues seem no longer relevant.

These audiences can frequently find such plays more escapist than disturbing because what seemed "real" in the nineteenth century seems distant—interesting historically but not immediately relevant—in the late twentieth century. If, however, a director decides to update them and, say, play Hedda Gabler as a man or give a contemporary setting to a Shaw comedy, then once again audiences will be disturbed by a dislocating theatrical experience and will be forced to consider the social or moral relevance of the drama.

Brecht's Influence on Modern Productions

Such dislocating theatrical experiences became, very explicitly, the subject of the influential plays by the modern German dramatist and director Bertold Brecht. Ibsen and Chekhov had tried to abolish the audience's sense that they were watching a play in a theater in order to get a sense of realism. But Brecht's "epic theater" goes out of its way to stress that a play is being acted in a theater in order, quite deliberately, to jar an audience's complacency and to make it respond to the issues that are raised in the play. Drama is seen not, in Brecht's words, as a "mirror" but as a "dynamo." He tries to achieve that effect by getting his audiences to respond questioningly, intellectually, not passively. His fundamental technique was to break the illusion by which audiences can become so involved with a performance that they forget themselves. Brecht's *Verfremdungseffekt* (or "alienation effect") tries to remind the audience that it is in a theater—by leaving the stage machinery visible or by having characters talk or sing directly to the audience.

Brecht was interested not so much in the development of actions as the presentation to his audience of its own social conditions. Rather than getting the audience to *identify* with his characters and their actions, he wanted it to respond as if in a debate with the production. So his characters are not rounded but deliberately inconclusive, with conflicting motives and interests. Brecht himself puts it this way in his notes to *The Threepenny Opera:*

> It is a sort of summary of what the spectator in the theater wishes to see of life. Since however he sees, at the same time, certain things that he does not wish to see and thus sees his wishes not only fulfilled but also criticized . . . he is . . . able to give the theater a new function.

Brecht's *Galileo,* first written in 1938–39 and revised in 1945–47, uses settings that Brecht notes "must not be such that the public believes itself to be in a room in medieval Italy or in the Vatican" where the historical events on which the play is based took place: "the public must remain always clearly aware that it is in a theater." Thus Brecht's goal is to refuse his audience the privilege of sitting back and passively watching. He wants his viewers to be profoundly disturbed by what they witness on stage and to apply what they see to their own lives. At the same time, he certainly wants to entertain—and one of the paradoxes of Brechtian theater is that it can be both intellectual and wonderfully entertaining. Later in his career, Brecht (rather belatedly) acknowledged that his plays did use the spectators' emotional involvement. On the following pages, we will present a detailed discussion of his play *Galileo,* and analyze some of the ways in which our students responded, both emotionally and intellectually, to the play.

Writing Suggestion

Choose a play or production you know and show either (*a*) how Brecht's influence can be seen in it; or (*b*) how a production might profitably use Brecht's influence to make it more effective.

Beckett's Influence on Contemporary Productions

Brecht's influence on contemporary theater has been immense. Staging techniques, alienation effects, productions that stress the theatricality of drama have all become commonplace—even in productions of classics like Shakespeare or Racine. Another major influence on recent drama and staging has been the Irish dramatist Samuel Beckett. His *Waiting for Godot* (1952) is now seen as both a dramatic masterpiece and a theatrical landmark. It brought **absurdist** drama into the mainstream and drew attention, as did Brecht's plays, to the highly entertaining and vividly theatrical power of an open, nearly deserted stage. It defined the naked exchange of actions and language as the essence of theater. But Beckett seeks to develop a combination of serious and comic theater that differs from Brecht's.

In *Waiting for Godot,* Beckett blends conventions from mime, burlesque, the films of Charlie Chaplin and Laurel and Hardy, as well as conventions from serious existentialist theater and Theater of the Absurd into a play that can be at once philosophically stimulating and wonderfully entertaining. The two main characters, Vladimir and Estragon, wait for two acts for someone named Godot who never arrives. Each act ends:

Let's go.

They do not move.

The dialogue proceeds by a brilliantly funny, nightmarish combination of absurd humor, literary references, and the kind of slapstick viewers now associate with Chaplin's movies or late-night television comedy:

VLADIMIR Moron!
ESTRAGON That's the idea, let's abuse each other.
They turn, move apart, turn again and face each other.
VLADIMIR Moron!
ESTRAGON Vermin!
VLADIMIR Abortion!
ESTRAGON Morpion!

VLADIMIR	Sewer-rat!
ESTRAGON	Curate!
VLADIMIR	Cretin!
ESTRAGON	Critic!
VLADIMIR	Oh!

He wilts, vanquished, and turns away.

In the next section, we provide a more detailed discussion of *Godot* and some of our students' responses to it.

Writing Suggestion

Choose a play or production you know and show either
(*a*) how Beckett's influence can be seen in it; or
(*b*) how a production might profitably use Beckett's influence to make it more effective.

The Open-Ended Nature of Drama

In setting before you the variety of ways scripts, directors, and audiences can interact, we want to stress the inherently open-ended nature of drama. You can have a situation where a play is produced solely as entertainment—as a light comedy in dinner theater, for example—and where some members of the audience will be content, while others find the production trivial. You can have a "serious" play produced to bring out the social issues or contemporary relevance—and, similarly, have members of the audience variously enthralled or bored. A tragedy can be treated farcically: some spectators will be intrigued, others indignant. Both script and production are inherently fragile—a performance of the same play may be quite different from one night to the next. What you as a reader and student of drama need to remember is that this fragility of the form means that you have an unusually active role in formulating the meaning of the plays you see, contemplate, and study. Perhaps at this point you should go back to the questions on *The Importance of Being Earnest* with which we opened this chapter (p. 216). Consider how many different answers could be given to them. "Which are right?" is not the correct question by which to approach them. "Which will work in the theater?" "Which will enhance your conception of the play?"—these are the right approaches.

It is often said, in the words of Hamlet, "the play's the thing." Yes—but how does Hamlet continue the phrase? "The play's the thing wherein I'll catch the conscience of the king." The play *in itself* is *not* the thing: what matters is what can be done with the play. Like any good director (or audience), Hamlet uses the script of his play to try to achieve certain effects in accord with his reading of it. And even he has no guarantees that it will work: his audience (the most important member of which is Claudius) may interpret his production differently. At the end of *The Tempest,* the dramatist-magician Prospero steps forward and addresses the audience directly, and in a speech designed in part to elicit applause, acknowledges that it is only when the members of the audience arise from their seats and go their separate ways into the world that the essential nature of drama is revealed. The script, finally, does not belong to the dramatist, or the actor, or the director. It belongs to the interaction between all these and you, the audience.

Entertainment and Seriousness in Brecht and Beckett

Peter Brook, one of today's most distinguished directors, speaks of how the best theater is both *rough* and *holy*. The best popular theater is *rough:* it is irreverent, profane, and vulgar. Thus it takes on a socially liberating role, enabling its audience to indulge in its anti-authoritarian feelings, its dislike of pomp and pretentiousness. But in addition, says Brook, theater should be *holy:* it should try to evoke in its audiences a yearning for significance, to present both "primitive situations disturbing the unconscious" (the rough) and "philosophical situations" (the holy), which together provoke spectators to reflect on their plight as men and women caught in history, living in a particular society, and wrestling in and with language.

When you read and write about dramatic texts, you should try to combine both the rough and the holy—the entertaining and serious aspects of the experience of drama. We want to end this chapter by briefly illustrating this mixture of reactions in our students' writing on two plays introduced here—Brecht's *Galileo* and Beckett's *Waiting for Godot*. In each case, our students were asked to become aware of how their responses were formed and to relate the plays to wider cultural issues.

Student Responses to Brecht's Galileo

Brecht encourages diverse audience reactions by the way he writes his play. Instead of seeing Galileo's trial by the Inquisition, the audience hears reports from various of Galileo's followers—and is asked to judge among these reports. Our students became aware that the subject of the play also involved them in matters of judgment in that it dealt with a famous historical personage about whom there was a great deal of controversy. So they were forced to grapple directly with the "serious" aspects of the play.

When you "read" the past, no less than when you "read" a text, you construct an interpretation out of your assumptions, predispositions, concerns, and needs, as you bring them to bear on what are perceived to be the "facts" of history. No less is this true of writers concerned with writing a "historical" play. Brecht wrote his play in the 1930s and 1940s, an era of war, violence, and terrible political events, including the Great Depression, the rise of Hitler, the Stalinist purges in Russia, World War II, and the explosion of the atomic bomb. He set his play in the early seventeenth century when the scientist Galileo Galilei was challenging the authority of the church over whether the earth revolved around the sun or the sun around the earth.

Thus to read Brecht's play some forty to fifty years after he wrote it provides you with three distinct historical layerings—your rereading of Brecht's rereading of Galileo. Today's readers can do some research into the life of Galileo *and* the life of Brecht to discover how Brecht's interpretation was colored by his own age and to determine whether they see the issues raised by the life of Galileo differently from the way Brecht saw them. Rather than finding a definitive and true account of Galileo in the history books that they could use as a measure of the "accuracy" of Brecht's play, however, most of our students discovered that accounts of Galileo vary and that history books seem as much a product of interpretations as history plays. The particular readings of Galileo, either by Brecht, historians, or students today are, finally, ideological constructs, created by their assumptions, values, and expectations.

Most people tend to think of Galileo as a heroic figure, nobly defending "truth" against the forces of ignorance. What our students discovered is that Galileo was regarded as an outcast by his society. From the viewpoint of the dominant ideology of his time, represented by the church, he was a very marginal figure—just as Brecht himself was in the 1940s. As one of our students wrote:

> During my years at school, I was always taught how great Galileo's achievements were, and what a benefit they were to humankind. I naturally assumed that Galileo in his time was thought to be a great man. Adjectives that I would use to describe the qualities of a great man include ethical, moral, and righteous. But Brecht portrays Galileo as just the opposite: he is portrayed as weak because he capitulates to the Inquisition.

Thus to see Galileo as a hero is to go against the dominant interpretation of his time: it is to rewrite history in ways that the most powerful authorities in the seventeenth century would have seen as wrong.

Interestingly the play does not present a unified view of Galileo. Indeed it seems to want its spectators and readers to become aware of the contradictions of history and thus to be caught up in the dramatic debate about Galileo. Nor is Galileo's society shown as a unified community, but as full of conflicting attitudes, values, and concerns. In this way, the plays asks its audience to consider very diverse views as they watch or read it. We found not only that students were sensitive to the contradictions in the seventeenth century when reading this play but also that they became acutely aware of conflicts within themselves and their society. One student found herself divided in her sympathies:

> I can't decide which side, if any, I'm on. On the one hand, I'm sympathetic to Galileo because, as a person living in a technological age and as an engineering major, I know how scientific advances and technological improvements can be advantageous to the individual. Yet, on the other hand, I also found it easy to relate to the concerns of the Inquisition. They were worried that the people would

become upset when they discovered that the earth or, in other words, human beings were not the center of the universe. Today's image of human beings has become what the Inquisition feared—one of nothingness and nowhere. It is very easy to think of oneself as not important in today's society. Brecht must have felt that too, especially after Hitler and the atomic bomb of World War II.

For this student, the ideological conflicts that Brecht interpreted as part of the seventeenth century also describe conflicts of the 1940s and the 1980s. She, like many students, finds herself in favor of scientific advancement but fears that science and technology threaten the status of the individual.

Our students did not come to many resolutions when they read this play, and we think that is good. What they discovered was that their attitudes toward science, authority, and the status of the individual helped to determine how they responded to the play. But they also discovered—and this is one of the implications of learning to read from a self-consciously ideological position—that their attitudes on these subjects are much more complex and contradictory than they had previously recognized.

But did they find the play entertaining? Most of them saw it as a play of ideas, involving its audience in a debate, and certainly not "escapist" entertainment. However, while a number of them found the play stimulating, many wondered how its ideas would communicate in the theater. For instance, one student wrote:

Many of Brecht's ideas belong in a book of philosophy or political science. I am not sure how they would "play." I can see many audiences being bored by so much philosophizing.

What is important here is not so much the correctness of this student's opinion but the assumptions behind it. Do you share them? Do you think that drama is primarily (or only) for entertainment? Or do you think plays like *Galileo* are more suited to a lecture than to the theater? It might be said that Brecht has succeeded with such a reader in that he feels "alienated" and so is likely to examine his own repertoire, but the play certainly seems (at least for this reader) to embody a narrow understanding of "entertainment."

In contrast some students responded to what they saw as the dramatic energy of narrative: "Brecht's play is like a compressed novel, acted out before the eyes," wrote one, who raised the question of how the ideas could be symbolized by means of the staging. Other students not only worked through the ideas of the play but also tried to imagine how they themselves would stage it. We discovered that the students who tried to read the play dramatically, that is, to visualize it, were those who found it "rough" as well as "holy." One of our students envisaged the scene in which the Pope was dressed in the robes of his office as particularly effective theatrically:

The Pope does not want to persecute Galileo. He is dressing as he argues with the cardinal who wants to have Galileo silenced, and his dressing is symbolic as well as literal. Gradually he all but disappears beneath the robes of his office. By the end of the scene, he is overcome by his robes as he becomes the spokesman for the oppressors of Galileo. As I imagined the scene, I was caught between thinking about the play's ideas and my feelings for the Pope. The play is about people who really existed, but the real people are also like actors in a play whose script they didn't write. The drama of this scene made me realize the power of ideology: once the Pope gets his costume on, he has to play his part. His script was written by his culture, and he couldn't deviate from it. I was moved both intellectually and emotionally. It is a very sad scene.

In such mixed reactions—acknowledging the power of the ideas as well as the theatrical effectiveness of the staging, and seeing how one might reinforce the other—you can see how an attempt to visualize a play can help you construct a reading that is both serious and entertaining.

Writing Suggestion

What aspects of our students' readings of *Galileo* do you agree or disagree with? Account for the influence of your own general repertoire on your own reading.

Student Responses to
Beckett's Waiting for Godot

Waiting for Godot is probably the most successful "experimental" play of the last forty years—so much so that it might be regarded as a "classic." It too is a play that has provoked widely divergent reactions: because its events are so odd, almost all readers feel compelled to naturalize it, but different readers focus on different cultural and intellectual references and therefore construct vastly different readings of the play. Among our students, some argue that Godot symbolizes God; others, that he symbolizes nothingness; still others, that he is a floating signifier and can mean whatever the reader or viewer wants him to mean. For some of our students, that Godot does not come indicates the hopelessness and ineffectual nature of Vladimir and Estragon's existence; for others, Godot's not coming makes the play optimistic since they see Vladimir and Estragon's purpose in life to be the waiting.

Many of our students have argued that they were able to naturalize the strange circumstances of the play by seeing it in terms of their own lives. One student wrote:

We're always waiting for something, whether it's grades, spring break, graduation, being "legal," getting a job. But when whatever you're waiting for happens, you're almost always disappointed. Gogo and Didi won't ever be disappointed. They'll always be caught up by anticipation—as we all are. When people meet one of their goals, they must make up another. Gogo and Didi won't have to do that.

What all of these widely divergent readings of the play have in common is a search for its "meaning," as if the play were being perceived only as a collection of ideas, and not as something that is meant to be staged, acted out before an audience. That is a problem with Beckett's work generally: he seems a "serious" artist rather than an entertainer. In support of Beckett's seriousness, another student wrote:

One idea that I became particularly curious about was its status as a play. One assumption that I hold about a play is that it should be performed, not read. However, I realized that *Waiting for Godot* was, perhaps, better in the written form.

This student argued that the play was better as a written text than as a production because she felt that it needed to be "studied." Note how these students are treating the play as a novel: they are doing an excellent job using their naturalizing strategies, but a poor job using their visualizing strategies.

In suggesting ways in which our students could develop their responses to the play, we emphasized that the play is meant to be performed: they should try to imagine the staging, costuming, and action of the characters (in ways we discussed earlier). Many of our students did not have in their literary repertoires the specific theatrical techniques Beckett was using, such as music hall repartee, but the mixture of farce and seriousness is something they—no doubt like you—are used to in *Saturday Night Live* or *Monty Python*. In this play, serious ideas are expressed as farce, and the endless talking at cross-purposes can be at once hilarious and frustrating, if it is read dramatically.

Students tended to discover that when they reread the play to imagine how it could be performed, they found it much more humorous than they had when they were reading it just for its ideas.

By visualizing the play, many students were able to focus on its theatricality. One student dealt with the scene in Act I in which Lucky and Pozzo enter, Lucky driving Pozzo with a rope around his neck. The stage direction reads: "Lucky is the first to enter, followed by the rope which is long enough to let him reach the middle of the stage before Pozzo appears." A student commented:

The scene must be hilarious with the two of them pulling at each other—a bit like an old Laurel and Hardy movie. I found a disturbing contrast between the humor and what it means, however. To see the blind, powerful master driving the slave makes me wonder what each stands for.

Another student took this kind of analysis even further by imagining an alternative staging:

What if instead of Pozzo becoming visible on the stage as Lucky goes off, the scene was played with both characters off, one to the left and one to the right, and only the rope shown. We could see a tug of war, with Lucky and all the goods he is carrying—the bag, the stool, the picnic basket, and greatcoat—suddenly being pulled back by the invisible Pozzo and collapsing onto the stage. Then Pozzo could enter, carrying the whip. I think that would be a perfect blend of visual comedy and quite sinister meaning.

Other students focused on the way they would dress Vladimir and Estragon. One commented:

> The effect of the play could be totally different depending on what Vladimir and Estragon were wearing. When I first read the play, I imagined them as kind of hoboes, dressed in old, tattered clothing. But the more I thought about how much their plight of waiting for Godot is like that of most people who are "waiting for their ship to come in," I thought it would be very effective to dress them in business suits, or tuxedos, or maybe even in chinos and Izod shirts. Imagine how funny it would be for all the yuppies in the audience if the boot with a hole in it was a Topsider! Dressing them like bums is a way of marginalizing them—of making them seem different from the audience and more removed from it. If I were directing the play, I'd like my audience to both laugh and squirm in their seats because the play would hit them close to home. Costuming is a way of producing a possible identification of the audience with these two characters.

Writing Suggestions

1. Do you find Beckett's *Waiting for Godot* optimistic or pessimistic? What in both the play's and your own repertoires influenced your reading?
2. Which of our students' comments on *Godot* do you agree or disagree with? Account for the influence of your own general and literary repertoires on your reading.
3. Which aspects of *Godot* lend themselves to theatrical performance?

Theatricality, as we have discussed it in this chapter, is an essential element of drama, and one of our aims has been to help you recognize that plays can bring out strong intellectual reactions in their audiences *and* simultaneously entertain. We hope you will enjoy theatrical performances and analyze the reading and viewing strategies as well as the wider cultural significance of your experiences in the theater. In the words of Vladimir's serious yet mocking, farcical yet provoking speech:

> What we are doing here, that is the question. And we are blessed in this, that we happen to know the answer. Yes, in this immense confusion one thing alone is clear. We are waiting for Godot to come.

To experience the pleasure as well as the point of those lines—that is an essential part of reading drama.

Checkpoints for Chapter 7

1. In reading and writing about drama, you should see yourself primarily as an audience, visualizing the theatrical possibilities of the dramatic script.
2. Script and audiences interact in drama in the way texts and readers do in other literary forms.

3. Different acting spaces, styles of direction, and audience preferences reflect the ideological contradictions of their society.
4. There is no "original" meaning or style of production of a play: plays are performed differently throughout their histories.
5. The distinctions between comedy and tragedy, entertaining and serious theater, are blurred, according to the ways in which the plays are produced and responded to by director and audience.

ℋ Chapter 8
Reading Media Texts

Expanded Definitions of "Reading" and "Texts"

"Reading" media? "Reading" television? "Reading" popular music? Or "reading" film? We read newspapers, magazines, and comics, certainly; perhaps we even read the lyrics of popular songs, although most people would prefer to listen or dance to the latest Springsteen song than merely to read the words. But in suggesting that students of literary texts also read and write about the texts of media, like television, radio, and popular music, clearly we are using terms like "reading" and "texts" in an unusual manner.

In what sense can one "read" television or rock music (the two kinds of media to which we will give most attention in this chapter)? Implied here is that "reading" isn't just something one does with written texts. In a broader sense, "reading" involves decoding the *sign systems* of our common culture, those messages and codes that continually bombard us and that constitute so much of our world. But it also implies that many of the strategies you use to read a novel are not essentially different from those you use to watch and interpret a song or television program.

Likewise, we are using the term "texts" in an extended way. It signifies something more than just the words that lie between two stiff (or paperback) covers of something you buy in a bookstore. If you can "read" television, then television programs are "texts" in this broad sense. When you can respond to and analyze a song by Peter Gabriel or Sting, then you are also reading a "text." Of course, you can simply relax, or dance, or try not to do anything so intellectual and self-conscious at all—much like indulging yourself in a novel that is just a "good read," a "page turner." But in order to understand the texts even minimally (even to dance to them!), you have to process information, produce mental images, look for consistency, match their repertoires with your own, even if you do this totally unself-consciously. Since they are such a vital part of everyday experiences, it becomes crucial to study the texts of media because in many ways these are the texts that most directly form and are formed by the dominant ideology of a culture.

It is the goal of this chapter to suggest ways in which you can see the reading of media texts as similar to the reading of literary texts. We want to show how your responses to them can be articulated and your interpretations deepened by the same strategies we have suggested you use with literary texts. The texts of today's media require just as careful "reading" and just as much awareness of the assumptions you bring to reading as literary texts. Moreover, writing about them is essentially no different from writing about literary texts.

Writing Suggestions

1. Give some reasons for and against including the study of media alongside literary texts.
2. What strategies do you think you habitually use with media texts that *differ* from the ones you use with literary texts?

A Media-Saturated Culture

People take television so much for granted that when anyone announces in a class that he or she does not have a television set, the common assumption is that either that person is somehow deprived or else has deliberately chosen to go against the dominant ideology of our society, as a part of a provocatively marginal style of life.

But like many things people take for granted as "natural" or "universal," television has a history, not just of technological changes but of the uses humans have made of it. Over the past sixty years, television has become a major focus within the family home. Television brings its messages into people's private worlds—into their living rooms, dens, recreation rooms, bedrooms. News, information, entertainment, and commercials come "in" from outside. Perhaps the overwhelming dominance of television as a medium of entertainment and news is based on its bringing the "public" world into the "private" world of the home. Until the widespread use of VCRs, movies were very different from television on this point: you go "out" to a movie, but television comes "in" to you. That difference produces important psychological and cultural characteristics.

"Media are/is all around us," one of our students wrote, showing in her confusion something of the very observation she was making. Her assignment was to analyze her response to a variety of television news programs, and in particular to consider whether television news was, or even could be, "objective." She was commenting on the omnipresence of the media in our world, the fact that ours is a media-saturated culture, in which we are all bombarded with constant and contradictory signs, messages, signals, and codes to an extent that is unparalleled in history.

Television is a major ideological apparatus of our culture: it gives us programs ("texts") that incorporate our society's dominant ideological values. Rather than presenting simple "reality," it gives us the complex, contradictory myths that make up our dominant ideology. The French critic Roland Barthes has studied how all the media—newspaper articles, photographs in magazines, and films—create people as what in Chapter 2 we called ideological **subjects.** He stresses (as we do) that it is the responsibility of the reader to demythologize such a process, to show how this process works.

What does it mean to say that *people* are created as *subjects?* Media give us all the languages by which we articulate ourselves. Movies, television, popular music, cartoons, all make up a constant part of people's conversation, thinking, and feeling—not just individual items communicated by the media, but the very media themselves. You don't just go to see *a* movie; you go "to the movies." You don't just listen to the Cars singing "She Comes"; you listen "to the stereo" or "turn on the radio." In the same way you "read the newspaper" and "watch the TV." Media are/is all around you.

Many sociologists have recognized that, although every culture has its characteristic communication systems, only in the past century have we witnessed this extraordinary phenomenon of different societies being interconnected so thoroughly and instantly by mass media systems. It is therefore not surprising that people today are so much more media-conscious than their ancestors. During the 1960s, the media theorist Marshall McLuhan argued that this new situation made the world a "global village." Our world could be, he argued, linked instantaneously by the same news, interests, and myths. Further, ours is an age of instantaneous communication, and we are all potentially part of the *same* community. Unlike in previous ages, the electronic media—the telegraph, telephone, radio, television, and computer networks—make up a total and almost completely interconnected environment. Virtually every home in this country has a television set; the average American watches six hours of television a day; at peak hours almost three-quarters of the television sets in the country are on, with over 80 percent tuned to one of the three national networks. Many people know the frustration (or sometimes the relief!) of being on vacation in another country and not being able to tune into their local TV station—or find out instantaneously the latest baseball scores or catch up with their favorite soap opera.

People from a variety of fields have worried about the enormous influence our communication system possesses over us. George Orwell's novel *1984* presents such a world as a nightmare, and long before the real 1984 came around, our society had developed many of the intrusive communication capacities envisaged in that book. Many of course weren't intrusive, but beneficent—or so most people in our society think. Of course, if you recall Chapters 1 and 2, it is possible they may think so only because they are caught up in their dominant ideology.

As you know, there is widespread concern today about the power of the media over people's lives, particularly of television, popular music, and movies. Such concern is often expressed in attempts to censor or certify movies or records, or to rate television shows or movies for some appropriate age group. There are also widespread attacks on consumerism and on the seemingly trivial content of the media by educational and religious leaders from both the political right and the left. One commentator suggests that to look at prime-time television one might think that America's greatest problems were not political integrity, nuclear survival, the environment, or poverty, but the smell, feel, and look of one's hair or skin!

Whether you take an optimistic or pessimistic view of the media's power, there can be no doubt that contemporary electronic media have changed today's society radically. Never before have so many people potentially shared a common system of messages, images, metaphors, and values. In short, never before have people all shared and "read" the same body of "texts."

Obviously people need to understand such a phenomenon. Becoming aware of the assumptions you bring to the media and the ways your assumptions are influenced by them is as vital in your reading of television, rock music, and film texts as it is in reading "literary" texts. Some might even think more so. In this chapter we will suggest some ways in which you can sharpen your understanding of as well as your writing about some of the texts of media. Although discussion is largely restricted to television and rock music, the principles of our discussion can be applied to other forms of media. For example, many of our students have written interesting response statements and more formal papers on comic strips like *Doonesbury* and *Peanuts,* films like *Desperately Seeking Susan* and *Blue Velvet,* and sitcoms like the *Cosby Show.*

Writing Suggestions

1. Discuss four or five different ways in which ours is a "media-saturated culture."
2. Do you think that television is a beneficial or destructive influence on our lives? Account for your answer by reference to your own repertoire.

Reading Television

"Reading television" seems to most people to be a "natural" activity. But, in fact, like reading fiction or poetry, it is a learned, culture-specific activity. Most people have learned to internalize the characteristic demands that television makes on them, and they take the "reading strategies" they have acquired pretty much for granted.

Now consider how you "read" television. We want you to become more self-conscious about the process by which you view and analyze television in the same way you can become more aware about reading literary texts. Every television text—whether drama, news, sports, commercials—has a particular repertoire by means of which it tries to construct you as a particular kind of reader. And likewise, as with other texts, you bring your own repertoire into play. Meanings are not found "in" texts; they are constructed in the interaction of viewers (or readers) and texts.

In their book *Reading Television,* John Fiske and John Hartley suggest that television has a "bardic" function in contemporary society. By *bardic,* they mean that like a bard in primitive civilizations, television has a number of unusual functions in our society:

- it *articulates* a consensus of cultural values
- it *implicates* individual members in the culture's values
- it *celebrates* and justifies their participation in the culture
- it *assures* them of the importance of their beliefs
- it *convinces* them that their status as individuals is guaranteed by society
- and it *transmits* a sense of how they belong in their culture

News programs are especially useful to analyze in these terms. What television news (like all other television programs) presents is not "events" or "facts," but *interpretations.* Viewers are given a selective reading of events from a distinct point of view, even though these are presented as objective or unbiased. As viewers, you watch a news summary that is presented authoritatively and (with the help of visuals) shows you apparent evidence for the meaning being "in" the event (the text). It is what we called in Chapter 3 an interpretation.

But as you saw when we discussed different modes of writing in Chapter 3, interpretations have certain costs. One cost is especially important: by presenting a particular reading as factual, interpretations fail to analyze the social, cultural, and historical factors that have influenced their development. As one of society's major instruments of socialization, most television programs, especially those on the major networks, are coded in the values of the dominant ideology of our society. In Fiske and Hartley's term, television tries to "claw" as many people into its grasp as possible. It does this, by and large, *not* by pursuing any deep cultural analyses but by articulating as many consensual values as possible—often quite contradictory ones. The major values of our television programs don't challenge the residual pattern of beliefs or habits of most Americans. Marginal or minority values have a decidedly subsidiary place, and some important though minority groups and beliefs in our culture have no place at all—or else are relegated to cable channels or to the public or minority networks.

Like poems, novels, plays, and other written texts, the electronic media express themselves as systems of signs—*signifiers* that are read and interpreted and assigned to *signifieds* by their readers. Of course, they are not coded exactly in the way a written text is: they incorporate elaborate visual and auditory as well as other non-linguistic sign systems. When you say you "read" television, therefore, you are focusing not only on the linguistic properties of a television program but on the whole experience of watching and listening to it, as well as on the repertoire you bring to your reading of it.

The Economic Motivation of Network Television

In America, at least, people take the "private" (as opposed to government) ownership of the media for granted, yet in most other countries the state has dominant control and, in some places, total control over television transmission. One consequence of our "free" system of communications is that a major motive behind television programs is profit. Whatever community- or state-imposed regulations there may be on television, the primary goal of television networks is to amass profits for their investors. The distinctive forms that television has assumed in the past sixty years grow directly out of the wider characteristics of American economic and social development. The effects can be seen in the much commented upon tendencies to show programs that will draw large audiences (and therefore advertising revenue), to avoid controversial issues, and to create a comforting and relatively homogenized set of values—in short, to embody and reinforce the dominant ideology of our culture.

At first it may seem strange to regard something as seemingly "universal" and neutral as the family television as an ideological instrument, part of the apparatus of the culture that creates, regulates, and reinforces the dominant values of society. Yet that has always been one of the major functions of any society's communication systems. Television transmits not just good stories and exciting games but also myths and ideologies.

Although many Americans may be unaware of the ideological impact of television on them, in other parts of the world there is no doubt about the embodiment of American ideology in American television. There has been an obvious penetration of many other countries by American television programs as part of what the communications commentator Herbert Schiller once called "the American Empire." Along with consumer goods and services, America exports television programs—and with them a picture of the way Americans (supposedly) live. When the people of other countries protest about the Americanization of their society (even in a seemingly friendly country like France or Britain), often what is being protested is American television—unfairly, it might be said, since television programs are just one part of a much more complex cultural exchange of goods and ideologies between countries.

Writing Suggestions

1. In what senses is television an "ideological instrument" of a society?
2. Do you think that television is the most important medium of our culture? Compare its impact with that of both literary texts and other media, for example, newspapers, radio, or film.

Analyzing the Effect of "Flow"
in the Television Text

The distinctive format of both radio and television is what the sociologist and critic Raymond Williams calls "flow"—its planned, ongoing sequence. You read a story or a novel as separate items, and a play is performed in a particular place and time. But television (like radio) is characterized by its continuing sequence—a flow of changing, yet linked, programs. Hence the very common expressions of "watching television" or "listening to the radio." Discriminating viewers, we like to think, pick out particular programs, switching on the television to watch the news or *Monday Night Football* or *Masterpiece Theater*, and switching it off when that program is over. But that is not how most people watch television. Most viewers experience television as a continuous flow. They may often move between channels, but the experience is still one of continuity. In the early days of television—and this is still true in some noncommercial modes of presentation like the *MacNeil-Lehrer Newshour*, on PBS—there were distinct intervals between programs or segments of a program that were distinguished by silent pictures or signs used to mark the boundaries between separate programs. But in network television today, the flow is continuous, linked by and built around commercials. The aim, of course, is to "capture" a viewing audience and hold its attention and thus influence its values, allegiances, and wallets for as long as possible.

As Marshall McLuhan once remarked perceptively, if perhaps overstating the point, "the medium is the message." What television communicates, as much as any individual "message," is—television. As you've all no doubt observed, when old movies are shown on television, you become irritated by commercial breaks. But commercial breaks fit neatly into the programs created specifically for television because these programs are pretailored, organized around those planned commercials. The most crucial breaks, in fact, are those designed to provide not interruption but continuity—the insertion of trailers for upcoming programs, or those anticipating a whole evening's viewing. Transitions between different segments of viewing are designed to discourage switching channels and to try to ensure the continuity of a viewer's attention.

Even when you aren't watching, it is always there. That is something else you know about television. At the flick of a switch, twenty-four hours a day, you can see what's "on," and with the advent of cable TV, what's "on" on multiple channels. What's "on" is primarily a homogenized flow, channels that are interchangeable. In Chapters 1 and 2, we introduced the idea that language pre-exists its users. It exists before each of us is born and gives us a picture of reality; people are "written" as well as writing subjects. Television is perhaps the clearest illustration of how this process functions. You turn on the television and find yourself inserted into a discourse that pre-exists you, that may even comfort you by its continuous accessibility. You can read *TV Guide* for separate programs, since broadcasting occurs formally as individual units. But your experience is one of continuity, a sequence designed to keep your eyes on the television despite the separateness of the programs.

Have you ever found that, inexplicably, your television doesn't work? Or your radio? For many people such an event creates a sudden severe nervousness: *You can't turn it on.* You have (temporarily) lost contact with something that provides part of your sense of reality. And if you have trouble literally "turning off" the television, imagine the difficulty of turning its messages off inside your head, the difficulty of resisting its powerful call to you to believe in and be enveloped by the dominant ideology it conveys.

What the Media Text and the Viewer
Bring to the Reading Process

In previous chapters, we noted how readers and literary texts interact in the reading process by an intersection of repertoires. Like stories or poems, media texts have their own repertoires of conventions and techniques by which they try to create preferred interpretations in their readers. Similarly, like the readers of stories or poems, readers of media texts can produce distinctively "strong" readings of them.

How can you produce **strong readings** of media texts? One way to find out is to focus on how they want you to interpret them. Advertisements on television are particularly useful texts to examine in this regard, because everyone is familiar with them. Most viewers assume that commercials are trying to sell them something, so if they are asked to analyze one, after noting its surface features—"a group of men drinking beer," or "a man in a white coat demonstrating how strong a garbage bag can be"—viewers are conditioned to go straight to the mode of reading that the advertisers want. The intended or preferred reading is usually best expressed by a summary: "The commercial wants us to drink Michelob or Stroh's or Heineken," or "It wants us to buy Glad garbage bags." Such texts bring to the foreground very strongly their preferred way of reading, and it is a low-level one. By summarizing the text, viewers come up with a message or *gist,* and the implications of such gists are also very clear: their viewers dutifully trot off to the grocery store or the beer store—and consume. Or they make a mental note to do so soon. Or they at least naturalize such acts as perfectly acceptable things to do, part of the American way of life.

But you can analyze your experiences of such texts in far more revealing ways. Analyzing television commercials gives you an excellent opportunity to develop some cognitive and cultural perspective and to produce strong readings—because you are attuned to recognizing the obvious (and often crass) demands made on you by television commercials. There is nothing subtle about most television commercials—at least about the level of their message. But they work upon viewers on a deeper level of appeal. They tune into the dominant ideological patterns of people's lives, making them feel comfortable with the underlying values they share—even if they don't buy the product being advertised. It is crucial to realize that commercials are selling ideology (or "the system" as a student put it) as much as any particular product.

Recall what we have frequently said about *ideology*. Its function is to make people feel at home, comfortable that they share their society's dominant and "natural" values. The ideological level of commercials, unlike that of many literary texts, is often very explicit. Commercials for pizza sauce that refer to a traditional (mom's or grandma's) recipe are clearly tapping into people's belief in family solidarity; commercials that stress that their product is "made in the U.S.A." appeal to the individual's sense of belonging to a national group; beer commercials that show a group of men in a tent or at a lake cottage invoke a whole complex of values—individualism, *machismo*, competitiveness. Consciously or unconsciously, you recognize these values and hence acknowledge your participation in your society's dominant ideology.

You can achieve interesting insights into the dominant ideology by working with soap and cosmetics ads. Foreigners often observe that Americans are obsessed with cleanliness, with teeth, hair, "body odor" (a concept invented by an advertising agency in the late 1940s). Why should this be? To many of you, it seems "natural" to be clean, to brush your teeth maybe six times a day, to use different shampoos, conditioners, or sprays that add body, bounce, shine, or glow to various parts of your anatomy. These values are not as "natural" or "universal" as they may seem but are, rather, very specific to our culture. Americans have a strong belief that they are free to choose a distinctive image and that because they have the shiniest hair, the brightest teeth, the nicest skin, they are unique—and almost immortal. Cleanliness is a way of keeping not only dirt but (almost) death itself at bay. Paradoxically this whole process gives Americans a group identity, a membership in a shared community that wears the "badge" of cleanliness, as one student put it. Such an analysis shows how both the television commercial and you as its viewers are part of a wider ideological interchange, and how your and the commercials' general repertoires overlap.

Writing Suggestions

1. Write an ideological analysis of a television advertisement of your choice.
2. Choose another television commercial. What ideological values do you *share* with it? Which values do you find yourself alienated by?

Ideological Analysis of Sitcoms

The ideological level of television commercials may seem obvious to you. But what about other kinds of television programs, sitcoms, for example? Ostensibly, their aim is to entertain their viewers, but again the relationship between viewers and program is one built on shared ideological values. As we've explained, this is part of the commercialization of television. On the commercial networks, most programming is carefully chosen to reinforce—not counteract—the values that the sponsors find conducive to selling their products. You can see this in the general avoidance of controversial topics or viewpoints, particularly in "family" viewing times. Commercials and programs share the same ideological values, as can be seen in the way they both use narrative closure. Commercials use vignettes of narrative in which closure is represented by the happy consumption of the product; sitcoms and dramas likewise typically use closure as a major device—the bringing together of plot strands, the parceling out of justice to most of the characters, and the reassuring return of normality or predictable and acceptable change. These are all part of the way ideology operates on the structure of television programs.

There are always exceptions to these generalizations (many early *Miami Vice* episodes, for instance), but sitcoms provide very few. One student analyzed why as a child she had found *The Brady Bunch* so powerful and why now (as a twenty year old) she finds it so transparently awful. Her response statement began:

> Now, many years later, whenever I turn on an old rerun of *The Brady Bunch,* instead of settling down and enjoying it like I used to, all I do is ridicule it—how dated the clothes are, how prissy the girls are, how unbelievably understanding the parents are. How could I have watched it for so many years without being offended? Well, that is the mystery I am going to solve . . .

This student recognizes that since the programs she sees are the same now as they were ten years ago, her very different reaction to them must be based on a change in her general repertoire: previously her repertoire had matched with the text's; now it clashes.

Her analysis developed by focusing first on the repertoire of the text, on the myths that the show now seemed to her to embody so blatantly—and then on how as an adult she had become aware of these myths and chosen to reject them. The program articulated a particular ideology that was prevalent in the 1960s—an ideal family, children who are all "good-looking, clean-cut, all-American kids." "This concept of the ideal family represents a dominant value of our society," she wrote. Surely not everyone, in fact almost no one, has such an ideal family life, but that is what the program encourages its viewers to strive for. In her view, *The Brady Bunch* upholds the view: "Come what may, family love is the bedrock upon which American society stands."

Having developed a sense of the text's repertoire, our student moved on to analyze those aspects of a typical viewer's repertoire that would find the show appealing.

> It is safe to say that *The Brady Bunch* is a myth. It is a fictional story that appeals to the consciousness of the viewers watching it by embodying the dominant ideology of our society concerning what the family should be. Those watching the program see this and wish their family was like this one.

As you can see, she was getting below the surface features of the television "text," asking questions about the ideological values that, no less than with commercials, were appealing to viewers and inviting them to feel at home and comfortable, part of the wider American family.

Our student then turned to her own involvement, to her own experience of "rereading" and recognizing the ways in which her repertoire had changed:

> Well, that may be why viewers, especially young ones, love the show, but what about my change of heart? Since *The Brady Bunch* is a myth, it exists in contradictions. No one who watches *The Brady Bunch* has the ideal family life. Not once did I ever see them have a good argument the way all normal families do.

This student, who had been doing some additional reading (see pages 267–270 for some suggestions), then likened the effect of *The Brady Bunch* to what the French psychoanalyst Jacques Lacan calls "the mirror phase." This refers to the phase of child development in which the child looks in the mirror and sees himself or herself seemingly as a whole "other" being. This vision of wholeness is both comforting and disturbing, because it presents a picture of an ideally unified self that jarringly contrasts with the dislocated set of experiences the child is beginning to have in life, such as separation from the mother. The child is struck by the contrast and experiences something like what we referred to in Chapter 6 while discussing "The Hitchhiking Game"—**decenteredness.** Our student's analysis was especially perceptive here:

> Children watch the show and for that brief thirty minutes they feel unified within themselves. The show lets them forget the fight with their mom and dad, or with their brother or sister. It reinforces the notion of the unified self. Unfortunately this is an illusion that lasts only for the duration of the show. When it ends, the viewers return to their not so perfect, fragmented lives, on the surface feeling happy but in a way more disconcerted than they might otherwise have been because they aren't one of the Brady Bunch.

This student's response statement is distinctive in that it focuses both on the ideological characteristics of the text she is studying and on her own participation in watching it. It is both cognitively aware and culturally speculative. She analyzes both the ideological contradictions of the show and her own place in those contradictions, which she can see more easily because she distances her present from her past self. She "reads" her former reading of *The Brady Bunch* and sees the very different repertoire of assumptions about family life and television that she now brings to it.

Writing Suggestions

1. (*a*) How do you respond to our student's comments on *The Brady Bunch?*
   (*b*) What parts of your own personal history and general repertoire influence your reading or viewing of such a show?
2. Analyze a prime-time television show of your choice (*Miami Vice,* for instance), emphasizing the extent of your own involvement in (and independence from) the show's expression of the dominant ideology of our society.

Developing Cognitive and Cultural Awareness:
How the Grinch Stole Christmas

Every *Who* down in Whoville
Down in *Who*-ville
Liked Christmas a lot . . .
But the Grinch who lived just north of *Who*-ville
did NOT!

Our students were asked to analyze a typical "family" television show traditionally shown a few weeks before Christmas, the animation of Dr. Seuss's children's book *How the Grinch Stole Christmas*.

The program is typically scheduled in a prime-time family viewing slot. It is therefore unlike the other main periods of purely children's programs, Saturday mornings and late weekday afternoons. The prime-time slot makes its influence all the more powerful.

But surely, you might say, *How the Grinch Stole Christmas* is only entertainment! How can we take it seriously as a value-laden text? How can we subject it to a symptomatic analysis? Is it really worth talking about how it articulates our culture's dominant ideology? Isn't it just a kid's program? The answer is that precisely because it reaches out to millions of viewers, because it *is* a children's program, it is worth studying. As with any interpretive situation, you have a text and readers (or viewers); the text possesses distinct conventional characteristics, a repertoire that serves to create a shared reading; similarly, each viewer brings his or her expectations and assumptions—about Christmas, children, the family—and (of course) about television as a medium of entertainment.

In writing about *How the Grinch Stole Christmas,* our students were asked to focus on the interaction of the text's repertoires with their own, and on the interpretive strategies that they used to develop their readings.

One student saw the program's primary aim as that of "creating an ideology of Christmas for the young and reaffirming it for the old." Another saw that ideology as inherently contradictory: "*The Grinch* evokes for viewers a quasi-spiritual myth of Christmas that clashes with the materialism of the holiday. American children, expecting Cabbage Patch dolls and Go-bots, identify with the little Whos coveting pantookas and wuzzles." The feasting and tree-decorating are similarly signs of both a kind of spiritual togetherness and the materialistic consumerism of Christmas. By means of these contradictions, the program tries to include as many responses as possible within its audience—"clawing back," to use Fiske and Hartley's term, its audience into sharable values.

Our students reported that their friends' and their families' most common reaction to the program was "identification" with the Whos. The family members watching became one with the Whoville community rather than allied with the Grinch (hence the common phrase that anyone who complains about Christmas is a Grinch). The Whos are shown decorating their tree as most viewers have been or will shortly. The Whos are constantly described as "little," living in "little houses"; as one student put it, "they are warm, secure, trusting, child-like—something a small child may identify with and an adult may want to."

In contrast, the Grinch is not to be identified with—except, perhaps, by the deliberately individualistic child who wants attention, or by an iconoclastic adult trying to expose the whole show! The program works explicitly with black-and-white morality, a characteristic of most children's television programs (and perhaps most "adult" television programs as well). "To be on the Grinch's side would be to challenge some of the most cherished values of America," as one of our students put it.

Yet the cutest Who of all, little Cindy Lou Who, is the one who confronts the Grinch when he is taking the Whos' tree:

> He turned around fast, and he saw a small *Who!*
> Little Cindy Lou Who, who was no more than two. . . .
> She stared at the Grinch and said, "Santy Claus, why,
> Why are you taking our Christmas Tree? WHY?"

Cindy Lou Who, the most innocent-looking of the innocent Whos, is already strongly influenced by her (and our) society's ideology: she embodies both the spiritual and the consumerist values that are contradictorily affirmed by the program. She believes in Santa Claus but also wants to have her own tree. One of our students pointed out that in the same way the Whos' singing is also a contradictory signifier, connoting, on the one hand, a sense of spiritual community, and on the other, a sense of materialism. After their presents have been stolen, what the Whos have left is their singing—signifying a sense of community in the face of loss and a new dedication, symbolized by the joining of hands. Moroever, as one student put it, "the audience knows that if the misguided Grinch hates singing, then the music must be Goodness." When the materialistic signs of Christmas, the tree and presents, are returned, however, the Whos continue the song in exactly the same religious vein, now celebrating the materialistic world that they and the viewers inhabit.

Santa Claus is another signifier with which viewers are all familiar—and it is as Santa Claus that the Grinch disguises himself. One student pointed to the interesting contradiction that it is the Grinch who represents "anticonsumerism" by "taking the presents away rather than giving them." This act not only identifies the spiritual significance of Christmas *with* the consumerism (Santa equals gifts), but it also reinforces the material togetherness of the consuming season (we are spiritually united to each other because we all buy and receive presents).

The need for consumption is further reinforced by the relationship of the advertisements that interrupt the program to the program itself. While the Grinch is stealing presents, various advertisements are offering parents and children alike presents that can be brought into their homes to make the holidays happy. Our student continued:

What of the production of the show itself? Is it not used as a vehicle for encouraging consumption, interspersed with advertisements aimed at children for possible Christmas presents, namely power wheels and gift certificates to McDonalds? Although they are breaks in the narrative, the commercials really become part of the show. They are not outside of the program but contained within it.

This student was clearly responding to the television "flow," noting how the experience of the program—commercials and all—was inserted into its viewers' experience.

Another student reading of the program focused on the question of the ending. One of the requirements for such a program is to reassure and comfort its audience, and so ensure as far as possible common responses. "If, at the end, the singing Whos connote a metaphysical *raison d'être* for Christmas, then why is it necessary for them to get their Christmas presents back?" asked one of our students. One could think of possible alternatives that would highlight the spiritual as opposed to the materialistic values of Christmas—the Whos could renounce their presents, having learned the "true meaning" of Christmas, or they could give them away to a less fortunate group of children—the Wheres of Africa perhaps. But no, this program reinforces American consumerism: the Whos want their presents back. The Whos' desire for material possessions, therefore, underscores a significant contradiction in the program. Paradoxically, the Grinch realizes what the Whos don't:

> "Maybe Christmas," he thought, "*doesn't* come from a store.
> Maybe Christmas perhaps . . . means a little bit more!"

In the overall program, "a little bit" is not defined, nor, said one student, "is it any more than a little, for the Whos get their presents back in order to fulfill the *viewers'* desire for their own presents." The "little bit more" is all very well, the student argued, but it was only a means of reassuring the families watching that the *real* meaning of Christmas is consuming. "Even the Grinch gets in on the act," she wrote, "when he carves the 'roast-beast' and is converted to the good side."

Another student raised an interesting question: "Where do the presents come from?" She pointed out that one of the very powerful *absences* in the text, and no doubt in most viewers' responses, was the production of the presents. She noted that the only actual material production we *see* ironically comes from the Grinch when he creates his costume from scratch—"possibly a nostalgia for pre-industrialist craftsmanship" and maybe reminscent of the way many consumer items are advertised as "old tyme," "original recipe," "all natural," and so forth. But the Whos' presents appear magically, as if they (literally) grow on trees.

Writing Suggestions

1. Which of our students' comments on *How the Grinch Stole Christmas* do you agree or disagree with? Account for your arguments in terms of your own repertoire.

2. Choose another "innocent" television program associated with an event like Christmas, Easter, or Thanksgiving, and write an ideological analysis of it.
3. Write an ideological analysis of the television presentation of the Super Bowl, the World Series, or some similar major sports event.

How the Grinch Stole Christmas
as Bardic Television

Such a program and the typical way it is viewed in its annual television ritual illustrate extremely well Fiske and Hartley's notion of "bardic" television. One student, in dealing with the program in detail, applied their categories, outlined above on p. 247. Here is a summary of her findings:

1. *How the Grinch Stole Christmas* "*articulates* the main lines of the established cultural consensus" about what Christmas really means—even if those meanings are culturally contradictory.
2. The program "*implicates* the individual members of the culture into its dominant value systems" by such devices as the black-and-white moralization, the appeal to identification with the Whos, and the invitation to the viewer to unite against the Grinch.
3. It "*celebrates,* explains, interprets, and justifies the doings of the culture," such as the Christmas celebration, the increased consumerism of the post-Thanksgiving period, and the ritual scheduling of good-will and togetherness during this special time.
4. It "*assures* the culture at large of its practical adequacy by affirming and confirming its ideologies"—against a world of threats to its lifestyle and its values. During the program, pictures of missing children were included among the commercial breaks. These ask for us to identify with these children and reinforce our sense of togetherness, of not being like these children, lost and cold, and without presents.
5. It "*exposes,* conversely, any practical inadequacies in the culture's sense of itself that might result from changed conditions in the world out-there." Such a function can be seen in the program's stressing the need to have both a prosperous Christmas season *and* a spiritual one—"the need to have an indeterminate metaphysical one-size-fits-all reason" for Christmas.
6. It "*convinces* the audience that their status and identity as individuals are guaranteed by the culture as a whole." Both the narrative and the linking commercials reinforce the place that the viewers have in their whole culture: their family and their Christmas celebrations are reinforced, and they are convinced that their individual practices of buying presents are important and valued, especially within the family setting.
7. It "*transmits* by these means a sense of cultural membership (security and involvement)." Whoville becomes Our Town—Who(ever)ville, perhaps. All viewers are invited to become members of the Whoville community, along with everybody else in their society, except of course for the Grinches. But even the Grinches further reinforce the sense of cultural membership because they do not have a coherent set of different values that could be

posed as an alternative to the Whos' and your own. If the ideology of being a Grinch were seen as a *real* alternative to that of the Whos, it would be threatening to an audience. So instead, "no one quite knows the reason" why the Grinch hates Christmas; it could be perhaps:

That his shoes were too tight
Or that his head
Wasn't screwed on just right
But I think that the most
Likely reason of all
May have been that his heart
Was two sizes too small.

In short, the Grinch didn't have the right (or enough) material goods, or he was deprived, or crazy. As one student pointed out, such reasons are suspiciously like those given by politicians when criticizing their opponents or other governments!

As you can see, our students had a great deal of fun demystifying *How the Grinch Stole Christmas*. They were aware that they were, for the most part, doing "strong" readings of a cherished Christmas institution. *How the Grinch Stole Christmas* is the American equivalent of Charles Dickens's *A Christmas Carol* (and one student suggested it might be interesting to analyze the Dickens in the same way). But even while they produced these readings against the grain and against the "intentions" of the program, many of them said how much, nonetheless, they loved it, how they thought Cindy Lou was "cute." *Especially* strong readings, those suggesting for instance that the Grinch was the real hero or that the Whos were blind to their own self-absorbed values, were uneasily rejected or put aside.

Analyzing Rock Music: Participation in Ideology

Analyzing television and film (media that have been treated for many years in the ways we are suggesting) is a legitimate and crucial extension of the theory and method we are advocating for reading and writing about literature. Another important kind of cultural text that can be usefully analyzed in this way is popular music.

In Chapter 5, we suggested that the social environment in which people listen to rock music—concerts in auditoriums, in the comfort of their own homes, or in the privacy of their own rooms—means that it is experienced in an emotionally rich environment. Once again, it is important not simply to concentrate on the surface meaning of the words of a song lyric but rather to look at the ways in which the song tries to integrate you into or alienate you from your culture's dominant ideology. In many cases, however, people are unsure about how to use their cognitive and cultural awareness to analyze their experience of listening to music, which, perhaps even more than watching television, seems to be "something you just do," not something you analyze. Just because you listen to music in a rich context doesn't mean that you can automatically put down on paper just why and how that context is so rich—and just why, perhaps, you like a particular song so much.

Writing Suggestion

Review the discussion of poetry and rock lyrics in Chapter 5. Which, in general, do you prefer, and why? Discuss the question in terms of your own repertoires.

Rock Lyrics and Ideology

From the best of our students' response statements, what emerges is an awareness of the way rock lyrics convey the dominant ideology of our culture. For instance, one student wrote on Bruce Springsteen's song "Cadillac Ranch":

> Myths carry broad, culturally based, values. *The car* is an American myth, inextricably bound up with key American values. It is part of what is often called the American dream, that "everybody, even the lowliest working man, deserves to have a car." The working-man voice of the song sees his car as a bright spot in his dull grind. The second myth referred to is that of Hollywood, of glamour. We all relate to Hollywood because we are part of a society that encourages us to be extravagant and glamorous.

Here the student is combining an acknowledgement of his participation in the excitement of American ideology with some penetrating analysis of how it works. He uses "myth" to mean the common patterns or stories that transmit a society's ideological values. Because they are often built out of verbal clichés and common experiences, popular songs frequently embody a wealth of such myths—desires for power, autonomy, individuality, identity. People associate certain songs with their personal desires, and these songs become meaningful for them because of their associations. But people also find that their experiences are collective ones: they are part of a common pattern (of growing up, initiation, emotional crises) that is shared by millions of others.

Just as the songs are the product of wider social and ideological forces, so too are their listeners. You think you have personal associations with, say, Sade's "Smooth Operator," but the reason that song appeals to you is in large part the reason it appeals to so many people; it evokes *common* experiences, all personal but nonetheless shared. Most people in our society, especially between the ages of thirteen and forty-three (and beyond, if one writer of this book is evidence), find in popular music an apparent objectification of their own lifestyles, their personal and public choices, as well as simple "entertainment." Most people— today almost anyone under forty-five—grew up with rock music as a "natural" part of their environment and associate particular songs with major crises, achievements, and losses in their lives. The popularity of "golden oldies" programs on the radio is evidence of the longevity of the "rock generation."

But don't forget that a song by Dire Straits or Elvis Costello or The Smiths is different in significant ways from a novel or poem. It is also different in significant ways from the music of "high culture"—symphonic or chamber music, or opera, for instance. Just as literary forms and television programs have distinctive text strategies, so do rock lyrics.

One distinctive feature of much contemporary popular music has been the rejection of the abstract, cerebral characteristics of much Western "classical" music. Jazz, rock, and blues have all moved away from the rational, nonpartic-ipatory tradition of high-culture music. Popular music provides, therefore, a focus for emotions and cultural urges that are not purely "aesthetic." There are consistent references to familiar feelings to which the audience can relate; words are usually kept relatively simple so that a message or a story line can be easily read; both words and music tend to be repetitive to encourage almost immediate participation; much popular music is dance music, and as such stresses rhythm and melody to the exclusion of complexity, though it will usually employ a recurring "hook," repeated phrases where the virtuoso lead guitarist or keyboard player demonstrates for a few bars his or her domination of the song. All of these text strategies help create a preferred "reading" of the song that is im-mediate and reassuring, and emphasizes participation within a cultural ritual. Such aims are not an invention of rock music: one function of all popular songs has been to create a sense of community, to give each individual a place within a broader context.

Since both readers (or listeners) and texts have particular strategies, rock lyrics are not essentially different from "literary" texts. We can therefore treat them in similar ways. Indeed, because these texts of popular culture are so powerful a part of people's lives, it is all the more important that you learn to analyze both your responses to them and the roots of those responses in shared sociocultural and ideological forces.

Writing Suggestions

1. What particular "text strategies" do you find most important in analyzing rock music?
2. What different kinds of popular music do you have in your repertoire? Do you find that any particular kind lends itself to promoting particular values?

Writing About Rock Music

When students are given response-statement assignments in which they are asked to analyze their experience of a favorite rock song, we find that they habitually choose the same range of task definitions that they pick for assignments on literary texts. Just as we suggested you compare your task definitions and mode of writing with those of our students after reading and responding to Robert Lowell's "Skunk Hour" (see pp. 59–60), we suggest you do the same with Laurie Anderson's "O Superman," recorded on her album *Big Science* (Warner Brothers, 1982). Laurie Anderson is well known as an "art rock" multi-media performance artist, and although in the United States she is seen as a "college-campus" rather than as a commercial or Top 40 performer, in Britain "O Super-man" was a Top Ten single in 1982:

LAURIE ANDERSON (b. 1950)

O Superman (For Massenet)

O Superman, O Judge. O Mom and Dad. Mom and Dad.
O Superman. O Judge. O Mom and Dad. Mom and Dad.
Hi. I'm not home right now. But if you want to leave a message, just start
    talking at the sound of the tone.
Hello? This is your Mother. Are you there? Are you coming home?
Hello? Is anybody home? Well, you don't know me, but I know you.   5
And I've got a message to give to you.
    Here come the planes.
So you better get ready. Ready to go. You can come as you are, but pay as
    you go. Pay as you go.

And I said: OK. Who is this really? And the voice said:
This is the hand, the hand that takes. This is the hand, the hand that
    takes   10
This is the hand, the hand that takes.
    Here come the planes.
They're American planes. Made in America.
Smoking or non-smoking?
And the voice said: Neither snow or rain nor gloom of night shall stay
    these couriers from the swift completion of their appointed rounds.   15
'Cause when love is gone, there's always justice,
    And when justice is gone, there's always force.
    And when force is gone, there's always Mom. Hi Mom!

So hold me, Mom, in your long arms. So hold me,
    Mom, in your long arms.   20
In your automatic arms, Your electronic arms, in your arms.
So hold me, Mom, in your long arms.
Your petrochemical arms, Your military arms,
In your electronic arms.

Summarizing, Free-Associating, Interpreting

In their response statements, our students found themselves performing a variety of tasks. Some **summarized** the text, treating it as if it contained some objective meaning, usually closely associated with what they saw as the "personal" insights of the author. The song was reduced to a few key points, and the response statements of this kind reproduced the gist of the song's "message"—as it was frequently put. In the words of one student:

The message of this song is a desire to find security—the kind of security represented by Superman, mom and dad, and the military power of America. Like Laurie Anderson, young people feel very powerless before the events of our time, and this song comments on some of the ways we try to find security.

Note how this student did not focus on the *experience* of listening at all. She wrote almost entirely on the "argument" as she perceived it rather than on the emotions evoked in her, especially ignoring the music, Anderson's voice, and the hypnotic effect many listeners feel the song has. Such a summary is easy to do, and it does give the reader a general orientation to the text, but it is superficial, uninvolved, and reductive. It ignores both the personal and the social context in which the song works. As a piece of writing, a summary like this is a good starting point, but it is only that.

Many students chose the technique of **free-associating,** in which the experience of hearing the song became a springboard for their own feelings and associations. Perhaps like these students, you too would find this kind of writing a strong temptation. One student wrote:

This song scares me. It reminds me of a time when I felt really oppressed by life and when I didn't think there were any answers—except from my parents or some exceptionally strong person who could take me over and look after me. My boyfriend was a kind of "Superman" figure: he always seemed to be so confident about his ability to plan my life as well as his. He was even good at things like cooking. What's more he came from a rich family, so we would often go to Boston and eat at the Ritz or at some elegant French restaurant. I just gave myself over to him.

This student was certainly talking about her reactions, but they become increasingly disassociated from the song. This approach would be fine if she came back to grappling with the specifics of listening to Laurie Anderson's song, but she doesn't. Although the pattern of associations is quite interesting, the associations at this point seem idiosyncratic and merely subjective.

Summarizing and free-associating are often useful starting points for a good response statement but no more; traditional *interpreting* is also an imperfect task definition (see Chapter 3, pages 67–69, for a discussion of traditional text-based interpretation). In such types of writing, what is often a personal reading is disguised as an "objective" reading, and any ambiguities seemingly present in the text are smoothed out. Clearly, an interpretation is not a very satisfactory means of analyzing media texts, since contradiction and ambiguity are major characteristics of such texts—as, we would argue, they are of any literary text.

When you are writing on media texts, we suggest that you avoid the extremes of summarizing and free-associating, and also avoid the seeming finality of traditional interpretation. Try to make your analysis sensitive to the interactive nature of the reading situation, stressing both the text's contributions and your own, and situating both within broader cognitive and cultural contexts. Here is a student response statement on "O Superman" in which he suggests an incipient awareness of the interactive nature of listening and responding to the song:

> I found this song required closer attention than I am used to giving an album cut. First, many contradictory things are going on. There wasn't merely a straightforward story line or a good hook. Most rock songs are easy to follow: here the background "ah-ah-ah" that goes throughout the song contrasts with the messages of the song. It's obvious that the song is supposed to evoke a sense of confusion in its listener. Whenever I listened to the song, I certainly felt disturbed and somewhat threatened. I was surprised that "O Superman" was a Top 10 single; that's not what I expect of a "pop" song. It's more the kind of song that would be heard on a campus radio station.

This student is beginning to examine the song's effects on him by comparing it to his repertoire of accumulated knowledge about rock music, that is, by comparing his expectations and reading strategies with the song's strategies. This student's reaction is still relatively undeveloped, but he is far more self-conscious about how the way listening proceeds than the students who simply summarized or free-associated.

Writing Suggestion

Review the material in Chapter 3 on summarizing, free associating, and interpreting and responding. Then choose a media text and analyze the costs and benefits of each kind of writing.

Response Statements: Cognitive and Cultural Awareness

With this assignment, some students were able to move to the level of response statement that extends an initial analysis into writing that is more cognitively and culturally self-aware. Throughout this book, we have suggested that you try to develop a "strong" reading by directly focusing on your strategies and goals. You can increase the pleasure of listening to rock music by becoming more conscious of what is involved in responding to it. You can focus on the way you bring cultural expectations about rock songs to bear on your listening experience. Setting your personal associations with songs in a wider cultural context helps you situate rock music within the larger dynamics of our culture. Here is part of a student's response statement in which both cognitive self-awareness and cultural references are starting to produce a most interesting strong reading of the Laurie Anderson song:

> "O Superman" evokes feelings of deep misgiving in me. First, it is not at all what I expect of a standard "pop" song. If this was a Top 10 single, then musical taste must be improving! I did not expect the variety of musical and vocal effects. The crying human voice in the background was reminiscent of a heartbeat in the form of a cry, and then the vocalist sang (or chanted) about many psychological, political,

and social issues that are usually not present in such songs, or else are just reduced to clichés. The result was that as I listened (and like a poem, this song demanded *re*listening!), I became a participant in an experience that was both emotionally and intellectually demanding. It was as if the singer was trying to give me insight—but not so much into a whole set of comforting answers as into a group of disturbing questions.

Listening to the song and thinking over my responses to it made me consider the social function of popular music much more closely. Most of it operates as part of our consumer society: it reproduces not just clichés but the clichés of our culture's dominant ideology. If one of the functions of ideology is to make us feel at home in our society, most popular songs do. They call up familiar feelings—even if those feelings are sad or lonely—and they convey the sense that these are natural and common to all of us, and that we can deal with them by just participating in the music—by listening, singing along, or dancing.

With this song, some kind of challenge to these dominant ideas starts to come through. There was no easy resolution, no answers: what emerges from this song (as perhaps in the best rock songs) are Laurie Anderson's thoughts on the contradictions of the modern world. There was no refuge in "personal" feelings: we are all part of the society that has been lulled to sleep by the "petrochemical arms" (a nice pun there!) of our culture. Finally, I am not sure whether I "like" this song. Its effects on me seem to go beyond liking and disliking. I am disturbed, haunted by it.

This response statement is characterized by a growing cognitive self-consciousness—an awareness of both text and reading strategies that have helped produce his response. He analyzes his initial responses, ponders why he had them, and recognizes the interaction of his own strategies with those of the text. He also shows a desire to relate what has clearly been an unexpectedly complex experience to wider cultural forces. It has the makings of a strong reading—even a research paper—on the ways in which rock songs and other media texts embody both the dominant ideology of our culture and also counter-dominant forces. Note how the three interrelated concepts we introduced in Chapter 2, language, history, and culture, implicitly enter into the analysis. The student is examining the text's strategies as well as his own (language); he is positioning his analysis about what rock music should be within his past experiences and expectations (history); and he is throughout relating his experience to wider ideological forces (culture). Note too how the different kinds of writing we discussed in Chapters 3 and 4 are present in his response statement. He includes a little summary and some personal association; he incorporates some standard interpretation but does not make it his final goal. His major emphasis is on becoming cognitively self-conscious and culturally aware; thus he starts to move towards that goal of all reading and all writing about texts—becoming a **strong reader.**

Writing Suggestions

1. To what extent do you agree or disagree with our students' comments on "O Superman"? Account for the influence of your own repertoires on your reading.
2. Write an analysis of another rock song that shows your cognitive and cultural awareness of your response.

Reading Other Media Texts

There are many other fertile media texts to work with in the ways we've demonstrated with television and rock music. Consider, for instance, how Walt Disney cartoons create very tightly organized signifying systems that are the bearers of ideology—in particular, a repertoire of values that are associated with the family, America, and traditional gender roles. Cartoons introduce young children to a framework of values that, particularly when reinforced elsewhere in their experiences, can often last well into adulthood.

A similarly interesting phenomenon is the way our society's dominant ideology is articulated by so-called women's magazines, such as *Seventeen, Glamour,* or *Mademoiselle.* These magazines are frequently geared to a preteen as well as a teenage audience, and they introduce their readers to a set of values that position them most frequently as consumers and as objects of beauty in society.

If you, like many of our students, know these magazines, you may find them particularly interesting to analyze. Such magazines offer their readers a tightly connected set of values and ideas of a particular group identity. Key values are "choice," "individuality," and "leisure," but, paradoxically, the magazines clearly prescribe what characteristics their readers should choose in order to become individuals and how they should spend their leisure—most frequently doing something that would make them more appealing to a man. Girls and women are told that they can best demonstrate their freedom by choosing clothes, cosmetics, and a "personal style" that is seen primarily in terms of visual appearance, a "natural" look that can be created only artificially by consuming the beauty products of the culture. The ideological contradictions are apparent: paradoxically, women have to conform in order to be free; they can choose but their choices are predetermined; and in order to enjoy their leisure and be free, they must work.

Women's magazines from *Seventeen* to *Redbook* to *McCall's* to *Self* to *Cosmopolitan* try to introduce their readers to a pattern that is presented as normal, one that progresses from an adolescent romance to the world of "free" consumerism, then to a more complex sexual world, and finally to marriage, childbirth, children—and, as one of our students sarcastically noted, to "real" love affairs, divorce, and remarriage. In these publications, the "girls" and "women" are addressed as if they were all the same, had no alternative choices, and belonged to a kind of false sisterhood. Such a pattern assumes that all women are born to date, catch a man, cook well, and that their careers will always be subservient to their personal lives.

Conclusion

"Reading texts," then, can include more than the texts you normally associate with literature or high culture. "Reading" is one of the basic ways by which people live in and create their world: human beings are readers. And they are all surrounded by "texts." Indeed, it might be said that we are ourselves both readers *and* texts—readers and writers, read and written.

Checkpoints for Chapter 8

1. People "read" media texts with many of the same assumptions and strategies they use for literary texts.
2. Reading television involves considering its particular ideological repertoire and "text" strategies, most especially the experience of "flow."
3. The experience of such television texts as sitcoms, soap operas, and commercials can all be analyzed in terms of cognitive and cultural awareness— just like literary texts.
4. Rock music, with its distinctive text strategies, also can be analyzed and written about—by summarizing, free-associating, interpreting, and (best of all) by cognitively and culturally aware response statements.

Brief Suggestions
for Further Reading

This is not a book on literary theory. It is a book designed to show how some of the most important recent thinking on reading and writing about literary and media texts can be adapted to classroom practice. But this brief chapter is included for those students who have acquired some curiosity about where "all this stuff comes from," as one of our students put it. Early in the period during which many of these notions were being tried out at Carnegie Mellon, one of our students wrote, "Now that all these existing ideas are around, where did they all come from?" and could she "get more of them"? These few pages are written for readers like her.

What is called *post-structuralism* in the higher circles of literary theory and criticism is a rather loose assemblage of ideas, concepts, methodologies, and feelings. In an American context, we should perhaps speak of *post-formalism,* the reaction against and developments since the New Criticism, a view of reading texts that stressed the objectivity of the text and the need to get away from the reader's "subjective" responses, feeling, and thoughts. Over the past decades, this movement has brought rapid changes in the meaning and status of many elements that students and teachers of literature took for granted—the nature of the text, the reader, the author, the act of reading. This is an exciting time to be working in the discipline of English—and to be learning. At least we hope our students think so!

Parallel to the development of the new literary theory, which deals with "reading" in the broadest sense, there has grown up a new rhetorical theory, which deals with "writing." New models of the writing process, especially those that focus on writing as a cognitive and social act, overlap with the new literary theory in some fascinating ways. In the next decade, students should increasingly benefit from the interaction of these two movements. In Chapters 3 and 4 you read and used some examples of such interaction.

For those of you who want to pursue these matters further, there are three main areas of work to which the authors of this book are especially indebted: *reader-response* criticism, *process-oriented* writing research, and *cultural* criticism. Reader-response, or reader-centered, criticism is closely allied to what in Europe is termed reception aesthetics. Reader-centered criticism focuses more on the act of reading than on the text as an object. It looks on reading as a process—an interaction between text and reader. To investigate some of the sources or expressions of this approach to reading texts, students might like to consult some of the following books and articles. Louise M. Rosenblatt's *The Reader, the Text and the Poem* (Southern Illinois University Press, 1970) was a pioneering work on the psychology of reading literary texts, as were David Bleich's two books, *Readings and Feelings* (National Council of Teachers of English, 1975) and *Subjective Criticism* (The Johns Hopkins University Press, 1978). Bleich's work on response statements and the accounts of his teaching have been very influential, as has the work of Norman N. Holland, in *Five Readers Reading* (Yale University Press, 1975) and many of his other studies, including one co-written with Eugene Kintgen, "Carlos Reads a Poem," in *College English* 46 (1984). Perhaps the best-known reader-response critic in the United States is Stanley Fish, the most interesting of whose work can be found in *Is There a Text in This Class?* (Harvard University Press, 1980). The theoretically more sophisticated (and difficult) German critics include Wolfgang Iser, *The Act of Reading* (English translation, Johns Hopkins University Press, 1979), and Hans Robert Jauss, *Towards an Aesthetic of Reception* (University of Minnesota Press, 1982). There is a useful survey of German work on reading in this area by Hans C. Holub, *Reception Theory* (Methuen, 1984).

Response statements (discussed in detail in Chapters 3 and 4) have proved to be perhaps the most distinctive legacy that teachers and students of literature have received from reader-centered theory and criticism. In addition to David Bleich and Norman Holland's work, you might look at Elizabeth Flynn's article "Comparing Responses to Literary Texts: A Process Approach" in *College Composition and Communication* 39 (1983), 342–48, and Bruce Petersen's "Writing About Responses: A Unified Model of Reading, Interpretation, and Composition," *College English* 44 (1982), 457–68. Parts of Chapters 3 and 4 of this book are based on Kathleen McCormick's article "Theory in the Reader: Bleich, Holland, and Beyond," *College English*, 47 (1985), 836–51.

A very influential aspect of the theory behind this book is process-oriented work on writing—in particular, the study of the cognitive processes of writing as set out in Linda Flower's *Problem Solving Strategies for Writing* (Harcourt, Brace, Jovanovich, revised edition 1985). For other work on the process of writing, see also the many articles by Linda Flower and John Hayes, especially "The Cognition of Discovery: Defining a Rhetorical Problem," *College Composition and Communication* 31 (1980), 21–32, and "Images, Plans, and Prose:

The Representation of Meaning in Writing," *Written Communication* 1 (1984), 120–60. Some of the research on the cognition of writing is to be found in both reader-response criticism and process-oriented writing research. For example, Douglas Vipond and Russell Hunt's "Point-driven Understanding: Pragmatic and Cognitive Dimensions of Literary Reading," *Poetics* 13 (1984), focuses on some cognitive aspects that underlie reading and writing about literature. Issue 14 of the journal *Reader,* edited by Kathleen McCormick, contains a series of articles on reading and writing that blend ideas from the new literary theory and the new rhetoric.

The approach to literature taken in this book is decidedly not that of reader-response criticism by itself. A major criticism of American reader-centered theory and practice is that it is far too tied to an old-fashioned notion of "subjectivity" or the "individual," and that it plays down the social, cultural, and historical dimensions of reading literature. A similar criticism is sometimes made of cognitive, process-oriented approaches to writing. Both readers and writers are, as we have said, "produced" in and through their cultures by the various literary and general ideological dynamics of their time. Our marriage of reader-centered criticism and cognitive study of writing to a wider social and cultural contextualism is, we hope, the distinctive mark of our approach.

Our concern with language, history, and culture comes from many sources. Those most relevant for readers who wish to pursue such matters further include the following works in what is increasingly becoming known as "cultural" as opposed to just "literary" criticism. Useful introductions are Catherine Belsey's *Critical Practice* (Methuen, 1978) and, dealing specifically with language, Kaja Silverman's *The Subject of Semiotics* (Oxford, 1983). The contributions of the French philosophers Louis Althusser and Pierre Macherey are thoughtfully adapted in *Criticism and Ideology* (Verso, 1970) by Terry Eagleton, whose *Literary Theory: An Introduction* (University of Minnesota Press, 1983) is the best overview of contemporary literary theory. Raymond Williams's *Keywords* (Oxford University Press, revised edition 1983) is a fascinating introduction to the historical dimension of language. John Fiske and John Hartley's *Reading Television* (Methuen, 1978) is the most accessible source for the study of media texts. Another useful study is Raymond Williams's *Television* (Fontana, 1974). Broader in scope and enormously influential (as well as highly readable) are the writings of Roland Barthes—*Mythologies* (Fontana, 1980) and *Images, Music, Text* (Fontana, 1977), for instance.

The combination of a reader-centered approach to reading with an insistence on the cultural context of both readers and writers is an unusual but, we believe, powerful one. Some suggestions for developing such an approach can be found in Tony Bennett's *Formalism and Marxism* (Methuen, 1979) and in his article "Texts in History: The Determinations of Readings and Their Texts," in *The Journal of the Midwest Modern Language Association* (Fall, 1985). The distinctive trio of language, history, and culture is given more detailed discussion by Gary Waller in "Post-Structuralist Practice: The Carnegie Mellon

Curriculum," *Bulletin of the Association of Departments of English* (Fall, 1985) and in "Powerful Silence: Theory in/of the English Major," in the same journal (Winter, 1986).

Some other studies, especially those that show the application of these theories to the study of literature, might be consulted. Raymond Williams's *Drama in Performance* (Penguin, 1972) was a pioneering study of the interaction of drama and society. Some of the ideas we put forward on Shakespeare can be supplemented by Ralph Berry's *Directing Shakespeare* (Croom Helm, 1977) or Jonathan Dollimore and Alan Sinfield's *Political Shakespeare* (Manchester, 1985). Bernard Sharratt's *Reading Relations* (Harvester, 1982) contains some amusing and insightful analyses of literature in the classroom. Gary Waller's *English Poetry of the Sixteenth Century* (Longmans, 1986) shows how a reader-centered approach can be combined with historical and cultural analysis. *Writing and Reading Differently: Deconstruction and the Teaching of Composition and Literature,* edited by G. Douglas Atkins and Michael L. Johnson (Kansas, 1985), contains a variety of essays in which recent literary and rhetorical theory are applied to the classroom. For some understanding of the institutional context in which many of these ideas are occurring, see Peter Widdowsen (ed.), *Rereading English* (Methuen, 1972), and Gerald Graff and Reginald Gibbons (ed.), *Criticism in the University* (Northwestern, 1985). For an anthology of literature—poetry, fiction, drama, and essays—in which the approach of *Reading Texts* is exemplified, see *The Lexington Introduction to Literature,* also published by D. C. Heath.

Most students reading this book will not be concerned with following up these references to literary theory and should not feel intimidated by them. A few will want to go much further. Whether or not you read any of these works, the fact that they exist shows you that the fields of theorizing and teaching about those two great basic skills—reading and writing—are presently in a state of great and exciting ferment and that all readers, experts or novices, can become part of the excitement. We hope that this book has helped you to do just that.

Documenting the Research Paper

Although the major form we recommend is the response statement, you will undoubtedly be required at some time to write a research paper, in which you develop your readings fully and, where necessary, quote other readers, critics, and authorities. We suggest you set out your research paper according to the following guidelines, which are in accord with the MLA documentation system (1984 version).

Sample First Page of the Research Paper

Jennifer J. Even
Professor McCormick
76-242
28 April 1986

''Unending Dream of Commentary'':
How Critics Engage with Doris Lessing's
Summer Before the Dark

As the reader drowns under the ever accumulating flood of criticism, he is justified in asking, why is there criticism rather than silent admiration? What ineluctable necessity in literature makes it generate unending oceans of commentary, wave after wave covering the primary textual rocks, hiding them, washing them, uncovering them again, but leaving them, after all, just as they were?

J. Hillis Miller

Criticism, according to J. Hillis Miller, is ''an ever-renewed, ever-unsuccessful attempt to 'get it right,' to name things by their right names'' (331). I would like to add to Miller's definition that criticism is a particular reading of the text based on the critic's literary, social and cultural repertoire, a reading that is often viewed as unacceptable only because the critic's repertoire differs from the reader's. In this paper I would like first of all to explain briefly the notion of repertoire, and secondly to examine several critical readings of Doris Lessing's <u>Summer Before the Dark</u> to illustrate how these critics often assume the universality of their particular repertoires and thus seem to come up with ''wrong'' interpretations in the eyes of readers with different repertoires. Then perhaps finally I can attempt to deal with Hillis Miller's question, <u>Why is there criticism?</u>

A person's repertoire is a subset of assumptions from the ideology which surrounds him or her--cultural, social, literary assumptions. One's literary repertoire contains strategies for reading a piece of discourse--traditional strategies, with expectations of full plot development, unity of details, and resolution and closure revolving around the author's intended meaning; and what we may call Hillis Miller<u>ish</u> strategies, deconstructionist assumptions

Document Sources Fully and Accurately

Although you need not acknowledge a source for generally known information such as the dates during which William Wordsworth lived or the nationality of Nathaniel Hawthorne, you must identify the exact source and location of each statement, fact, or idea you borrow from another person or work. There are many different ways to acknowledge sources, but one of the simplest and most efficient is the MLA system, which requires only a brief parenthetical reference in the text of the paper, keyed to a complete bibliographical entry in the list of works cited at the end of the essay. For most parenthetical references, you will need to cite only the author's last name and the number of the page from which the statement or idea was taken; if you mention the author's name in the text of your paper, the page number alone is sufficient. This format also allows you to include within the parentheses additional information, such as title or volume number, if it is needed for clarity. Documentation for some of the most common types of sources is discussed in the sections below.

References to Single-Volume Books

Response statements do not normally incorporate documented references to other works. In research papers, articles and single-volume books are the two types of works you are most likely to refer to. When citing them, either mention the author's name in the text and note the appropriate page number in parentheses immediately after the citation, or acknowledge both name and page number in the parenthetical reference, leaving a space between the two. If punctuation is needed, insert the mark outside the final parenthesis.

Author's name cited in the text

Terry Eagleton has argued that Literary and Cultural Studies should "look to the various sign-systems and signifying practices in our society, all the way from *Moby-Dick* to the Muppet Show" (207).

Note that the period ending the sentence occurs *after* the parenthetical reference, not before.

Author's name cited in parentheses

Literary and Cultural Studies should "look at the various sign-systems and signifying practices in our society, all the way from *Moby-Dick* to the Muppet Show" (Eagleton 207).

Corresponding bibliographic entry

Eagleton, Terry. *Literary Theory: An Introduction.* Oxford: Basil Blackwell, 1983.

If the work you are citing has two or three authors, cite all their last names in parentheses, following the conventions for spacing and punctuation noted above. If there are more than three authors, use the last name of the author listed first on the title page, plus the abbreviation et al.

Sample parenthetical references

(Dollimore and Sinfield 153)

(Barker et al. 111)

(McCormick, Waller, and Flower 65)

Corresponding bibliographic entries

Dollimore, Jonathan, and Alan Sinfield. *Political Shakespeare: New Essays in Cultural Materialism.* Manchester: Manchester UP, 1985.

McCormick, Kathleen, Gary Waller, and Linda Flower. *Reading Texts.* Lexington: Heath, 1987.

Barker, Francis, et al. *Confronting the Crisis: War, Politics and Culture in the Eighties.* Colchester: U of Essex, 1984.

References to Articles

In text, references to articles are handled in exactly the same way as references to single-volume books. The bibliographic citations, however, are somewhat different in that you don't cite a publisher, but must cite the volume in which the article appeared. Scholarly journals generally appear four to six times annually, and each year of the journal has a volume number (that is, Volume 12 for all of 1986). Each individual issue within a given year is also numbered or labeled with a month or a season (that is, Volume 12, Number 3; or Volume 12, Spring 1986).

Journals with Continuous Pagination

If the journal you are citing paginates its issues for a given year continuously (for example, Volume 12, Number 3 begins with page 467, where the previous issue left off), you need not cite the issue number, month, or season in your bibliographic entry.

Bibliographic entry for article in journal
with continuous pagination

Booth, Wayne C. "Pluralism in the Classroom." *Critical Inquiry* 12 (1986): 468–79.

Journals That Page Each Issue Separately

If the journal issues for a given year are not paginated continuously (that is, issue number 3 of Volume 12 begins with page 1), they you must cite the issue number, month, or season as well as the volume number in your bibliographic entry.

Bibliographic entry for article in journal that pages
each issue separately or that uses only issue numbers

Fish, Stanley, "Why No One's Afraid of Wolfgang Iser." *Diacritics* 11 (Spring 1981): 2–13.

Lyon, George Ella. "Contemporary Appalachian Poetry: Sources and Directions." *Kentucky Review* 2.2 (1981): 3–22.

References to Works in an Anthology

When referring to a work in an anthology, either cite the author's name in the text and indicate in parentheses the page number in the anthology where the source is located, or acknowledge both name and page reference parenthetically. Only in the full citation in your bibliography do you give the name of the editor of the anthology.

Author's name cited in text

One of the most widely recognized facts about James Joyce, in Lionel Trilling's view, "is his ambivalence toward Ireland, of which the hatred was as relentless as the love was unfailing" (153).

Author's name cited in parentheses

One of the most widely recognized facts about James Joyce "is his ambivalence toward Ireland, of which the hatred was as relentless as the love was unfailing" (Trilling 153).

Corresponding bibliographic entry

Trilling, Lionel. "James Joyce in His Letters." In *Joyce: A Collection of Critical Essays.* Ed. William M. Chace. Englewood Cliffs: Prentice, 1974.

References to More Than One Work by an Author

When you paraphrase or quote from more than one work by an author, give the title as well as the name of the author and the page reference so that the reader will know which work is being cited. If you mention the author's name in the text, you need not duplicate it in the parenthetical reference. Just cite the title (or a shortened version of it), skip a space, and insert the page number, as in the second example below. If you do not mention the author's name in the text, cite it first in the parenthetical reference, put a comma after it, skip a space, and insert the title. Then skip a space again and insert the page number (see the third example below).

Title cited in text

Siegfried J. Schmidt argues in his article "On Writing Histories of Literature" that the seventies "will go down in the history [of literary studies] as a period concerned with the writing of new histories of literature" (279).

Title cited in parentheses

Siegfried J. Schmidt argues that the seventies "will go down in the history [of literary studies] as a period concerned with the writing of new histories of literature" ("Histories" 279).

In the words of a major critic of the field, the seventies "will go down in the history [of literary studies] as a period concerned with the writing of new histories of literature" (Schmidt, "Histories" 279).

Corresponding entries in the list of works cited

Schmidt, Siegfried J. *Foundations for the Empirical Study of Literature.* Trans. Robert de Beaugrande. Hamburg: Buske, 1982.

_____. "On Writing Histories of Literature. Some Remarks from a Constructivist Point of View." *Poetics* 14 (1985): 279–301.

References to Works of Unknown Authorship

If you borrow information or ideas from an article or book in which the name of the author is not given, cite the title instead, either in the text of the paper or in parentheses, and include the page reference.

Title cited in the text

According to an article entitled "Sidney at Kalamazoo" in the *Sidney Newsletter,* planning is now under way for next year's Kalamazoo sessions (43).

Title cited in parentheses

Planning is now under way for next year's Kalamazoo sessions ("Sidney at Kalamazoo" 43).

Corresponding bibliographic entry

"Sidney at Kalamazoo." *Sidney Newsletter* 2.2 (1981): 27.

References to Multivolume Works

When you borrow from one volume of a multivolume work, cite the volume of your source in parentheses as an arabic number *without* the abbreviation Vol., and put a colon after it. Then skip a space and insert the page reference.

Sample references

Frazer points out that scapegoat rituals have been common throughout history, not only in primitive societies but also "among the civilized nations of Europe" (9: 47).

Scapegoat rituals have been common throughout history, not only in primitive societies but also "among the civilized nations of Europe" (Frazer 9: 47).

Corresponding bibliographic entry

Frazer, Sir James G. *The Golden Bough: A Study of Magic and Religion.* 3rd ed. 12 vols. New York: Macmillan, 1935.

References to Information Gathered from Interviews

When citing an oral source, either mention the informant's name when you introduce the quotation or paraphrase or give the name in a parenthetical reference.

Informant's name cited in text

When asked about her response, Debra Bernstein, one of our students, said that "it grew out of my belief that all contemporary fiction should be disruptive."

Informant's name cited in parentheses

When asked about her response, one of our students said that "it grew out of my belief that all contemporary fiction should be disruptive" (Bernstein).

Corresponding bibliographic entry

Bernstein, Debra. Personal interview, July 4, 1987.

References to Literary Works

When citing works of literature, observe the following guidelines for each genre.

Novels and Other Prose Works
Subdivided into Chapters or Sections

Begin the parenthetical reference with the author's last name and the page number (the author's name may be omitted if it is mentioned in the text of the paper or if the authorship is evident from the context) and insert a semicolon. Then skip a space and give the number of the chapter (with the abbreviation Ch.) as well as the number of any other subdivisions.

Sample reference

At the beginning of *The Great Gatsby,* Nick Carraway characterizes himself as someone who has "a sense of the fundamental decencies" (Fitzgerald 1; Ch. 1)—a trait that he displays throughout the novel.

Corresponding bibliographic entry

Fitzgerald, F. Scott. *The Great Gatsby.* New York: Scribner's, 1925.

Poems

When quoting or paraphrasing a poem that is divided into sections, cite the number of the book, part, or canto plus the line number(s). There is no need for abbreviations such as bk. (book) or l. (line), but the first time you cite the work write out the word line or lines so that the reader will not mistake the line numbers for page references. If the poem you are citing has no subdivisions, line numbers alone are usually sufficient to identify the source—provided that the author and title are identified in the text of the paper.

Sample reference to a poem with subdivisions

One of Byron's satiric techniques is to juxtapose the comical with the serious, as in this passage from *Don Juan:*

> But I am apt to grow too metaphysical:
>   "The time is out of joint,"—and so am I;
> I quite forget this poem's merely quizzical,
>   And deviate from matters rather dry.
>   (9. lines 321–24)

Note: If you omit the word lines, put a period after the number of the section (in this case Canto 9) and, without spacing, insert the line number(s): (9.321–324).

Sample reference to a poem without subdivisions

One of the questions that might be answered in any analysis of Jeffers's "Hurt Hawks" is whether the author's viewpoint is reflected in the narrator's statement "I'd sooner, except the penalties, kill a man than a hawk" (line 18).

Corresponding bibliographic entries

Byron, George Gordon, Lord. *Don Juan.* In *Lord Byron: Don Juan and Other Satirical Poems.* Ed. Louis Bredvold, New York: Odyssey, 1935.

Jeffers, Robinson. "Hurt Hawks." *Selected Poems.* New York: Random, 1928.

Plays

When citing a play, give the act and scene number without abbreviations, plus the line numbers if the work is in verse.

Sample reference

Shakespeare repeatedly describes Denmark in images of unnaturalness, as in Horatio's comparison of Denmark with Rome just before Caesar's murder, when "The graves stood tenantless and sheeted dead/Did squeak and gibber in the Roman streets" (I.i.115–6).

Note: Upper-case Roman numerals are traditionally used for act numbers and lower-case Roman numerals for scene numbers.

Corresponding bibliographic entry

Shakespeare, William. *Hamlet.* In *Shakespeare: Twenty-Three Plays and the Sonnets.* Ed. Thomas Parrot. Rev. ed. New York: Scribner's, 1953.

Bibliography

In preparing the bibliography (or list of Works Cited) for your research paper, arrange all the works cited alphabetically.

Works Cited

Barker, Frances, et al. *Confronting the Crisis: War, Politics, and Culture in the Eighties.* Colchester: U of Essex, 1984.

Byron, George Gordon, Lord. *Don Juan.* In *Lord Byron: Don Juan and Other Satirical Poems.* Ed. Louis Bredvold. New York: Odyssey, 1935.

Dollimore, Jonathan, and Alan Sinfield. *Shakespeare: New Essays in Cultural Materialism.* Manchester: Manchester UP, 1985.

Eagleton, Terry. *Literary Theory: An Introduction.* Oxford: Basil Blackwell, 1983.

Fitzgerald, F. Scott. *The Great Gatsby.* New York: Scribner's, 1925.

Frazer, Sir James G. *The Golden Bough: A Study of Magic and Religion.* 3rd ed. 12 vols. New York: Macmillan, 1935.

Jeffers, Robinson. *Selected Poems.* New York: Random, 1928.

Lessing, Doris. *Summer Before the Dark.* New York: Knopf, 1973.

McCormick, Kathleen A., Gary F. Waller, and Linda Flower. *Reading Texts.* Lexington: Heath, 1987.

Miller, Hillis. "Stevens' Rock and Criticism as Cure, II." *Georgia Review* 30.2 (1976), 330–48.

Schmidt, Siegfried J. *Foundation for the Empirical Study of Literature.* Trans. Robert de Beaugrande. Hamburg: Buske, 1982.

——. "On Writing Histories of Literature: Some Remarks from a Constructivist Point of View." *Poetics* 14 (1985): 279–301.

Shakespeare, William. *Shakespeare: Twenty-Three Plays and the Sonnets.* Ed. Thomas Parrot. Rev. ed. New York: Scribner's, 1953.

"Sidney at Kalamazoo." *Sidney Newsletter* 4.3 (1982): 43.

Trilling, Lionel. "James Joyce in His Letters." In *Joyce: A Collection of Critical Essays.* Ed. William M. Chace. Englewood Cliffs: Prentice, 1974. 143–165.

Glossary
of Terms

absurd The *theater of the absurd* refers to plays written primarily in the 1950s and 1960s by dramatists such as Samuel Beckett, Eugene Ionesco, and Jean Genet. These works explore the tension between humankind's desire for purpose and the apparent purposelessness of the world. Rather than adopting realism's conventional assumption that the theater should mirror life and present a unified, coherent view of characters and situation, the theater of the absurd calls attention to the theatricality of drama and the incoherence of characters and situations, and to illusion, lack of communication, and futility. Nonetheless, these plays are frequently hilarious and uplifting in their brilliance. Ionesco's *The Gap* and Pirandello's *Six Characters in Search of an Author* are examples. The adjective *absurd* is also used to describe literary forms other than drama.

analysis With respect to discussion of literary text, a term used interchangeably with *explication*. Analysis focuses on studying textual characteristics in isolation, rather than integrating those characteristics with the overall effects of the text. Such an approach, which is associated especially with *formalism*, tends to ignore the vital place of the reader in the making of meaning; it isolates the text from the contexts in which it is written and read and tends to promote the notion that "true" or "objective" meanings somehow exist "in" texts.

argument The line of reasoning that holds a piece of writing together and that readers often reproduce in a *summary* or *interpretation*. Although readers' reproductions of a work's argument may differ widely, they will generally reflect the effect of *text strategies* used in the writing to direct the readers' attention to particular aspects of the text at the expense of others.

assumptions The prior knowledge, values, and beliefs a reader brings to his or her reading experiences. Assumptions may be conscious (for example, strategies designed to produce a specific kind of reading), or they may be unconscious (for example, preexisting ideological values that deeply influence the reader).

authorial intention Many readers assume that the author is the only person who knows what his or her text "really means." This assumption implies that (1) authors are unified beings who always know what they mean, (2) authors have the ability to imbed their intentions and meanings in a work, and (3) readers have the ability to discover these intentions when reading. The approach advocated in this anthology rejects this assumption on the grounds that it is based on a naive objectivism regarding readers, writers, and texts. Although the life of the author may be of interest and may have an intimate connection with the literary work, it is important to remember that a literary text does not "belong to" the author. Even the author's use of the first person

"I" in a work does not guarantee that the work is autobiographical. Unconscious as well as conscious factors influence the writing of a text, and thus the intentions of the author are not authoritatively recoverable from the text and should not be the major concern of criticism. A work's meanings are always the product of what a reader brings to his or her reading and what the author has encoded in the text. What is thought to be the dominant meaning of a text changes from one historical period to another. Authors can be seen as the first readers of their own works, perhaps even privileged readers, but certainly not final authoritative readers.

blanks As defined by Wolfgang Iser in *The Act of Reading* (Johns Hopkins University Press, 1978), those absences or *indeterminacies* in a text that must be completed or resolved by a reader. Blanks, or gaps, can be filled in a number of ways and hence are one of the major sources of readers' different interpretations of texts. Blanks cannot be said to exist in an objective sense in any given text because various readers, depending on their *repertoires,* will "discover" different blanks in the text.

canon The tradition of literary works generally held to be the best or the greatest in the language. Although the works of some writers (for example, Shakespeare) are held to be universally canonical, the canon is continually changing to reflect the values and concerns that different ages bring to their assessment of literature.

character The fictional representation of a person. In many fictional and dramatic texts written between the eighteenth and twentieth centuries, characters are constructed so as to encourage "realistic" and coherent readings. The characters are developed to be psychologically consistent. In most earlier and a great deal of recent literature, there is less inclination to encourage "realistic" readings of characters. In non-realistic (or non-illusionist) texts—for instance, Shakespearean drama, fairy stories, and much contemporary fiction—there is no such encouragement. Characters can be read as stereotypical or inconsistent since the focus is not on creating the illusion of coherence, but on providing a set of verbal codes that the reader experiences in the continuous process of reading. As the German dramatist Berthold Brecht said, "When a character behaves by contradictions, that's only because nobody can be identically the same at two unidentical moments . . . the continuity of the ego is a myth." The notion of a unified character, therefore, belongs to a particular type of literature known as classic realism. Although classic realism is no longer the dominant literary form, the habits it spawned remain residually powerful today in the intepretation of character.

cognitive style The general ways in which a person takes in, processes, and reacts to what he or she perceives. For example, some people seem by temperament to have a much higher tolerance for ambiguity than others. They enjoy employing reading strategies that open up multiple meanings of a text and feel no compulsion to reduce responses to a single meaning. Other people seem always to seek resolution in their reading, as well as in their lives in general. Similarly, some people read more connotatively than others. These are the people who notice double entendres and discover multiple meanings in poetry and in general conversation; perhaps they themselves like to make puns. In contrast, there are those who tend always to read literally; whether they are reading a poem or a letter from a friend, it does not occur to them to "read between the lines." This book advocates that you become self-consciously analytical about your cognitive style in order to understand why you read the way you do; it also suggests that by expanding your repertoires you can develop and enrich your cognitive style so that you will be able to control it rather than letting it control you.

connotation, denotation The associations we bring to a word or phrase—emotive, social, cultural, ideological—are its connotations. Although the term is most commonly applied to poetry, all words can be read for their connotations. Words that carry cultural values—for example, love, duty, democracy, freedom—can be a particularly powerful focus of connotations. Connotations may be contradictory, as the associations we bring are produced by the wider cultural forces of our society. Connotation is conventionally contrasted with denotation, which is considered to be the "real," "true," or "literal" meaning of a word. Connotation and denotation may also apply to visual, olfactory, and and other experiences.

consistency building A reading strategy described by Wolfgang Iser in *The Act of Reading* (Johns Hopkins University Press, 1978) whereby readers at various points in their readings seek to combine into a meaningful, consistent whole the diffuse and often inconsistent material they are reading. To build consistency is to place closure on the text, to decide, temporarily what it is "about." Iser suggests that in the process of reading, readers alternately open up and close off interpretive possibilities. In the consistency-building phases of reading, readers synthesize materials, which necessarily involves excluding some of what they have read. Although this synthesis should never be seen as final, it is necessary for readers to take stock so that they can once again open up to the text as they continue their reading. See also *wandering viewpoint*.

context The surrounding situation. Both reading and writing occur in linguistic, social, cultural, and ideological contexts. The interpretation of any language unit depends on the context in which it is read. See also *cultural situatedness*.

convention Structural patterns or similarities occurring frequently in a large number of works. Such patterns become so widely used that they are taken for granted, often either becoming clichés or becoming thought of as "natural." For example, the division of a play into acts, the telling of a story from a particular unified perspective, and the division of a poem called a sonnet into fourteen lines are all conventional strategies of literary texts. These conventions encourage certain prescribed ways of reading. An awareness of the conventions of writing and reading can enable readers to read a text more self-consciously "against the grain."

couplet In English poetry, two lines of equal length, linked by rhyme: for example,

> Had we but world enough, and time,
> This coyness, lady, were no crime.
> (Andrew Marvell, "To His Coy Mistress")

criticism A generic term used to cover the act of analysis, interpretation and judgment, usually associated with close reading. The term is often qualified by an adjective describing a particular attitude toward the text under review: for example, structuralist criticism, formalist criticism, Freudian criticism.

cultural situatedness A person's (or subject's) place within a particular culture with its presuppositions, values, and *ideology*, all of which deeply influence assumptions about reading and writing. Readers and writers alike are the products of (situated in) specific cultures.

culture A complex word, the dominant meanings of which encompass the relationships between works and practices of literature, art, music, etc., and the whole way of life of the people producing them. It can point to a discriminating or elitist view of human aesthetic productions (that is, "high" culture), but it is used more broadly to refer to the totality of practices and institutions of human society.

decentered Refers more to the experiences of our own lives than just to readings. It implies that rather than having a stable "center" to our lives, we experience continual change, unpredictability, and movement. As Jacques Lacan puts it, the self or *subject* is not a point but a process.

discourses The innumerable ways, or structures, by which a society's knowledge and hence language are collected, organized, and controlled. In order to function within a particular discourse, we learn its rules, concepts, and problems and so become a member of that discourse community. Because a society is made up of many and frequently contradictory discourses, we are all subject to (or written by) many different discourses.

dominant Any society contains many contradictory values, practices, and beliefs that are also reflected in the language and literature current in that society. Those cultural practices that are more powerful than others and exert more influence are termed dominant. Because a society is continually in flux, meanings dominant in any one age may become marginalized in another, and vice versa.

explication See **analysis.**

fiction Broadly and somewhat crudely defined, a mode of writing that gives us imaginative or mental experiences that are not literally true in that they did not occur in the "real" world. Thus fiction is often opposed to fact, or what is equally crudely called "reality." Historically, certain puritanical views have often led to a distrust of fiction as deceptive or even immoral. In another sense, fiction refers to any mental activity whereby we construct models of reality or explanations for ourselves, shaping material in our minds the way a novelist or artist does in order to make sense of phenomena by imposing interpretations upon them. In its narrowest and perhaps most common sense, fiction is often identified with narrative (usually prose) compositions such as novels or short stories.

foreground (verb) To bring to explicit consciousness; to make explicit (used with *assumptions,* concerns, implications).

formalism A mode of analysis that focuses on what are considered to be objective, even scientific, descriptions of the devices (especially stylistic) of a literary text—particularly those that highlight its supposedly distinctive "literary" use of language. Formalism has much in common with *New Criticism.*

free association A kind of writing that stresses the personal relevance of the work. Rather than focusing on the interaction of the *repertoires* of text and reader, it is characterized by "subjective" experiences.

free verse A loose descriptive term for poetry that has no recognizable metrical pattern and closely resembles ordinary speech. The fact that readers must establish their own intonation, speed of reading, and stresses tends to intensify their involvement. Much modern poetry is written in free verse.

gaps See **blanks.**

genre A term used loosely to mean the "kind" or "form" of literature, vaguely analogous to the biological term "species." Standard genres include poetry, fiction, drama, and essay, but within each category sub-genres are conventionally distinguished. For example, fiction is divided into novel, romance, story, and so on. There are no fixed or absolute distinctions among genres. They are largely the product of reader assumption and expectation, and as such are useful conventions rather than real categories.

historicism An approach to criticism that focuses self-consciously on the placing of a text within a historical context—that is, the ideas, material practices, or conventions of its time. An earlier historicism held that because such criticism was based on a detailed, objective reconstruction of the past, it revealed the "true" meanings of texts. A more recent version of historicism acknowledges that history is of necessity written from the perspective of the present, and so, rather than being objective, historicism is the product of questions, preoccupations, and issues important to the historians themselves.

ideology The conscious or unconscious beliefs, habits, and social practices of a particular society. These often seem true, correct, and universal to members of that society, when in fact they are relative and specific to the society. Ideology pervades every aspect of our lives from our table manners to our politics; it is reflected in the kinds of clothes we wear just as much as in our religious and educational practices. We are most likely to become conscious of our own ideology when we visit or study a foreign culture whose lifestyles and customs are radically different from our own. Ideologies are continually in conflict within any society; at a given point, however, certain ones are always *dominant*. Ideology can be divided usefully into literary ideology (beliefs, assumptions, and ideas about literature) and general ideology (beliefs, assumptions, and ideas about all other matters, including politics, religion, and lifestyle). See also *repertoire*.

indeterminacy An ambiguity or a blank in a text that requires the reader's active involvement to supply or determine the meaning. (See *blanks*.)

interpretation Used loosely to signify any act of textual analysis, usually with a stress on meaning. The fact that perceived inconsistencies in the argument are ironed out and personal or "subjective" associations are avoided tends to give interpretations an apparent (though false) objectivity. See also *free association, response statement,* and *summary*.

intertextuality The implicit references to one text that occur in another; alternatively, the influences of one text on another. In one sense all texts are intertextual, since none is written in a vacuum, unaffected by those written previously. But the term is generally applied when influences are more specific. For example, an intertextual relationship exists between Tom Stoppard's *Rosencrantz and Guildenstern Are Dead* and William Shakespeare's *Hamlet*. Your reading experience of *Rosencrantz and Guildenstern Are Dead* will be enhanced if your repertoire includes the earlier text.

irony Verbal irony is often used to emphasize a clash between what words say and what they "really mean." It is invoked when a person uses words that, literally interpreted, express the opposite of what he or she intends. For example, "I had a great day," stated ironically, means the day was terrible. Dramatic irony occurs when an audience has relevant information of which the character is unaware, and thus can derive from the character's words or actions meanings unintended by the character. For example, the audience sees irony in Hamlet's assertions that he will immediately avenge his father's death, as they know that his fate is to continually delay. Situational, or circumstantial, irony arises when the opposite of what one expects happens. For example, you work all night to finish a paper, only to have your disk crash an hour before you are supposed to hand it in. Nothing is inherently ironical. Irony in literature depends on the matching of repertoires—the matching of a text that can be read ironically with a reader who is attuned to irony.

literature An ambiguous term pointing to a historical, not a universal, category of writings. What one society calls literature, another may not. As printed books became more accessible from the Renaissance onward, the word came increasingly to stand for specialized "imaginative" writing, usually of a high quality. The particular texts that should be accorded the title, however, cannot easily be agreed on. Thus literature is an evaluative category, not a scientific one.

lyric A short, concentrated, songlike, and evocative poem, usually written in the first person. Originally a lyric was a song sung to the lyre.

matching of repertories The interaction that occurs between the **repertoires** (general and literary) of the reader and those of the text when a text is read.

metaphor A word or phrase that brings different meanings together, usually either abstract and concrete or literal and figurative. Although it is sometimes argued that *all* language use is metaphorical, it is generally assumed that metaphor is the particular mark of poetry. According to Aristotle, "metaphor consists in giving the thing a name that belongs to something else," thereby forcing the reader to consider one in terms of the other. "Love is a disease," "his heart shattered," "a Calico Cat," and "her facial rash broke out" are all examples. A *mixed metaphor* occurs when the concrete example conjures up (deliberately or not) incongruous associations: for example, "he bulldozed his way through the bottleneck."

meter The regularities of rhythm in poetry that create, often in complex and attractive ways, expectations of pattern, regularity, and surprise. In most English poetry the rhythm is based on the stressed syllables in a line of verse. Although each reader will bring slightly different reading patterns to a poem and so there will inevitably be debate about its exact meter, a well-written poem will direct the reader to a preferred or dominant reading, usually through the interaction of meter with meaning. Meter is measured in units called feet, the principal types of which in English are as follows:
iambic, in which a stressed syllable is preceded by an unstressed syllable, as in the word *ağaińst.*
trochee, in which a stressed syllable is followed by an unaccented syllable, as in the word *híghĕr* or *céntĕr.*
anapest, in which two unstressed syllables are followed by a stressed one, as in the word *iñtĕrcépt* or the phrase *ăt thĕ córe.*
dactyl, in which a stressed syllable is followed by two unstressed syllables, as in the word *déspĕrăte* or the phrase *hére tŏ ă.*
spondee, in which two syllables are accented, as in the phrase *jump iń* or *áll díes.*
A line of poetry with two feet is called a *dimeter;* with three, a *trimeter;* with four, a *quatrameter;* with five, a *pentameter;* and with six, a *sexameter. Iambic pentameter,* with five feet each consisting of a stressed syllable preceded by an unstressed syllable,

is the most common English metrical pattern. Its dominance is due to a long-established assumption that it is close to the rhythm of "natural" human speech. In any good poetry, the meter will vary according to the sense. A poem will include among its textual strategies directions to its readers on how it might best be read, and meter is one of these strategies. We judge the effectiveness of the poem not by how well it keeps to some set pattern, but by its effect in opening us up, in our readings, to the possibilities of various meanings.

monovalent reading A reading in which the reader tries to avoid ambiguity and find only one plausible meaning. Some texts (such as instructions, recipes) encourage the reader to read monovalently, although there is nothing to prevent a reader from playing with the language and reading *polyvalently.*

mood The atmosphere—frightening, calming, oppressive—created for the reader by a text. The manner in which the characters and the setting are described contributes to the mood.

myth In one sense, ancient stories that set out a society's religious or social beliefs. The Greek myths, for example, recount the exploits of the Greek gods. In another sense, myths are narratives used by a society to try to make sense of or account for the common patterns of social life in that society. This second sense of myth is close to *ideology:* Myths may be said to be the narratives of a culture's dominant *ideology.*

naturalization The process by which readers reduce what is strange, disturbing, or out of the ordinary in a text by interpreting or assimilating it so that it fits within acceptable cognitive and cultural norms. For example, readers often try to naturalize Gregor Samsa's metamorphosis into a bug in Franz Kafka's story "The Metamorphosis" by arguing that his becoming a bug is really no different from his becoming disfigured in a car accident or suffering a serious physical ailment, since in any of these instances the victim may be ostracized from his family. To develop such an interpretation in order to assimilate the strangeness of this text into more easily negotiable terms is to deny the oddness, the absurdity, the impossibility of Gregor's becoming a bug. All acts of reading involve some degree of naturalization, but it is important to recognize that naturalizing is a learned, conventional reading strategy that you can choose when and when not to employ.

New Criticism The dominant mode in American literary criticism and education between the 1930s and the 1960s, characterized by an intense focus on "close reading" of the text, to the exclusion of the effects on or contribution of the reader (termed by its theorists the "affective fallacy") and the intentions of the author (the "intentional fallacy").

open text A text that encourages its readers to take up different, even contradictory attitudes toward the issues it raises; alternatively, a text that is deliberately incomplete, either stylistically or structurally, with major *blanks* for readers to fill.

overdetermined A term used to describe an event when its causes and interpretations are multiple, interconnected, and perhaps unanalyzable, so that one single cause cannot be isolated without distortion.

paradigm A model of reality or of a field of inquiry constructed to explain, as exhaustively as is possible at the time, the phenomena that appear to be significant. A *paradigm shift* occurs when the model of reality changes.

plot The sequence in which the events of a story occur. Plots frequently follow the pattern *exposition* (background information), *rising action* (the building of tension), *climax* (resolution), *falling action* (untangling of tensions), *conclusion*. Although most readers assume that this five-part organization of action makes for realism, actually it is simply the most conventional way of telling a story; it does not in fact parallel the way events occur in real life. Experimental fiction frequently plays with readers' expectations about plot; for instance, tension may be left unresolved or a story may have little or no action.

point of view The perspective from which a story is told. A story may be told in either the first person or the third person. A *first-person observer* tells the story but is not involved in it. A *first-person participant* both tells and is involved in the story. A naive first-person storyteller, such as a child, is frequently called the *innocent eye*. Third-person perspectives are classified according to the amount of information the narrator posseses regarding the characters' inner thoughts. *Third-person omniscience* implies that the narrative voice knows all the characters' thoughts. If the narrative voice comments on the story or characters, the point of view is *editorial omniscience*. If the voice has access to the thoughts of only one or a few of the characters, the point of view is *third-person limited*. Some third-person narratives have an *unreliable narrator*. If the narrative voice does not have access to any characters' thoughts and does not comment on the action of the story, but simply records the facts, the point of view is said to be *objective*. Readers should keep in mind that a point of view is a convention of storytelling, a particular type of textual strategy, not an objective fact about stories.

political unconscious According to Fredric Jameson in *The Political Unconscious* (Cornell University Press, 1980), that level of historical meaning—usually expressing historical contradictions—that underlies all reading and all texts.

polyvalent reading A reading that recognizes that multiple readings are possible, even desirable. Some texts (most of the texts we term "literature") encourage polyvalent readings, and in some people's eyes, reading polyvalently is a distinguishing mark of reading literature.

reader-centered criticism The mode of criticism, in part advocated by *Reading Texts*, that stresses the active role played by readers in the construction of readings of texts. Readings, however, are not merely "subjective," since readers are themselves "constructed" by ideological and other factors in their society. Reading, that is to say, is not just a matter of cognition but is deeply affected by cultural factors as well.

reading strategies The techniques used by a reader to process a text, such as creating themes, identifying with characters, looking for a consistent point of view, creating literal/figurative distinctions, filling in gaps, relating the text being read to other texts, relating the text to personal experiences, responding to certain *text strategies* (such as viewpoint, tone, meter, mood) in particular ways, reading playfully for multiple meanings, and relating "personal" responses to the text to larger aspects of the culture. Although some of your reading strategies will evolve as a response to certain text strategies that you encounter, this book suggests that, regardless of what kind of text you are reading, you adopt strategies that will "open" the text up as much as possible in terms of exposing multiple meanings and setting it in a larger cognitive and cultural context. To do this with texts that employ traditional text strategies which encourage you to create closure, it is often necessary to read "against the grain"—that is, to use reading strategies that defy the text strategies.

realism A term used loosely to describe a mode of writing that creates the illusion that "reality" is represented in language. It might more accurately be called "illusionism." Realism presupposes that the world of natural objects and events is unproblematic, clearly given, and available for objective observation and description. It assumes that literature "reflects" life or "expresses" reality rather than being a verbal construction of an interpretation of life. What literature and art "reflect," in the final sense, is not "reality" but *ideology*.

referential Referring to the real world. Referential discourse has as its dominant or preferred meaning a "literal" or "factual" set of events or circumstances.

repertoires The particular sets of beliefs, assumptions, values, ideas, and practices distilled by each text and each reader from a society's *ideology*. One's repertoires can be usefully divided into a literary and a general repertoire. The repertoire of every reader, like that of every text, is different in particular respects from all others (otherwise everyone would think and feel the same), but all are drawn from the same ideological background. See also *ideology*.

response statement An informed record of a reader's initial or predominant reaction to a text. As used in *Reading Texts,* response statements require that readers analyze the assumptions underlying their responses to texts—that is, that they explore their own cognitive strategies, the strategies of the text, and also the literary and general *ideology* of both reader and text. This involves an analysis of the readers' own *repertoires* and those of the text and calls for the development of cognitive and cultural awareness. Response statements also require that readers explore the implications of their assumptions, not only for future reading experiences, but for other areas of their lives.

rhyme The echo of sound that ties two or more lines together in a poem. Rhymes encode a pattern of repetition of identical or similarly stressed sounds, often in a very elaborate organization. Rhyme was one of the dominant devices of poetry until this century; now it tends to be used only for isolated, local effects.

satire A literary form that uses wit or humor to attack a particular object or person. Reading a work for its satirical impact involves a close match of reading strategies with textual strategies. It may also require becoming aware of the object of attack and being familiar with some of the normal standards assumed by the satire. Satire tends to become dated quickly, as the objects of attack lose their relevance. But some satires or satirical aspects of a work can be given renewed life by generalization; for example, parts of *Hamlet* can be read as satirical attacks on corrupt politicians and hypocritical civil servants in general.

scansion The convention by which the rhythms of poetry are described. In ordinary speech, the syllables of words are given different emphasis to show particular meanings: for example,
Andrew, are you coming *in* for dinner? (as opposed to staying *out*)
Andrew, are you coming in for *dinner?* (as opposed to coming in for some other purpose)
Andrew, are *you* coming in for dinner? (as opposed to Michael's coming in)

In poetry, strong and weak emphases on different syllables have traditionally been the basis for distinguishing different *meters*. Strong syllables are stressed more than weak syllables: for example,

> Aš vírtŭoŭs mén páss, mildlў ăwáy,
>
> Aňd whíspĕr tó thĕir soúls tŏ gó

Although many poems, especially those written before the twentieth century, are relatively regular, some variation of emphasis is always possible; it is rare for a line to be absolutely regular in its meter. No two people will scan a poem in exactly the same way. The best guide is to read a poem in your natural voice and listen to where the emphasis falls. See *meter*.

setting The locale, including the place as well as the historical time period, in which a story takes place. The setting often contributes to the *mood* of a literary word.

simile A rhetorical device that compares two phenomena using "like" or "as": for example, "O my Luve's like a red, red rose."

site of struggle Language is a site of struggle in that conflicting meanings (and, behind them, ideological positions) struggle for dominance—for the "right" to be seen as natural or "true." Texts or people, as well as individual words, can be described as sites of struggle.

soliloquy An important structural device in drama, particularly that written in the time of Shakespeare, whereby a single character, alone on the stage, addresses his or her words (usually some personal or intimate revelation) directly to the audience.

strong reading A reading or response that attempts to be very self-conscious about its assumptions and goals. Such a reading may go "against the grain" of a text for any of a number of reasons: the reader's *ideology* differs vastly from that of the literary work; the reader perceives significances in the work that could not have been part of the author's repertoire; the reader deliberately tries to read from an alternative perspective, such as a feminist or a religious perspective.

subject We often think of ourselves as individuals, with unique rights and an "essential" nature that is "ours." But we are all produced by our society's distinctive ideology, constituted by the many discourses of society. The "I" that speaks and acts in the world is subjected to these discourses, which offer the "I" various positions as a subject. The "individual" or "person," then, is not a free or fixed category, but an ensemble—as Lacan puts it, the "I" is not a point, but a process. To recognize that we are all subjects, historically and socially produced, is to recognize that we are all deeply affected by social and historical forces, that character is not a fixed but a continually changing or "decentered" entity.

summary Writing that paraphrases the argument the writer perceives "in" a work. Summary tends to be reductive and to present itself (falsely) as objective. See also *free association, interpretation, response statement,* and *strong reading.*

symbol A linguistic device that uses vivid language to compress a complex or abstract idea into a representation such that any discussion or explication of its significance inevitably leads the reader into a longer, often very elaborate process of explanation.

A symbol is like an expanded *metaphor,* working by the accumulation of associations. An idea whose explanation might be lengthy, difficult to understand, or even unintelligible can be rendered vivid and powerful by a symbol.

symptomatic analysis A mode of analysis that probes the text not for its surface or preferred meaning, but for symptoms of the pressures and concerns that brought the text into being, of which even the writer may have been unaware. Symptomatic analysis is usually only possible in a time period different from that in which the text was originally written and thus relatively independent of the original ideological pressures.

text In one sense, the work—that is, the novel, poem, play, story, etc.; in another sense, that which is produced by the interaction of the work and the reader. Whereas the work can be seen as a finished object enclosed within the covers of a book, the text is an unstable product or process that changes from reading to reading. This distinction, articulated by Roland Barthes and other writers, is a somewhat esoteric one, but it does usually draw attention to the fact that the text is produced anew by each reader.

text strategies The formal techniques used in writing a text, including rhyme, meter, metaphor, plot, setting, character, theme, flashback, flashforward, point of view, description, dialogue, introduction, rising action, climax, falling action, and various techniques of realism. From your experience of reading, you have acquired certain *reading strategies;* when these match the text strategies, you generally feel very comfortable reading the text. When you encounter texts with whose strategies you are unfamiliar (such as Pirandello's *Six Characters in Search of an Author,* in which characters call themselves characters and do not pretend to be "real"), you may reject the text as "nonsense," but this is only because you do not have in your literary repertoire the reading strategies by which to process it. The approach to reading advocated in *Reading Texts* involves expanding your repertoire of reading strategies both so that you can match the strategies of traditional and untraditional texts and so that you can choose when to read texts "against the grain" (that is, to self-consciously employ strategies that counter those of the text in order to do a *strong reading*).

theatricality The distinctive quality of being acted, or played, in a theater. Frequently avant-garde theater defies the conventions of *realism* by overtly calling attention to the fact that a play is a play, not "real life."

theme Loosely defined, what a literary work is "about," in the sense of its main idea or its message. Although many readers believe that they *find* themes in literary works, in fact they *produce* those themes by paying attention to some details and ignoring others. Themes such as appearance and reality, society's attack on individuals' rights, women as an oppressed majority, or love conquers all are so general that they can be applied to almost any text one chooses. The term is therefore not an especially precise one.

theory The philosophy of or self-conscious thought about a discipline or subject.

voice The "person" construed by a reader of a literary work (usually a poem) as being the speaker, sometimes identified with the author. Voice in this sense is a creation of the reader, who is imagining that a lyric or other kind of poem is a direct "speaking" communication. A work's voice, like a person's, is inevitably overdetermined—that is, made up of conflicting voices.

wandering viewpoint A reading strategy described by Wolfgang Iser in *The Act of Reading* (Johns Hopkins University Press, 1978) whereby readers maintain an openness to the text by allowing themselves to revise their ideas on what they think the text is "about." Readers are thought to move back and forth between *consistency building* (placing closure on texts) and modifying their perspective about the text as they read further and gain more information. To maintain a wandering viewpoint is to be willing to reassess what one remembers as having occurred in a text and to revise expectations of what should happen later in the text. See *consistency building*.

Index

Note: Author's name in SMALL CAPITALS indicates that a writing selection (or excerpt) appears in text.

Absences, 47–48, 199, 256
Absurdism, 26
Absurdist drama, 234
Advertising. *See* Commercials
"Against the grain," 27, 28, 29, 202
Allegory, 204
All Morning (Gregory Orr), 38
Ambiguity, 26
ANDERSON, LAURIE, 260
  O Superman, 261
And Ut Pictura Poesis *Is Her Name* (John Ashbery), 39–40
  student comments on, 40
Antigone, 20, 220
Argument, poem's, 39, 40–41, 161, 164, 165, 167
ASHBERY, JOHN, 39
  And Ut Pictura Poesis *Is Her Name,* 39–40
Associations:
  personal, 166–167
  of words, 160
As You Like It, 218–219
Audience involvement, 228–234

Balloon, The (Donald Barthelme), 196, 197
Barrett, Lynne, 210
Barth, John, 27, 191, 194–195
  Lost in the Funhouse, 27, 194–195
Barthelme, Donald, 188, 196–197
Barthes, Roland, 183, 245
Because I Could Not Stop for Death (Emily Dickinson), 3–5
Beckett, Samuel, 52, 74, 234, 239
Belsey, Catherine, 182, 190
BLAKE, WILLIAM, 29, 168
  London, 168–170
Blanks, 24–25, 165–166
Bradley, A. C., 121, 122

BRADSTREET, ANNE, 20, 21
  To My Dear and Loving Husband, 21
Brady Bunch, The, 252–253
  student comments on, 252, 253
Brecht, Bertold, 223, 233–234, 236
Brontë, Emily, 186
Brook, Peter, 236
Bunyan, John, 48

CALVINO, ITALO, 95
  The Canary Prince, 95–104
Canon, 151
Capote, Truman, 151
Canary Prince, The, 95–104
  student comments on, 107–117
Capote, Truman, 151
Cartoons, 265
Cask of Amontillado, The (Edgar Allen Poe), 196
Cather, Willa, 186
Characters, fictional, 185–186, 191–194
Charlton, H. B., 122
Chekhov, Anton, 14, 199, 200–202, 232
Cognitive response, analysis of, 81–82
Coleridge, Samuel Taylor, 121
Collage, 189, 195
Comedy, 228–229
Commercials, 250–251
Connotations, 38, 154, 160, 161, 163
Consistency:
  building, 184
  plot, 184
  point of view, 186
Contradictions, 167–168, 225, 227
Conventional reading, 184–188
Counter-dominant view, 10, 20
CRANE, STEPHEN, 7
  The Open Boat, 7
Critical Practice (Catherine Belsey), 190
Criticism, literary, 118–128, 267–268
Cultural response, analysis of, 84–86, 162

Culture:
criticism, 268, 269
effect on reading response, 84–86, 90
influence on history of dramatic production, 225–226
as monolithic, 51
textual practices of, 49–53
Culture and Anarchy (Gary Waller),
63–65

Decentered, 185, 193
Denotations, 38, 160, 163
Dickens, Charles, 18
DICKINSON, EMILY, 3, 8, 170–171
Apparently With No Surprise, 170
*Because I Could Not Stop for
Death,* 3
Discourses, 34
Doctor Faustus, 225
Dominant view, 20, 22, 119
Donne, John, 151, 162, 165
A Valediction: Forbidding Mourning,
162–165
Double entendres, 26
Doyle, Arthur Conan, 190
Drama, 215–242, 270
absurdist, 234
audience involvement, 228–234
comedy vs. tragedy, 228–229
history, 220–227, 237–239
social realism, 232–233
theaters, 219–222
Dylan, Bob, 49

Eagleton, Terry, 38
Easter 1916 (Yeats), 42–44
Eliot, T.S., 122
Expressive realism, 182

Fairy tale, 102–104, 205
Fantasy, 204
Fiction, 181–214
characters, 185–186, 191–194
conventional reading, 184–188
mixed reading strategies, 198–206
plot, 184–185, 188–190
point of view, 186–187, 194–196,
200
post-modern, 189, 198
theme, 187–188, 196–198

traditional, 198
unconventional reading, 188–198
Fictional vs. factual, 44
First-person point of view, 186, 196
Fiske, John, 247
Fowles, John, 28
Free-associating, 65–67, 76, 77, 78, 88,
262
Free verse, 152
French Lieutenant's Woman, The
(John Fowles), 28
Freud, Sigmund, 48, 51, 127

Galileo, 233–234, 236–239
student comments on, 237, 238–239
Gaps, 24–25, 165–166
García Márquez, Gabriel, 203–206
Gardner, Helen, 125, 126
Gender, influence on reading, 200–202,
210–213
General ideology, 15, 16, 18, 32–54
culture, 49–53
history, 41–48
language, 34–41
General repertoire, 15, 19–24
dominant vs. counter-dominant views,
21–22
and literary repertoire, 206–210
Genre, 151–152, 204
Gist, 41, 62
Goethe, J. W. von, 121
Go, Lovely Rose (Edmund Waller), 9–10
Granville-Barker, Harley, 122–123
Great Figure, The (William Carlos Wil-
liams), 12

Hamlet, 19, 24, 119–120, 235
review by John Jump, 120–127
student comments on, 127
Hanmer, Thomas, 120
Hartley, John, 247
HASS, ROBERT, 176
Meditation at Lagunitas, 176–180
Hawthorne, Nathaniel, 25, 48, 187,
207–210
Hedda Gabler, 28, 217, 232
Hemingway, Ernest, 184
History:
historical perspective, 20–33, 41–42,
44–46
of language, 269
literary references, 41–48

plays' changes throughout, 224–227
research, 174–175, 207–209, 237–239
of theaters, 219–222
Hitchhiking Game, The (Milan Kundera),
52, 191–194
Horace, 11
How the Grinch Stole Christmas (Dr.
Seuss), 254–258
students comments on, 256, 257–258
Human subject, 34, 212, 245
Hunger Artist, The, 26

Ibsen, Henrik, 28, 217, 232
Ideology, 16, 227, 254–258
general, 15, 16, 18, 32–54
literary, 15, 16, 18–19, 32
and rock lyrics, 259–260
of sitcoms, 251–253
of television commercials, 251
Importance of Being Earnest, The (Oscar
Wilde), 216–217, 235
*Incredible and Sad Tale of Innocent
Eréndira* (García Márquez),
203–206
student comments on, 204, 206
Interpretation, 7, 14, 44, 45, 67–69, 85,
88, 127, 193
limits to, 29–30
reader-centered, 5, 6–7
television, 247
text-centered, 5
traditional, 88, 161
See also Strong reading
Inventory, 210
student comments on, 211
I Wandered Lonely as a Cloud (William
Wordsworth), 70

Jones, Ernest, 122, 127
Joyce, James, 152
Jump, John:
review of *Hamlet,* 120–127

Kafka, Franz, 26, 94, 101
Keats, John, 11
King Lear, 8, 19, 226
Knights, L. C., 125
KNOPFLER, MARK, 156, 162
Money for Nothing, 156–158
Kundera, Milan, 52, 191, 212

Lady with the Dog, The (Anton
Chekhov), 199, 200, 201
Lady with the Pet Dog, The (Joyce Carol
Oates), 199, 200
Language, 34–41, 269
indeterminacy of, 38
as overdetermined, 38
as value-laden, 36–37
Life Story, 191
Limited narrator, 186–187
Literal vs. figurative, 74
Literary criticism, 118–128, 267–268
Literary ideology, 15, 16, 18–19, 32
Literary repertoire, 15, 24–27, 181
blanks or gaps, 24–25
general repertoire, 206–210
texts, 24–25
Literary texts, 10–11
Literary theory, 267–270
Literary Theory (Terry Eagleton), 38
Literature. *See* Texts; specific types of
literature
London (Blake), 168–170
Lost in the Funhouse (John Barth), 27,
194–195
LOVELACE, RICHARD, 172
To Lucasta, Going to the Wars,
172–173
LOWELL, ROBERT, 59
Skunk Hour, 59–60
Lyrics, 156–159, 258–266

Macbeth, 12, 45–46, 229
Magazines, 265
Mailer, Norman, 151
Marlowe, Christopher, 225
Marriage, 20–21
MARVELL, ANDREW, 82
To His Coy Mistress, 82–83
Maypole of Merry Mount, The (Nathaniel
Hawthorne), 207, 208
student comments on, 209
Meanings:
made by readers, 8
multiple, 11–12, 81, 151, 198
McLuhan, Marshall, 245, 249
Media texts, 243–266, 269
Meditation at Lagunitas (Robert Hass),
176–180
Metaphor, 6, 40, 153, 197
Merchant of Venice, The, 46
Messenger (Dave Smith), 24, 78–80
student comments on, 74–75

Metamorphosis, The (Franz Kafka), 94, 101–105
  student comments on, 104, 107–117
Miller, Hillis J., 131, 133, 146
Money for Nothing (Mark Knopfler), 156–158
Monovalent reading, 13, 154
Mood, 154
Multiple meanings, 11–12, 38, 74, 81, 129, 151, 155, 198
Music. *See* Lyrics

Narrator, limited, 186, 187
  third-person omniscient, 195
  third-person unreliable, 195
Naturalizing, 151, 187, 189–190, 203
Novels. *See* Fiction

Oates, Joyce Carol, 14, 51, 199, 200–202
Open Boat, The (Stephen Crane), 7
ORR, GREGORY, 38
  All Morning, 38
O Superman (Laurie Anderson), 261
  student comments on, 262, 263
Oral presentation, 3
Overdetermination, 15, 32, 34

Papers, research, 94, 128–147
  sample student papers, 131–147
Papers, writing of, 93–147
  sample student paper, 107–117
Paul's Case, 186
Personal associations, 166–167
Pilgrim's Progress, 48
Plays. *See* Drama
Plot, 184–185, 188–190
Poe, Edgar Allan, 196
Poetry, 38–41, 151–180
  argument, 40–41
  associations, 178–179
  interpreting, 4–5, 12
  issues raised, 40
  lyrics, 156–159, 258–266
  mood, 154
  subjects, 177–178
  voice, 154
Point of view, 24, 186–187, 194–196, 200, 201

Polyvalent reading, 8, 12–13, 38, 154
Porcupines at the University (Donald Barthelme), 197
Pynchon, Thomas, 195

Readers:
  cognitive style of, 26
  context of, 33–54
  general repertoire of, 22–24
  literary repertoire of, 25–27
  reading strategies of, 26–27, 184–206
Reading:
  conventional, 184–188
  dominant, 30
  of drama, 215–242
  experience, 41
  of fiction, 181–214
  gender, influence on, 200–202, 210–213
  as interactive process, 8
  of literary criticism, 118–128
  media texts, 243–266
  mixed strategies, 198–206
  monovalent, 13
  of poetry, 151–180
  polyvalent, 8, 12–13
  process, 77, 161
  strategies, 26–27, 88–91 (tab.), 184–206
  strong, 27–30, 183, 223, 226, 250–251, 264
  symptomatic, 47, 170, 173, 190, 199
  television, 246–258
  of texts, 3–31
  unconventional, 188–198
  and writing response statements, 57–90
Reading Television, 247
Realism, 26
  expressive, 182
  social, 232–233
Realistic plot, 185
Repertoires, 14, 154, 170–172, 211–212
  general, 15, 19–24
  literary, 15, 24–27, 181
  matching of, 16, 25
  symptomatic, 47
Research papers, 94, 128–147
Response statements, 57–90, 262, 268
Rock music, 156–159, 258–266
Romeo and Juliet, 20, 223–224
Royal Shakespeare Company, 223, 226

Scarlet Letter, The, 25, 48, 187–188, 208
Semiotics, 36
Seuss, Dr., 254–258
SHAKESPEARE, WILLIAM, 8, 11, 12, 19, 20, 24, 29, 119–120, 218
  comedy and tragedy, 228–229
  "entertaining" plays, 230–231
  historical perspective of, 41, 45–46
  problem plays, 231
  Sonnet 65 (William Shakespeare), 161
  staging of plays, 221–231
Shakespearean Tragedy, 121
She Dwelt Among the Untrodden Ways (William Wordsworth), 87
Short Happy Life of Francis Macomber, The (Ernest Hemingway), 184–185
Short stories. *See* Fiction
SIDNEY, SIR ROBERT, 67
  Song 17, 67
Signifieds, 6, 35–36, 247
Signifiers, 6, 35–36, 247
Sitcoms, 251–253
Skunk Hour (Robert Lowell), 59–63, 66–67, 69–71
  student comments, 62, 65, 68, 76, 81, 84–85
SMITH, DAVE, 24, 78
  Messenger, 78
Social realism, 232–233
Song 17 (Sir Robert Sidney), 67
Sonnet 18 (William Shakespeare), 29
Sonnet 65 (William Shakespeare), 161
Sophocles, 20, 220
Springsteen, Bruce, 49
STAFFORD, WILLIAM, 159
  Traveling Through the Dark, 159
Strategies, 57
  narrative, 201
  naturalizing, 187, 189–190
  reading, 26–27, 75, 152, 154, 184–206
  text, 24, 184–206
Strong reading, 27–30, 46
  of fiction, 183
  of lyrics, 264
  of media texts, 250–251
  of plays, 223, 226
Subject, human, 34, 212, 245
Summary, 40, 41
Summarizing, 61–63, 88, 120, 261
Symbolism, 77, 187–188, 197
Symptomatic reading, 47, 170, 173, 190, 199

Task definitions, 88–90
  interactive, 61, 71–72, 76–90
  text-based or reader-based, 61–71
Television, 49, 244–258
Texts:
  didactic, 11
  form of, 18, 49–51
  general repertoire, 19–22
  literary, 10–11, 24–25, 51–53
  meaning "in," 5, 48, 128
  media, 243–266
  message of, 11
  reading, 3–31
  strategies for reading, 24, 184–206
Theater. *See* Drama
Theaters, 219–222
Theme, 20–22, 45, 187–188, 196–198
Theory, literary, 267–270
Third-person point of view, 186, 200
Thomas, D.M., 52
Thoreau, Henry David, 57–58
To His Coy Mistress (Andrew Marvell), 82–83
To Lucasta, Going to the Wars (Richard Lovelace), 172–173
To My Dear and Loving Husband (Anne Bradstreet), 20, 21
Tone, 204
Tragedy, 228–229
Traveling Through the Dark (William Stafford), 159–161
Twelfth Night, 228
Tyger, The (William Blake), 29

Unbearable Lightness of Being, The, 212
Unified self, 192
Universal theme, 20–22

Valediction: Forbidding Mourning, A, 162–165
Views of My Father Weeping, 188–189
  student comments on, 189
Voice, 154

Waiting for Godot (Samuel Beckett), 52, 74, 234
  student comments on, 74, 239, 240, 241
Walden, 57–58
WALLER, EDMUND, 9
  Go, Lovely Rose, 9

WALLER, GARY, 63
  Culture and Anarchy, 63–65
White Hotel, The, 52
Wilde, Oscar, 216
Williams, Raymond, 249
WILLIAMS, WILLIAM CARLOS, 12
  The Great Figure, 12
Wilson, Dover, 122–123
Wilson Knight, G., 124–125
Wordplay, 152
WORDSWORTH, WILLIAM, 70, 87
  I Wandered Lonely as a Cloud, 70
  *She Dwelt Among the Untrodden
    Ways,* 87
Writing:
  conventions, 58
  formal papers, 92–147
  free-associating, 65–67, 88, 262

goals, 88–91 (tab.)
interpreting, 67–69, 88
papers, 92–147
research into, 268–269
response statements, 57–90
about rock music, 260–264
sample student papers, 107–117,
    131–146
summarizing, 61–63, 88, 261
Wuthering Heights, 186–187

Values, student, 14

YEATS, WILLIAM BUTLER, 42
  Easter 1916, 42–44

3 4 5 6 7 8 9 0